A PLUME BOOK

THE INSTANT ECONOMIST

Courtesy of the author

TIMOTHY TAYLOR has been managing editor of the prominent *Journal of Economic Perspectives*, published by the American Economic Association, since the journal's inception in 1987. The AEA makes the journal freely available to the public at www.e-jep.org. Taylor is the lecturer for several recorded economics courses marketed by the Teaching Company, based in Chantilly, Virginia, including *Economics* (3rd edition), *America and the New Global Economy, Legacies of Great Economists*, and *History of the U.S. Economy in the 20th Century*. He is the author of an introductory economics textbook, *Principles of Economics*, published by Textbook Media. He has won student-voted teaching awards at Stanford University and at the University of Minnesota. He blogs at conversableeconomist.blogspot.com.

Founded in 1990, THE TEACHING COMPANY produces DVD and audio recordings of courses by top university professors in the country, which they sell through direct marketing. It is a nine-figure-a-year business and they distribute forty-eight million catalogs annually. They offer more than four hundred courses on topics including business and economics; fine arts and music; ancient, medieval, and modern history; literature and English language; philosophy and intellectual history; religion; social sciences; and science and mathematics.

THE INSTANT ECONOMIST

Everything You Need to Know About How the Economy Works

TIMOTHY TAYLOR

A PLUME BOOK

PLUME
Published by the Penguin Group
Penguin Group (USA) Inc., 375 Hudson Street, New York, New York 10014, U.S.A. • Penguin Group (Canada), 90 Eglinton Avenue East, Suite 700, Toronto, Ontario, Canada M4P 2Y3 (a division of Pearson Penguin Canada Inc.) • Penguin Books Ltd., 80 Strand, London WC2R 0RL, England • Penguin Ireland, 25 St. Stephen's Green, Dublin 2, Ireland (a division of Penguin Books Ltd.) • Penguin Group (Australia), 250 Camberwell Road, Camberwell, Victoria 3124, Australia (a division of Pearson Australia Group Pty Ltd.) • Penguin Books India Pvt. Ltd., 11 Community Centre, Panchsheel Park, New Delhi – 110 017, India • Penguin Books (NZ), 67 Apollo Drive, Rosedale, Auckland 0632, New Zealand (a division of Pearson New Zealand Ltd.) • Penguin Books (South Africa) (Pty.) Ltd., 24 Sturdee Avenue, Rosebank, Johannesburg 2196, South Africa

Penguin Books Ltd., Registered Offices: 80 Strand, London WC2R 0RL, England

First published by Plume, a member of Penguin Group (USA) Inc.

First Printing, February 2012
10 9 8 7 6 5

LIBRARY OF CONGRESS CATALOGING-IN-PUBLICATION DATA

Taylor, Timothy, 1960–
The instant economist : everything you need to know to about how the economy works / Timothy Taylor.
p. cm.
Includes bibliographical references and index.
ISBN 978-0-452-29752-4
1. Economics. I. Title.
HB171.T36 2012
330—dc23 2011033416

Printed in the United States of America
Set in Berling • Designed by Chris Welch

PUBLISHER'S NOTE
While the author has made every effort to provide accurate telephone numbers and Internet addresses at the time of publication, neither the publisher nor the author assumes any responsibility for errors, or for changes that occur after publication. Further, the publisher does not have any control over and does not assume any responsibility for author or third-party Web sites or their content.

To Kimberley, always, and to Nathaniel,
Isabel, and Emery, as they grow up

Contents

Introduction

Talking about the wisdom of economists in polite company is like talking about the honesty of politicians or the lips of chickens. Yet in the face of this prejudice, I maintain that economics has useful lessons for understanding the world. My wife says I hold this belief because I am an evangelist, with economics as my religion. Perhaps so, but I have also been asked many times, by many people—at venues as diverse as conferences and cocktail parties—to recommend "just one book" that explains economics. These people aren't looking for a treatise on the beauty of the free market, or for a lecture on the need for government regulation. They have their own views on politics and policy, but they are self-aware enough to recognize that at least some of their views are built on a shaky or nonexistent understanding of economics. I can sympathize. There are dozens of books out there on economics—freaky and otherwise—but I'm hard-pressed to point to a readable non-textbook that would give a soup-to-nuts understanding of the key principles of economics. I hope that the book you're reading will impart a working understanding of both micro- and macroeconomics, not enough to prepare you for setting up your own economic forecasting business, but enough that you can read and speak about economics topics with greater confidence and conviction.

I know what you're thinking. You're wondering if I'm out to push a certain set of economic policies, and if so, whose side of the political fence I'm on. Such skepticism is understandable, but here's the honest truth: If you're wondering whether this book's contents are slanted toward liberal or conservative economic policy—or toward the Democratic or Republican Party—the short answer is *no*. Professional economists of all political leanings use the tools and concepts I will discuss here. Economics is not a set of answers, but a structured framework for pursuing those answers. For example, we can divide the study of economics into two big chunks—microeconomics and macroeconomics. Microeconomics is the view of the individual actors, whereas macroeconomics takes an overall view of the economy. To refer to an old but apt metaphor, macroeconomics is looking at the forest and microeconomics is looking at individual trees. The trick is to build up an overall understanding that encompasses both the forest and the trees. The first eighteen chapters of this book are largely devoted to building up a microeconomic understanding of the economy. To begin, I'll discuss how markets work in the context of goods, labor, and financial capital. Then I'll broaden the lens to discuss situations in which unregulated markets may run into issues, including monopoly and lack of competition; pollution and environmental harms; lack of sufficient support for new technology, innovation, and infrastructure; persistent or rising levels of poverty and inequality; and dysfunctional insurance markets. Each of these issues provides a potential rationale for government action, but to temper such enthusiasms, the final chapter of the microeconomics discussion is a reminder of the possibilities that democratic government can also fail when seeking to address these issues. In the second half of the book, I'll tackle topics in macroeconomics, including economic growth, unemployment, inflation, international trade, and monetary and fiscal policy.

Whatever your beliefs about the respective roles of markets and government, I hope this book will challenge them. I hope it will also give you language and structure for articulating your beliefs more clearly and for becoming a more sophisticated participant in the economic disputes of our time.

THE INSTANT ECONOMIST

CHAPTER 1

How Economists Think

Economists don't have much of a reputation as delightful company. Victor Fuchs—a preeminent health care economist at Stanford University—likes to say, "Some people talk in their sleep, but economists talk in other people's sleep."

With that kind of encouragement, why study economics? Economic issues are central to many elements of our lives, including not only jobs and income, but also health care, education, retirement prospects, and America's future position in the world economy. If you're going to participate in the great social conversation about economics, a conversation that is happening all around us, you need the ability to "talk the talk." Maybe you've already discovered this the hard way: You're having a friendly argument over the minimum wage, or the budget deficit, or national health insurance, and at some point the other person sniffs and says, "Well, even the most basic economics shows that . . ." and then repeats whatever his or her argument is. Now, in my experience, people who make assertions about what "basic economics" shows have only a fifty-fifty chance of being correct. But if you don't know any economics, basic or otherwise, you can't dispute the claim. All you can do is nod or shrug. As British economist Joan Robinson (1978, p. 75) once wrote, the reason to study economics is "to avoid being deceived by economists."

How much economics do you really need to know to participate in such conversations, whether socially or professionally? Brace yourself for a shock: Herb Stein (1991, p. 6), who worked in various roles as a U.S. government economist for almost fifty years, noted that "Most of the economics that is usable for advising on public policy is about at the level of the introductory undergraduate course." All right, maybe that advice wasn't a huge shock: we do live in cynical times. But the point is that you don't have to be eligible for that tenured chair in economics at Harvard or Stanford to hold your own in most everyday economics debates. You just need to understand the economist's way of thinking.

Let's lay some groundwork, beginning with the three basic questions of economics:

- What should be produced by a society?
- How should it be produced?
- Who gets to consume what is produced?

These three questions are fundamental to every economic system and indeed every society: capitalist or socialist or communist, low-, middle-, or high-income. It's useful to think of the possible answers to these questions as falling along a spectrum. At one end of the spectrum is total government control: government institutions determine what is produced, how it's produced, and who gets it. At the other extreme, you can imagine a society in which individuals make all the decisions about what, how, and who. In the real world, of course, very few societies occupy either extreme.

Let's think about what it would mean to move along this spectrum. Putting aside pure anarchy, we could start at one end with a society in which the government provides only the basics for a market economy: prosecuting theft, enforcing contracts, and providing minimal infrastructure such as national defense. This is sometimes called the "night watchman state." Farther along the spectrum, you can imagine a society with a slightly broader scope for government, adding public services such as roads and education to the night watchman's responsibilities. The next step might be taking on what's sometimes called a social safety net: a system of national pensions (such as Social Security) and nationalized health care. An even broader government might be responsible for supporting or even partial ownership of certain industries, such as steel or agriculture; it might control the distribution of food or basic consumer goods, such as housing. At the other extreme, you could imagine a government that hands out all the jobs, all the housing, all the food; one that determines what everyone makes and what everything costs.

In the great debate between government control and individual freedom, there's a long tradition of treating the people at the other end of the spectrum as if they were idiots—or monsters. But modern economics recognizes both that markets have their strengths and that, in some situations, markets don't work especially well and the government may have the ability to do something genuinely helpful. Modern economics also recognizes situations in which government intervention hasn't worked well and in which it would probably work better to let the market have a go. To think like an economist, you have to step beyond the ideological arguments about market versus government and get pragmatic. It's necessary to dig down into understanding how markets *really* work and what to do, in practical terms, when they don't work well.

With this idea of what economics is, it's useful to clear away some misconceptions about what economics is not. For one thing, economics is not about predicting the future. It's a common complaint that economists can't say when a recession is going to start or end, or when the stock market will rise or fall. But economists aren't fortune-ellers, able to predict every factor that might affect consumption or production in an economy.

Economics is also not about taking political sides. A lot of people ask me (often in a polite and coded way!) whether I'm a Republican or a Democrat or a Libertarian or a Green, but in teaching basic economics, political affiliation isn't relevant. Economics is not about supporting business or labor, or Democrats or Republicans. Economics is a framework for thinking about the questions.

As an entrée into how economists think, let's consider some statements that most economists would view as obvious but many non-economists wouldn't.

Trade-offs should be taken seriously. Well, everybody believes that, right? Actually, no, they don't. Think about the question of whether, if a government needs to raise additional revenue, it should raise the tax on individuals or on corporations. In public discourse, this tends to boil down to asking, "Which do you care about, corporations or people?" But an economist sees the bigger picture. If you raise taxes on corporations, where do the corporations get the money? They could raise the prices of their products sold to consumers; they could cut the bonuses of top executives; they could cut the dividends they pay to stockholders—all of which would mean less money in the pockets of some actual person. My point here is not that corporate taxes should or shouldn't be raised, but that any sensible discussion of corporate taxes should focus on which actual people are likely to end up paying the tax. Similarly, when the media report on economic issues, they tend to start their stories with a person. Perhaps it's Joe, who just got laid off from a job at a failing company, or Susan, who depends on a social program that's being cut. This is sometimes called "putting a face on the news," and it's effective journalism. But when I hear about Joe or Susan, I always wonder about all the people who aren't in the news story but who are affected in one way or another by the same issue. As economists sometimes say, the plural of "anecdote" is not "data." Many economic choices have the characteristic that they help some people and hurt others. Economists care about all the statistical people who are hurt or helped, not just the individual faces in a news report.

Self-interest can be an effective way of organizing a society. If you ask a number of people, "What would happen if everyone in a society behaved in a purely selfish way?" most of them would reply that it would lead to chaos. But many everyday market exchanges rely on self-interest: shopping around for the best deal, waiting for a good price before selling your house, and so forth. Adam Smith (1776, pp. 484–85), arguably the founder of the discipline of economics, wrote:

> Every individual . . . generally, indeed, neither intends to promote the public interest, nor knows how much he is promoting it. . . . He intends only his own security . . . only his own gain, and he is in this, as in many other cases, led by an invisible hand to promote an end which was no part of his intention. Nor is it always the worse for the society that it was no part of it. By pursuing his own interest he frequently promotes that of society more effectually than when he really intends to promote it.

The idea of the "invisible hand" is that in pursuing your own self-interest, you may benefit others. By producing a better product, for example, you're improving the life of the person who uses it. Adam Smith knew perfectly well that the invisible hand is not a magical cure for all an economy or a society's woes. But economists view self-interest as a powerful force, which when appropriately directed, can provide broad social benefits.

For example, if you wanted to get people to conserve energy, how might you go about it? You might develop a huge public relations campaign and get the word out on TV and in the school curriculum. But an economist is more likely to say, "You want people to use less oil? Tax it; they'll use less. You want firms to develop more fuel-efficient cars? Subsidize that technology; the firms will then do the research and development that will make it happen. You want people to use more solar power in their homes? Give them a tax credit; they'll put the extra money toward the installation." If there's something you want less of, discourage it with a tax; if there's something you want more of, encourage it with a subsidy. Such choices in any individual case may be wise or unwise public policy for a variety of reasons (discussed in more detail later in this book), but at least they work with incentives, rather than ignoring them.

All costs are opportunity costs. When you make a choice, the thing you didn't choose is what economists call an "opportunity cost." For example, if you want to hire someone to clean your house, let's say it will cost you $150 per cleaning, two cleanings per month. So you could say it costs you $3,600 a year to have your house cleaned, or you could say it costs you a week's vacation at a beach resort in Mexico to have your house cleaned. The true cost is not the money you've spent; it's the thing or things you give up. Thinking in terms of opportunity costs includes costs that aren't measured in terms of money. If you attend college full time, you are giving up time you could spend doing something else—including working for pay. That opportunity cost is part of the cost of attending college.

Prices are determined by the market, not by a producer. In everyday conversations, you've probably heard someone make a comment such as "my landlord raised my rent" or "those big oil companies raised fuel prices" or "the banks raised my interest rate." But when, say, gasoline prices drop, you probably don't hear anyone say, "Oh, those generous oil companies. So nice of them to give us hardworking folks a break!" Or when interest rates are low, people don't say, "Those generous banks—how sweet of them to give me more for my money." To an economist, the basic premise behind both the blame and the praise in these statements is faulty. Economists certainly agree that landlords and gas companies and bankers are greedy and are trying to make the most money they can, but they're greedy all the time. They raise rents and prices and rates not because they want to—they always want to—but because market conditions of supply and demand shift in a way that allows them to do so.

No person can have everything he or she wants. No society can have everything it wants. Trade-offs are unavoidable. In a modern economy in which people have a wide variety of skills and desires, the question is how to coordinate the decisions about what is produced, how it is produced, and for whom it is produced.

CHAPTER 2

Division of Labor

In our modern world, even seemingly simple consumer goods are often produced through a complex process that reaches across the world. Let's take the pencil, for example. In 1958, an economic educator named Leonard Read wrote an essay, "I, Pencil," that described the remarkable process of pencil production. The wood comes from Northern California, where it must be logged, then shipped and milled. The lead is a mixture of graphite produced in Ceylon and clay mined in Mississippi, which are combined in a process performed at yet another location. The yellow paint on the outside is made from castor beans—that's three more steps: growing, shipping, and paint making. The brass sleeve that holds the eraser is made from zinc, copper, and nickel, which must also be mined, shipped, and refined. The eraser is a mixture of vegetable oil from the Dutch East Indies, pumice from Italy, and various binding chemicals—imagine how many steps that is for the eraser alone. In the essay, Read claims that there is no single person in the world who could make a pencil from scratch, and he may well be right.

A pencil is disposable. If you drop one on the floor, you may well let it roll away without thinking twice. But what it takes to make a pencil, considered closely, is awe-inspiring. What's even more awe-inspiring is that almost everything in the economy is the result of this kind of near-miraculous economic coordination.

This division of labor creates substantial economic gains, both at the level of a firm that's producing a good and at the level of a national economy. How does it do that?

Division of labor allows workers to focus on the things they are best suited to do and allows firms to take best advantage of local resources. If you run an ice-cream business, odds are the person who designs the labels won't be the same person who tends the dairy cattle. Similarly, you may be able to raise dairy cows in Wisconsin, but you'll need a warmer climate to grow your sugar. Bringing the right workers and the right resources from many locations means more productivity.

Workers who specialize typically become more productive with practice. In the automobile manufacturing business, assembly line workers are often the best at coming up with new ways to perform their tasks. When receiving a service, we all want an experienced and specialized person for the job, whether we're looking for a doctor or a hairdresser. Some organizations develop specializations, too. Firms that focus on one or just a few "core competencies," as they are called, often do better jobs than firms that try to do everything.

Division of labor allows a firm to take advantage of economies of scale. "Economies of scale" is the jargon for saying that, in certain cases, a larger firm can produce at a lower average cost than a smaller firm. A tiny factory that produces only one hundred cars a year will have much larger production costs per car than a factory making ten thousand cars, which can take advantage of specialization and assembly line production. The concept of economies of scale helps make sense of how the world works. Without economies of scale, every little city and town would have tiny little factories for making very small numbers of cars, refrigerators, clothing, and other products. But in a world that takes advantage of economies of scale, regions produce one kind of thing in large numbers and trade with other regions that produce something else. The division of labor doesn't happen only within a firm; it happens also within economies and even across countries. For example, auto manufacturing is not spread evenly across the United States, but happens mostly in a north–south corridor reaching from Michigan to Alabama.

A high-income economy typically has a greater division of labor than a low-income economy. The average citizen of a wealthy nation doesn't need to know anything about, say, electronics or weaving or dairy farming. You don't need the knowledge or the skills to produce everything you need because specialization and trade provide access to smartphones and cheddar cheese. Instead, you can buy goods that embody all that different knowledge, and then you pay for those goods by working at a highly specialized job of your own. The economy is the social mechanism that coordinates this extraordinary division of labor. As the economist Robert Heilbroner (1968 [2009], p. 2) once wrote:

> The overwhelming majority of Americans have never grown food, caught game, raised meat, ground grain into flour, or even fashioned flour into bread. Faced with the challenge of clothing themselves or building their own homes, they would be hopelessly untrained and unprepared. Even to make minor repairs in the machines that surround them, they must call on other members of the community, whose job it is to fix cars or repair plumbing. Paradoxically, perhaps, the richer the nation, the more apparent is the inability of its average inhabitants to survive unaided and alone.

Division of labor increases production in firms, national economies, and the global economy. Nations, like workers or firms, can develop specialized skills and expertise. One recent major trend in world trade is sometimes called "breaking up the value chain"—meaning that the parts of production are becoming more widely separated. People sometimes talk about "American cars" or "Japanese cars," a distinction that used to make sense, because just about all the parts of those cars were made in America or Japan. Today, the seat cover for a car might be made in one nation, its inner springs in another, and the parts installed in yet a third place. The parts move back and forth across national borders so frequently that there may be no clear answer to the question of where the car was made. If America wants to take advantage of division of labor, we don't want to focus on undertaking every step of production ourselves. There are, of course, complex issues of both gains and losses involved in international trade, which we'll look at in depth later. But on the whole, division of labor—in which every nation specializes in certain goods and even certain services—can make all parties better off.

One useful metaphor for understanding an economy with a high division of labor is to imagine that all the goods produced by an entire economy could be collected in one storehouse. When you produce something, you bring it in the front door. When you want to consume something, you go around to the back door to pick it up. The division of labor means we're all producing different things and bringing them to the storehouse, and so a problem arises: The stuff that goes in the storehouse needs to be the same as what comes out of the storehouse. It would be pointless to produce or store products that no one ever used or that had no particular function, and you'd want to avoid a situation in which lots of people were waiting at the back door of the storehouse for something that wasn't available.

So how can we coordinate what goes in and what comes out of the storehouse? Unfortunately, the honor system is not a practical solution. Think about what happens in a dormitory refrigerator. If a dorm has a common fridge, you put things in and you hope that everyone will replace what they've used and that you'll always have milk for your morning (or midnight) coffee. But as anyone who has opened a common fridge to find it full of sour milk and stale pizza knows, this never works in a dormitory. It won't work well in the economy at large, either.

A society needs a system for placing value on what people bring to the storehouse and what they take out, as well as some way to link the two. If somebody brings a product to the storehouse that nobody wants, it won't have any value. If someone brings something to the storehouse and there's already a lot of it in there and no one wants much of it, then its value will be small. Conversely, if someone brings something to the storehouse that people are eager to have and there's hardly any of it available, then that product will have a higher value.

In a market economy, the value of what goes into and comes out of the storehouse is determined by supply and demand. The value of a product in a market economy is its price—and paying a price for goods offers an incentive for people to make careful choices about what they take out of the storehouse and not to take more than they will actually consume. The value of labor in a market economy is shown by the wage or salary that is paid, which in turn provides an incentive to provide goods and services that are valuable to others. The price mechanism and those forces of supply and demand—which will be the focus of the next chapter—are how a market economy coordinates the division of labor and matches up what goes into the great storehouse of the economy and what comes out the other end. Of course, the storehouse metaphor is limited. It doesn't take into account issues such as fairness, poverty, pollution, taxes, or regulation. We'll discuss these issues and others later.

In theory, decisions about what is brought in and what's taken out of the storehouse could be made by the interactions of individuals in markets, or by government, or by some combination of the two. But in any case, every society has to answer those three basic questions of economics: What is made? How is it made? Who is going to consume it?

A decentralized market economy, with its division of labor, works so marvelously well at providing a wide array of goods and services that, for practical purposes, people in high-income countries often take it for granted. One sometimes hears about people who come from places without market-oriented economies, where government rations most goods and where the variety and price of what is available in the stores is dismal. When those people stand in the aisle of a modern supermarket or giant retail store in a high-income country, they gape in wonder. One part of economics is to understand and analyze—and maybe marvel at just a bit—the feats of coordination that a market-oriented economy accomplishes every day.

CHAPTER 3

Supply and Demand

You should be starting to glimpse how economists see the world: the division of labor leads to exchange of goods and services; somehow a society has to coordinate all that production and consumption. All high-income societies of the world such as the United States, Canada, Japan, and the countries of Western Europe primarily coordinate their economies through market arrangements, influenced to a greater or lesser extent by government. Let's take a deeper look at how markets work together in the economy as a whole.

We're going to start with a circular flow diagram, which pictures the economy in terms of flows of goods, services, and payments between two groups, households and firms, through three markets: goods, labor, and financial capital.

The goods market includes all the items that households buy: food, clothes, furniture, haircuts, phone service, computers, and so on. In the goods market, goods flow from the firms, which produce the goods, to the households. Households make payments for the goods, which flow back to the firms. In the jargon of economists, firms are the suppliers of goods and households are the demanders of goods.

In the labor market, labor flows from households—that is, from people who work—to the firms who hire those workers. For example, the Target Corporation has about 350,000 employees. Payments flow

THE CIRCULAR FLOW DIAGRAM

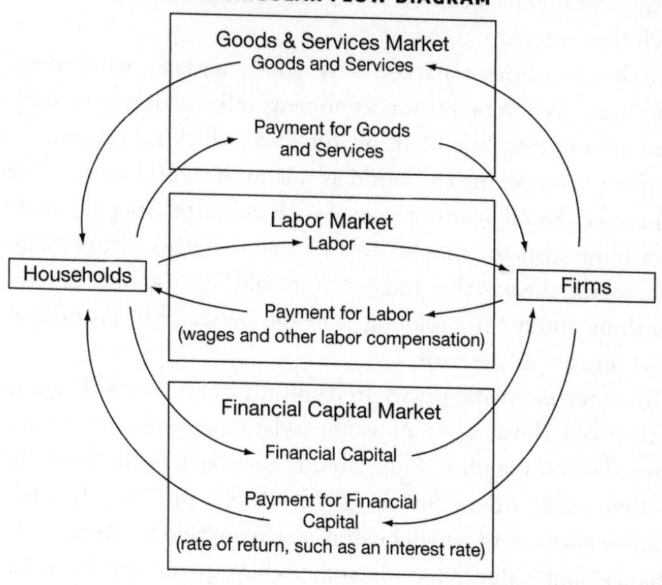

from the company to the workers and their households in the form of wages and benefits. In this market, the roles of supply and demand are reversed from the goods market; firms demand labor, while households supply labor.

In the financial markets, households invest money—either directly by buying shares of stock or indirectly by putting their savings in a bank, which in turn invests in or lends to firms. The households are paid for those investments by the firms in the form of interest and dividends. Thus, households are suppliers of financial capital and firms are demanders. (It should be noted that firms may also supply capital, but they invest on behalf of their owners and shareholders—that is, households again.)

The circular flow diagram shows how all three circles run through households and firms, and thus, how all three markets are part of a larger, integrated macroeconomic whole. Later on we'll look at how government and other nations interact with these three loops, but for starters, let's focus on these two sets of actors and three markets in which they interact.

In the first of three markets—the goods market—where do prices come from? When many noneconomists talk about prices, they talk about prices being "too high" or "too low," which is best understood as a way of comparing the world as it is to the world as they think it ought to be. You'll hear statements such as "nurses are paid too little" or "gasoline costs too much." To an economist, this sort of judgment is like saying the weather today is "too cold" or "too hot." It tells you something about the preferences of the person, but nothing about why things are as they are.

To noneconomists, prices are typically value-laden. Economists try to avoid those sorts of value judgments, which we call the diamond water paradox. This paradox goes back to the forefather of all economists, Adam Smith (1776 [1994], pp. 31–32), and *The Wealth of Nations,* in which he draws a distinction between "value in exchange" and "value in use." Diamonds have great value in exchange. If you have one to trade, you can get a lot for it. But diamonds don't have much value in use—you can't eat them, they don't trim your hedges for you, and they make lousy paperweights. They're basically frivolous, a luxury. Water, on the other hand, is one of the basic necessities of life, not to mention water's not-so-basic uses, such as transport and steam power. It has very high value in use. But water is also extremely cheap. In most places, it falls out of the sky for free, and in normal circumstances its value in exchange is correspondingly low.

Clearly, value in exchange and value in use don't always line up. So when we look at the price of an item, which of these values are we talking about? When economists talk about price, we're talking about the exchange value. The exchange value of a good is tied to its scarcity—how much of the good there is relative to how many people want it. Diamonds have a high price because, compared with how many diamonds there are, lots of people want them enough to pay a high price. Water has a low price because, compared with how much is available, people aren't willing to pay much for it. You can imagine a situation in which someone dying of thirst would be willing to trade diamonds for water, but that's not the norm!

The dramatist Oscar Wilde (1891) once defined a cynic as "a man who knows the price of everything and the value of nothing." That's also a good description of economists, who focus on the price of everything and the intrinsic value in use of nothing. To think about price like an economist, you need to purge your mind of preconceptions about a good's value in use. When you get used to it, separating prices from judgments about value is emotionally liberating. You don't have to think about whether a price is "right" or whether it's an accurate reflection of your personal values. Price is what happens out in the world from the interaction of supply and demand, from what's available and what people want.

I've been tossing the terms "supply" and "demand" around rather loosely, but they actually have quite specific meanings. When economists talk about demand for a good, they're referring to the relationship between the price of a good and the quantity of that good that's demanded. For most goods, most of the time, as the price of the good goes up, the quantity demanded tends to drop.

This is easy to visualize with a graph. The quantity of the good is on the horizontal axis, and the price of the good is on the vertical axis. The curve representing demand slopes downward. That downward slope tells you that as the price drops further and further, the quantity demanded gets bigger and bigger.

At the gut level, this pattern makes sense, but what's the actual cause? Economists have offered two specific reasons. One is the "substitution effect." As the price of a good goes up and up, people tend to substitute other goods for it. For example, as the price of orange juice goes up, people substitute other drinks, or perhaps vitamin C pills. As the price of gasoline goes up, people might drive less, they might join carpools, or they might buy cars that have higher gas mileage.

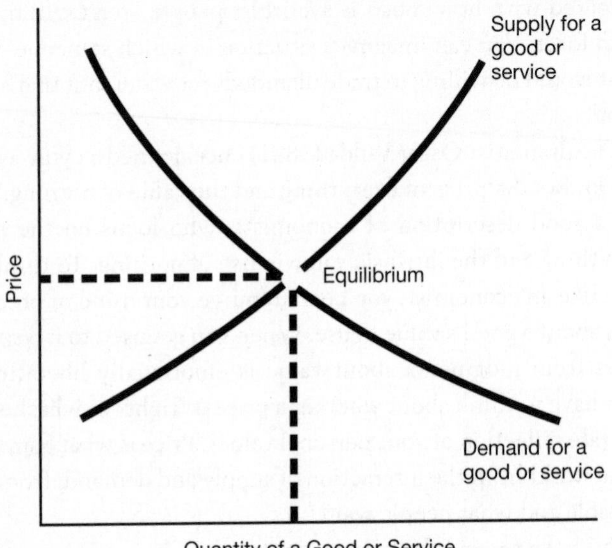

The other reason is called an "income effect." As the price of a good rises, your income has less buying power, so you can't buy everything you did before—you buy either fewer things or less of the same things. For example, if you're someone who likes to buy fancy coffee every morning on your way to work, and the price of your favorite beverage goes up to $100 a cup, you probably can't buy that cup of coffee every morning. The buying power of your income in terms of coffee is reduced. Even if the price rises only a little bit, the buying power of your income is diminished, and the income effect forces you to buy less of that good or other goods.

It's important not to confuse the terms "demand" and "quantity demanded" as economists use them. "Quantity demanded" refers to the specific amount of a good that is desired at each given price. In 2009, about 120 million bags of coffee were sold at a price of $1.15 per pound. "Demand" refers to the relationship between price and quantity demanded. It refers to how much is desired at any possible price or at every price. As the price of coffee rises, the quantity of coffee demanded will decline. In terms of our graph, quantity demanded is a point, but demand is the curve.

So here's a trick question: What makes demand rise or fall? The answer is not price; price affects the quantity demanded, but it doesn't cause the demand relationship itself to move. When economists talk about "demand" shifting, we're not talking about one point moving up or down; we're talking about the whole demand curve shifting up or down by the same amount. We're talking about a situation in which, at every given price on the axis, the same larger or smaller quantity is demanded. What could cause such a change?

- What if income rises for society as a whole? If everyone had more money, there would be greater quantities demanded for most goods across the board at pretty much every price.
- What if a society has a population boom? If you have more people demanding goods, that equates to higher quantities demanded at every price.
- What about tastes and fads? Certain things become more or less popular all across a society—such as people consuming more chicken and fish and less beef. In that example, the quantities of chicken and fish go up and the quantity of beef demanded goes down at any given price. The demand for chicken and fish rises, and the demand for beef declines.
- What about a change in the price of a substitute good? In the previous scenario, if most people think chicken is the best substitute for beef, its price goes up, and in response, people move away from chicken and demand more beef. Conversely, if the price of chicken goes way, way down, people buy more chicken, and the demand for beef goes down.

Now let's turn to supply. Supply refers to the relationship between the quantity of a good supplied and the price of a good. As the price of the good goes up, the quantity supplied tends to rise, too, because as the good's price rises, firms become more willing to supply that good. So whereas our demand curve sloped downward, the supply curve slopes upward.

Once again, this probably makes some intuitive sense, but economists have tried to spell out specific reasons behind the pattern. First, existing firms want to produce more as the price rises because they can earn higher profits. Second, new firms decide to enter the market and start producing the good if the price rises enough.

Just as there's often confusion between "demand" and "quantity demanded," there's a parallel confusion between "supply" and "quantity supplied." Quantity supplied refers to the specific amount produced at a given price. Supply refers to how much is produced at every price. Quantity supplied is a point, and supply is a curve.

Here's that trick question again, this time from the supply perspective: What makes supply rise or fall? Again, it's not price. Price causes the quantity supplied to change, but it doesn't shift the entire supply curve. For supply to increase, the whole supply relationship has to move, so that at every given price, a larger quantity will be supplied. Conversely, for supply to fall, at every given price, a smaller quantity must be supplied. What are some examples of factors that could move supply in this way?

- What if there's a change in technology? A cheaper production method could mean that a greater quantity of a certain good could be supplied at every given price.
- What if production is affected by weather? This factor is particularly important in agriculture. Better weather means greater crop yields, which means more of a good supplied at every given price; bad weather means lower yields, which means less of a good supplied at every given price.
- What about a change in input prices? An input price is the cost that goes into making a good. If a firm uses a lot of oil or a lot of steel to make its product, and the price of oil or steel goes up, then the quantity supplied of their product at every given price is going to fall.

Now we're ready to look at how supply and demand interact. Let's start off by thinking about a basic good, such as pizza. Let's first consider the situation with a low price. At a low price, the quantity supplied is correspondingly low because nobody wants to produce the good, but the quantity demanded is likely to be relatively high because many people want to buy lots of pizza at that low price. As the price of pizza rises a little, the quantity supplied increases; restaurants want to produce more of the good. But when the price rises, the quantity demanded drops off; people are less willing to buy the pies. As quantity supplied rises and quantity demanded falls, at some point the quantity of pizza demanded is equal to the quantity supplied. That point is called the equilibrium.

What does equilibrium mean in practical terms? If a good's price is higher than the equilibrium, then the quantity supplied of that good will exceed the quantity demanded. Stuff starts piling up on the shelves. To get rid of it, the seller has to start cutting prices until people are willing to buy. The price starts to drop toward that equilibrium point, where the quantity supplied and the quantity demanded meet. Equilibrium is the point at which price and quantity are efficient in the specific economic sense that nothing is being wasted. Just as an efficient machine has no wasted motion, or no extra parts, an efficient market has no extra products sitting around, or no extra demand for products that are not there.

If the price of a good falls below the equilibrium, then quantity demanded will exceed quantity supplied. In that situation, people are practically lining up to buy that good before supplies at the local store run out. Suppliers notice this, and they begin to raise prices. As a result, quantity demanded begins to fall and quantity supplied starts to rise, until again, the two quantities are equal and the price reaches equilibrium.

Equilibrium is the point toward which a market economy tends—but that's not to say that markets are always at equilibrium. There are long-standing disputes over how long it takes markets to reach equilibrium, how close they usually are to equilibrium, and when or whether market prices will overshoot equilibrium and need to bounce back. In the mid-2000s, housing prices in the United States clearly veered well above equilibrium for a period of several years before the pendulum began to swing the other way. But over time, markets typically *tend* in the direction of equilibrium.

Any change in demand or supply—remember, that's a change in the whole curve—will cause the equilibrium point to shift. Consider, for example, the market for beef. If income rises, then the demand for beef rises. The result would be a situation in which the new equilibrium has a higher price and quantity sold in the market. Now imagine the opposite situation. Let's say there's an outbreak of cattle disease, and the supply of beef drops as a result. The outcome would be a lower quantity and a higher price sold at equilibrium. A lot of an introductory economics class is devoted to thinking through the consequences of these demand and supply shifts. The specific goods and examples change, but the basic pattern is the same: Think about demand, think about supply. Start at equilibrium; think about what would happen if demand or supply shifted. Think about what new price and quantity would result at the new equilibrium. Supply and demand is a framework for discussing how prices and quantities are determined in markets and why those market prices and quantities are going to change. Understand this, and you're on your way to a solid grasp of the basics of economics.

In the real world, equilibrium means only that quantity demanded and quantity supplied are in balance; it doesn't mean that people feel content with the result. Some buyers will always say, "I think I'm paying too much." Some sellers will always say, "I can't believe it's selling for so little." Sometimes buyers or sellers will go to the government and lobby for a change in the price of a good, even when the market for that good is at or near equilibrium. In the next chapter, we'll talk about some consequences that arise when this happens.

One common complaint about the supply-and-demand model is that "real people don't think that way." At one level, this is obviously true: most people don't use these terms or draw graphs in their heads. But as long as buyers search for what they prefer at the lowest possible price, taking their desires, their finances, and their possibilities for substitution into account, and as long as firms adjust their production in response to changes in price, the supply-and-demand approach will work reasonably well. The reality of supply and demand may not always be likable, or morally attractive, or desirable in any deep philosophical sense, but it is a useful tool—a powerful and accurate way of describing and understanding why prices are at the levels they are and why prices might be rising or falling. It works as a way of describing markets all over the world, at all different times in history, and for all sorts of products—from pencils to pizza.

CHAPTER 4

Price Floors and Ceilings

If you have ever tried to rent an apartment in New York City or San Francisco, you know that the prices can be jaw-droppingly high. Demand for real estate is so strong that even unimpressive dwellings can command high rent. What should happen when the market-determined price seems unreasonably high to many people? On the flip side of the coin, some years, when conditions are exceptionally favorable, farmers grow so much that they receive very low prices for their crops. What should happen when the market-determined price seems unreasonably low to many people? Supply and demand are inevitable forces, but not all outcomes of supply and demand are desirable. Even the most enthusiastic free market economists don't agree that nothing can or should ever be done about the outcomes of supply and demand. It is certainly possible for the government to intervene and affect the prices of what can or will be charged in particular markets. The question for price-control legislation is whether the methods used accomplish the desired goals, or might the result be counterproductive?

Disagreements about price and quantity in a market are impossible to avoid. Suppliers will always say if they just had a little more money, they could create new jobs, build new factories, hire more people. Demanders will always talk about the difficulties of trying to get by at their income level. Both sides will appeal to fairness. Businesses will say they just want a "fair" price—by which they mean a higher price. Individuals will talk about how the price of rent or electricity or gasoline is "unfair"—by which they mean the price should be lower. If a group is politically powerful enough, it can sometimes push a government into changing the law to enshrine its advantage.

When politicians are persuaded to enact a law to keep the price of a good low, they create a price ceiling—a maximum price for the product. Rent-control laws are one common example of a price ceiling. The political argument for rent control is that shelter is a need, not a want, and that the unregulated equilibrium point for housing is too high for a significant number of people to afford.

But a price ceiling doesn't prevent the forces of supply and demand from working; in fact, these forces enable us to predict the consequences of the price ceiling. If you set a price ceiling lower than the equilibrium price would have been, people who are buying the good will be enthusiastic about that low price, but suppliers of the good are not going to be so enthusiastic. Quantity demanded will rise, but quantity supplied will fall. The result is a shortage.

Let's look at rental housing again as an example. Rent control has led to housing shortages at many times and in many places, including the two hundred or so U.S. cities that have adopted rent-control laws at one time or another since World War II. One result is that in cities with strict rent-control laws, a consumer may not be able to find an apartment at the legal price; there are too many potential renters looking for too few apartments. Landlords, unable to meet their rising costs by raising rents, may skimp on maintenance; they also know that with demand so high, potential renters won't be too fussy. As a result, the quality of rental housing diminishes. Owners might convert their rental apartments to condominiums, exiting the rental market altogether. Construction of new rental apartments will likely decline. The apartment owner may extract extra money from tenants through various ancillary fees, and from "deposits" that you pay when you move in but somehow don't get back when you leave. Price ceilings also enable a gray market in which people who obtained the good cheaply resell the good to someone willing to pay more—in this case, one could sublet part or all of a rent-controlled apartment at a not-so-controlled rate. Finally, consumers who get into price-controlled apartments have a tendency to stay there for a longer time, thus preventing others—some of whom might have a greater need for a low-price apartment—from finding a rental.

The government can hold down prices, but in a free society, it can't force sellers to produce more, and it is very, very hard to regulate all these possible ways of getting around a price ceiling.

Let's consider the opposite case. When those who supply a good are a politically powerful force, that group can sometimes get the government to set a minimum price, or price floor. In the United States, for example, there are laws that have the effect of providing farmers who grow certain crops a guaranteed minimum price for their goods. The argument for price floors in agriculture is that the nation needs a stable and an expanding supply of food—we need to keep farmers in business—but the equilibrium price is sometimes just "too low," so we need a law to guarantee the farmers a "fair price" (notice those value judgments). Whatever the political intent, the forces of supply and demand are unavoidable, and price floors have consequences.

If you set a price above equilibrium, suppliers will be delighted at the high price, and quantity supplied will be high. However, quantity demanded will be low. The result is a surplus: quantity supplied exceeds the quantity demanded. The government might act to avoid a surplus through quotas—limiting how much a producer is allowed to sell—or through buying and storing the excess product. In the United States, surplus agricultural products have historically sometimes been shipped to low-income countries as food aid.

The counterproductive effects of farm price floors go beyond the surpluses. The price of farmland will rise with price floors, because the products produced there are worth more. People who own the land benefit, but lots of farmers who rent their land will pay more, thus negating any benefit to them from the price floor on the crops they grow. Agricultural price floors may also have environmental consequences when they encourage the use of marginal land or potentially toxic chemicals to increase yields. The shipment of surplus product as food aid can be positive when it staves off a famine; however, food aid may also injure the farming economies of the recipient countries when their domestic farms can't compete with an influx of free food aid.

Moreover, price regulation draws no distinction between who's needy and who's not. Price regulation changes the price for everyone. Some people who need help will receive it, but many who don't need help will receive it, too.

What if the government simply tried to help everyone, with price floors for all producers and price ceilings for all consumers? Actually, that scenario is roughly how the Soviet Union tried to manage its economy. In the 1980s about a quarter of the central Soviet government's budget was subsidies, because the government simultaneously subsidized high prices for producers and low prices for consumers. The Soviet Union suffered the costs of shortages, and surpluses, and black markets, and all the rest. As Soviet premier Nikita Khrushchev is reputed to have said, "Economics is not a subject that greatly respects one's wishes."

At about this point, some people get grumpy with economists and accuse them of having a concealed agenda. "You might say you're open to different kinds of economic policies," they grumble, "but it sure sounds like you're dictating a policy, and that policy is noninterference. This whole riff about price floors and price ceilings and equilibrium is just an excuse for fatalism and inaction."

But criticizing one set of policies doesn't mean that no other policies are acceptable. Let's start by considering some alternatives to rent control. One could give money directly to the poor by raising welfare payments, or by giving housing vouchers. This kind of demand-side help is more targeted than price controls, going straight to those who need it. On the supply side, a government could subsidize the construction of low-cost housing or adjust zoning laws to allow and encourage the construction of more low-cost housing. Either of these actions should result in a higher equilibrium quantity of affordable housing without causing shortages or surpluses.

What about agricultural subsidies? Imagine that the policy goal is to ensure a decent standard of living for farmers with small- and medium-size operations. Instead of implementing price floors, a government could subsidize buyers of food through food stamps, school lunch programs, and so forth. Encouraging demand should help farmers sell more of their product. On the supply side, the government could supplement the income of farmers whose farms are below a certain size, thus targeting the assistance to those in need. Both of these choices avoid the problems of accumulating surpluses of farm products at home or dumping the surpluses on developing nations abroad.

Ironically the political system tends to choose price floors and price ceilings precisely because they're not especially good public policy tools. Whereas economists force themselves to acknowledge the trade-offs in any scenario, politicians often prefer to hide the costs of their policies. Price floors and ceilings look like policies with a zero cost because they don't require a spending increase or a tax cut. Price controls sweep the costs under the rug.

Economists also believe in taking all the costs—not just the budgetary costs, but also the opportunity costs—into account. Rent control, for example, benefits some people because they get lower housing costs, but others suffer because they can't find an apartment, and some construction businesses suffer because they can't turn a profit. Similarly, when a government keeps crop prices high, the farmers producing those crops benefit, but poor and middle-class families face a higher price for basic food necessities such as milk or bread, and farmers in low-income countries may be living in dire poverty because food aid from heavily subsidized countries is pushing them out of the market. The waste from shortages and surpluses in these situations doesn't show up on the government's balance sheets as explicit taxes or subsidies, but it is a real cost nonetheless.

Economics as a subject is not hostile to the poor, nor does it require a vow of noninterference in a free market. Economists differ in their political beliefs, and so they will argue over whether certain kinds of interference are desirable policy. But where economists stand united, regardless of their political beliefs, is that they insist on acknowledging all the trade-offs of any policy.

CHAPTER 5

Elasticity

Smoking is an expensive habit. The federal cigarette tax is roughly $1.00 per pack, and on top of that, the average state cigarette tax is $1.45 per pack. Are these taxes aimed mainly at discouraging the use of cigarettes? Or are they intended to collect government revenue? Answering this kind of question requires us to think about how cigarette taxes affect the quantity of cigarettes demanded, which economists refer to as "elasticity." Many public policy disputes, as well as many issues of pricing strategies, rely on understanding the concept of elasticity.

Imagine that the price of a good, such as a pack of cigarettes, rises by 10 percent. Does the quantity demanded fall by 50 percent or 2 percent? The elasticity of demand is defined as the percentage change in quantity demanded divided by the percentage change in price, so in these two examples the price elasticity of demand would be either 5 or 0.2 (that is, 50/10 or 2/10). Similarly, imagine that in response to a 10 percent rise in price, the quantity supplied of cigarettes in the market rises by 40 percent or only 5 percent. The elasticity of supply is defined as the percentage change in quantity supplied divided by the percentage change in price, and so in these two examples the price elasticity of supply would be either 4 or 0.5 (that is, 40/10 or 5/10).

It's useful to think about elasticity in three broad categories, which can be applied to both elasticity of demand and elasticity of supply.

Goods with inelastic demand have an elasticity of less than 1. In a situation of inelastic demand, the percentage change in quantity demanded is smaller than the percentage change in price; for example, a 10 percent rise in price might cause the quantity demanded to fall by 5 percent. Goods that are highly inelastic are often ones for which it is difficult to substitute a less expensive good; if you have a cold, you can choose the generic cough medicine over the name brand, but a diabetic can't cut back on insulin use just because the price goes up. Demand for insulin is inelastic. Demand for cigarettes from smokers who are well and truly hooked is inelastic.

Goods with elastic demand have an elasticity of greater than 1. In terms of the formula, the percentage change in quantity demanded is greater than the percentage change in price. Here, a 10 percent rise in price might cause a 20 or 30 percent fall in the quantity demanded. The quantity demanded is highly stretchy; it moves a lot in response to changes in price. A classic example is orange juice. If the price of orange juice goes way up, people can easily substitute other drinks and vitamin C pills. Demand for orange juice is elastic. Demand for cigarettes from teenage smokers, who are not yet well and truly hooked, may well be elastic.

Goods with unitary elasticity of demand have an elasticity equal to 1. When the percentage change in the quantity of a good demanded is exactly equal to the percentage rise in its price, we say it has unitary elasticity. This means that if the price goes up 10 percent, the quantity demanded falls 10 percent.

Goods with inelastic supply have an elasticity of less than 1. Here, a given percentage change in price will bring a smaller percentage change in the quantity supplied, so a 10 percent rise in price might cause a 5 percent rise in supply. A classic example of a completely inelastic supply is the paintings of Pablo Picasso: no matter how much the price goes up, we aren't getting any more of them! But in general, in any industry where it's difficult for firms to expand their supply of raw materials or skilled labor quickly, those firms will produce goods with an inelastic supply.

Goods with elastic supply have an elasticity of greater than 1. In this situation, a given percentage change in price will bring a larger percentage change in the quantity supplied, so a 10 percent rise in price might cause a 20 percent rise in the quantity supplied. These are products for which it's pretty easy for a firm to ramp up production very quickly, perhaps because they were running below capacity.

Goods with unitary elasticity of supply have an elasticity equal to 1. In this situation, a given percentage change in price would cause an equal percentage change in the quantity supplied, so a 10 percent rise in the price would bring a 10 percent rise in the quantity supplied.

Why is elasticity calculated by using percentage changes in price and quantity? The great advantage of this approach is that it allows comparisons across a variety of different markets in which quantities might be measured in different units or where prices might be measured in different currencies. Imagine, for example, comparing the elasticity of demand for gasoline in the United States and Japan. By using percentages, we can avoid the complication of calculating the exchange rate between U.S. dollars and Japanese yen and converting imperial units to metric. We can also compare across goods in every market. We can compare the elasticity of demand for gasoline with the elasticity of demand for beef with the elasticity of demand for haircuts in a way that doesn't depend on how the quantities of these goods are measured.

Knowing whether demand or supply is elastic, inelastic, or unitary has a wide range of practical applications for how prices should be set and how markets react to shifts in demand and supply. Here are some examples:

Raising price brings in more revenue if demand is inelastic, but not if demand is elastic. Imagine a band on tour booked to play an indoor arena that has 15,000 seats. To keep this example simple, assume that the band keeps all the money it gets from ticket sales and pays all the costs for its appearance, such as travel and lodging and equipment and so on—fixed costs that are the same no matter how many people are in the audience. Let's also assume, for simplicity, that all the tickets are the same price. The band knows that if it raises the price of tickets, it will sell fewer tickets. The band has to decide whether to set a high price and sell fewer tickets or a lower price and sell more tickets. So how does the band maximize its revenue—that is, the ticket price times the quantity of tickets sold?

Let's first discuss a moderately popular band for which the demand for tickets is elastic, because this band isn't a "must-see." This band should think about cutting the ticket price as long as a certain percentage drop in price will result in an even larger percentage rise in quantity demanded, which will increase the overall revenue for the band. But for a superstar band that expects to sell out the venue, the demand is probably inelastic; certain fans will pay almost any price. In that case, the band can raise ticket prices significantly with little or no drop in quantity demanded and quantity sold. If you're a music fan, you've probably noticed over the past ten or fifteen years that the biggest bands are doing just that.

Of course, in the real world, this problem is more complex—different prices for different seats, promos and giveaways and VIP passes, T-shirt sales, and even ticket scalpers all complicate the issue. But the key lesson is that when a band—or a firm—is setting prices, it shouldn't simply charge as much as possible. Any firm needs to consider the elasticity of demand for its product, which it can learn about over time by experimenting with slightly higher or lower prices, and seeing how its customers react.

Demand and supply are often inelastic in the short run and elastic in the long run. Think about demand for gasoline. In the short run, if the price of gasoline goes up, what can you really do? You pay because your options are limited in the short term—combining errands into single trips, doing a little more walking or bicycling for short distances, and so on. For the most part, your demand will be inelastic in the short run. In the long run, if the price of gasoline stays high, you have more options. When your car needs replacing, you can buy a more fuel-efficient model. You can organize a carpool at your office. You can get yourself in shape and ride that bike regularly. You might consider moving nearer to where you work or taking a job that's closer to home.

On the supply side, producers of goods and services often find it easier to expand production in the long term of several years than in the short term of a few months. In the short run, the response of quantity supplied to price might be fairly inelastic, but over time, as firms have a chance to adjust, supply can become quite elastic indeed. In this way, elasticity explains why the prices in an economy tend to jump up and down a lot in the short run—because demand and supply are both somewhat inelastic. But in the long run, both quantities adjust, and prices become more stable, although of course not fixed in place.

When demand is inelastic, increases in the cost of production can be passed along to consumers, but when demand is elastic, increases in the cost of production have to be carried by the producers. If the price of energy goes up, we know there will be higher prices and lower quantity for all the goods that require energy for their production (basically, just about everything). But will the result be *mostly* higher prices; in other words, can producers pass on that higher cost? Or will it be *mostly* lower output, in which the producers have to carry the costs themselves? Let's look at some examples.

Coffee shops use coffee beans, but they don't control the world market price of coffee. If the cost of coffee rises, can they pass the cost on to consumers in the form of higher prices? Well, is the demand for coffee elastic or inelastic? Can buyers get a less expensive caffeine fix, such as tea? Or can buyers cut out the cost of skilled barista labor and make coffee at home for less money? Unfortunately for the coffee shop, the answer to both questions is "yes." As a result, demand for those coffee drinks is elastic, and only a modest portion of the increase in coffee prices can be passed to consumers.

Let's return to the example from the start of the chapter: What is the result of raising the tax on cigarettes? A tax, like the cost of ingredients, is an input cost. It's a price that's charged to the producer as it makes the product. Now, on some level, smoking is a choice; it's certainly not a necessity any more than a double-shot extra-foam cappuccino. But for many people, smoking is also an addiction with few substitutes. We'd expect the demand for that group to be inelastic, and in fact, the evidence is that increasing the price of cigarettes by 10 percent will lead to a mere 3 percent reduction in the quantity of cigarettes smoked. As a result, if society increases taxes on companies that make cigarettes, the companies can pass most of these taxes along to consumers in the form of higher prices.

The enforcement of antidrug laws offers another application. Laws against illegal drugs raise the cost of producing and distributing those drugs; as a result, many of the arguments over legalization are essentially arguments about elasticity. Some say that strict enforcement will cut drug use because demand is elastic, and so higher prices and higher penalties will discourage use. Others say that strict enforcement only puts more money in the pockets of drug dealers; it pushes up the price, but dealers can pass that along to consumers because addiction makes demand inelastic. Because the drug market is illegal, it's been quite difficult to gather enough evidence to support one position or the other.

The concept of elasticity stretches to cover many other situations. For example, we can ask whether trimming Social Security payments will encourage older people to work rather than retire. In terms of elasticity, the question is "What is the percentage change in hours worked that would result from a certain percentage change in Social Security payments?" Or it is sometimes stated that cutting income taxes will encourage people to work more. These are questions about elasticity—about how quantities respond to changes in price.

Sometimes laws are proposed to increase the quantity of savings by offering tax breaks for saving, such as through individual retirement accounts, 401(k) plans, and the like. Will such accounts increase saving? In elasticity terms, the question is "What is the percentage increase in saving that would result from a certain percentage increase in the rate of return?" The evidence on the supply curve of financial capital is controversial, but at least in the short run, the elasticity of saving, with respect to interest rates and rates of return, is pretty inelastic. In plain English, this means that tax breaks for saving cause people to move their existing savings into the tax-free accounts, but at least in recent decades, they don't seem to increase overall levels of saving by very much.

Many of the confident assertions you hear about the results of various policies or strategies are actually assertions that there will be a large response to a change in price—perhaps a large response in quantity demanded of some good (in the case of cigarette taxes) or quantity supplied of some good (in the case of subsidies for alternative energy sources) or hours worked (in arguments over tax policy) or amount saved (in arguments over encouraging personal saving). When you don't feel well equipped to rummage through old economics journals in search of statistical estimates of elasticities, it can be intimidating to try to guess what the result of any particular policy might be—whether it's a sin tax on alcohol or an incentive to buy a hybrid car. But if you think about the basic concepts of whether demand and supply are likely to be elastic or inelastic in any given situation, you'll have a strategy for making a defensible prediction.

CHAPTER 6

The Labor Market and Wages

Economies are commonly described in terms of the goods and services they produce, but it's equally valid to say that the U.S. economy is what happens when 140 million or so Americans get up and head off for work in the morning. Supply and demand is the key to understanding labor markets, just as it is with markets for goods. In the labor market, instead of talking about the price of each good, we talk about the wage or the salary that each worker receives. Just as there are markets for many different goods and services produced by firms, the market for labor is really many different markets. There is a labor market for nurses, a market for firefighters, a market for computer programmers, a market for every different kind of job. But there's one major distinction: In goods markets, firms are the suppliers and households and individuals are the demanders. But in the labor market, household and individuals are the suppliers and firms are the demanders.

Demand for labor is a relationship between the wage or salary and the quantity of work that employers demand. A higher wage will tend to make businesses demand a lower quantity of labor, just in the same way that a lower price tends to make consumers demand less of a good. At an intuitive level, this ought to make some sense. Firms are trying to make money; if the cost of labor goes up, firms try to cut back on labor. How much an increase in wages reduces the quantity of labor demanded depends, as you might now expect, on the elasticity of demand for labor.

Demand for labor is often fairly inelastic in the short run. Firms have hired whom they've hired; they're going to work with whom they've got. But the demand for labor can be much more elastic in the long run, when firms have a chance to reorganize production. For example, firms might come up with new capital equipment or a new technology that allows them to reduce their number of employees if they have the time and the incentive to do so.

So, back to our trick questions (similar to those asked back in chapter 3): What moves demand for labor? The answer is *not* "wages." The wage changes the quantity of labor demanded but not the entire demand curve. What sorts of factors could change the demand for labor at every wage that could be paid?

Changes in demand for outputs—that is, different goods and services—will alter the demand for labor. A classically trained musician will have difficulty finding work if no one is attending concerts and symphonies are disbanding; an auto mechanic who specializes in repairing German cars will be in less demand in a city where most consumers drive American cars; and so forth.

For the past several centuries, workers have feared that new technologies would diminish the demand for their labor and drive down wages. The historical data show that while new technologies have made certain industries and jobs obsolete, they have also helped to create new industries and jobs. Moreover, the use of that new technology has made labor more productive, which results in higher wages.

Ultimately, the willingness of firms to hire workers depends on productivity: how much the labor is going to produce. If workers don't produce enough to justify their wage, firms won't hire them. If workers produce a lot more than their wage, then in a market economy we would expect some other firm to come along and hire that worker for a higher wage. Over time, and on average, wages are going to be determined by the value of what labor produces.

Now, let's think about supply of labor. Again, supply is a relationship—in this case, between the wage and the quantity of work supplied. A higher wage would typically mean a higher quantity of labor supplied, because a higher wage makes it more attractive to work. Precisely how much will an increase in wages increase the quantity of labor supplied? Once again, that depends on elasticity.

For many full-time workers in the economy (that is, workers who put in about forty hours of labor a week), the labor supply is pretty inelastic; a 10 percent increase in their wages leads to less than a 10 percent increase in their work hours. (Many full-time workers don't have the ability to adjust their hours of labor, so it's not clear how to estimate how they would prefer to respond to a rise in wages.) However, for part-time workers or for the secondary wage earner in a family, labor supply is more elastic; for that group, a 10 percent increase in wages often leads to more than a 10 percent increase in hours of work.

What causes the supply of labor to shift? A shift in labor supply might be caused by something like a rise or fall in the population; with more people available to work, more labor is supplied at a given wage, and vice versa. A demographic shift within a population can also alter labor supply. For example, in an aging population, more laborers will be leaving the workforce than joining it, and the supply of labor will fall. Social trends will affect labor supply as well, such as expectations about who should work. In the 1970s many American women who had been working in the household sector decided to take paying jobs outside the home, which caused a shift in the supply of labor at every given wage or price.

The markets for different types of labor require different skills and characteristics, which is what distinguishes a market for nurses, a market for hairstylists, a market for engineers, and so forth. In each market, the equilibrium wage will be determined by where the quantity of labor supplied is equal to the quantity of labor demanded in that particular market. With this supply-and-demand framework for labor in our minds, let's contemplate several issues that often arise in discussions about labor markets: the minimum wage, labor unions, discrimination, and employee benefits.

Since the 1930s, when a minimum wage was first adopted at the national level, there have been perennial arguments over whether to raise the minimum wage and by how much. The minimum wage is a form of price floor, in the sense that the law forbids an employer to pay less than that rate for labor. Knowing what we know about price floors, we would expect a national minimum wage to lead to a decreased demand for labor; that is, in response to a higher minimum wage, fewer employers would offer jobs for unskilled or low-skilled labor. Meanwhile, more people would be willing to supply this labor. Indeed, there's some evidence that in the United States, a 10 percent rise in the minimum wage can lead to 1 or 2 percent more unemployment for low-skilled workers. But that effect is quite small, and in other studies, the effect of a higher minimum wage on employment is indistinguishable from zero. This pattern suggests that in the United States, the minimum wage has not been much above the equilibrium wage in recent decades.

The public policy surrounding the minimum wage, however, is complicated because, like everything else, it involves trade-offs—trade-offs that can make both advocates and opponents of a higher minimum wage uncomfortable.

Here's an insight for opponents of a higher minimum wage to mull over: Let's say a 20 percent rise in the minimum wage leads to 4 percent fewer jobs for low-skilled workers (as some of the evidence suggests). But this also implies that a higher minimum wage leads to a pay raise for 96 percent of low-skilled workers. Many people in low-skill jobs don't have full-time, year-round jobs. So perhaps these workers work 4 percent fewer hours in a year, but they get 20 percent higher pay for the hours they do work. In this scenario, even if the minimum wage reduces the number of jobs or the number of hours available, raising it could still make the vast majority of low-skilled workers better off, as they'd work fewer hours at a higher wage.

There's another side to the argument, however. The short-term costs to an individual of not being able to find a job are quite large, while the benefits of slightly higher wages are (relatively speaking) somewhat smaller, so the costs to the few who can't find jobs because of a higher minimum wage may be in some sense more severe than the smaller benefits to individuals who are paid more. Those costs of higher unemployment are also unlikely to be spread evenly across the economy; instead, they are likely to be concentrated in communities that are already economically disadvantaged. Also, low-skill jobs are often entry-level jobs. If low-skill jobs become less available, the bottom rung on the employment ladder becomes less available to low-skilled workers. Thus, higher minimum wages might offer modest gains to the substantial number of low-skilled workers who get jobs, but impose substantial economic injury on those who can't.

There are alternatives to price floors, and economists often tend to favor such alternatives because they work with the forces of supply and demand. For example, if a government wants to boost wages for low-skilled workers, it could invest in skills-training programs. This would enable some of those workers to move into more skills-driven (and better paying) positions and would lower the supply of low-skilled labor, driving up their wages as well. The government could subsidize firms that hire low-skilled workers, enabling the firms to pay them a higher wage. Or it could subsidize the wages of low-skilled workers directly through programs such as the Earned Income Tax Credit, which provides a tax break to workers whose income is below a certain threshold. This policy increases the workers' net income without placing any financial burden on the employers.

Labor unions are another controversial aspect of labor markets. People tend to have strong emotional reactions to unions. Here, let's try to step back from the emotions and look at how unions function in an economy. Labor unions serve two basic functions. First, they seek to raise the wages of their members through contract negotiations, with the threat of a strike looming in the background. If the union is particularly hard-nosed in negotiations, odds are that the industry's employers will, over time, find ways to shrink the unionized workforce. The employer might do this through labor-saving machinery, through subcontracting and outsourcing to nonunion labor, and so forth. As a result, the size of militant unions will usually diminish over time; to some extent, that's what happened with the steel- and auto-workers' unions in the United States.

The second function of a union is to build a better, more productive workforce. The union accomplishes this through some obvious means, such as apprenticeships, and some more subtle ones, such as giving workers a sense of community and an emotional investment in the quality of their work. The union acts as a voice for the workers, communicating their concerns and needs to employers. These two functions of unions can seem contradictory—the cooperative Dr. Jekyll and the militant Mr. Hyde—but most unions act each way at different times.

Asking whether unions are "good" or "bad" for the economy will oversimplify the question. Unions clearly can coexist with high-income market-based economies; for example, many European countries have very high levels of unionization compared with the United States. The percentage of the workforce that is unionized in the United States has fallen from about 33 percent in the 1950s to about 13 percent in the 2000s. In the United Kingdom and Italy, for example, about 40 percent of the workforce belongs to a labor union. In some Scandinavian countries, unionization is closer to 70 or 80 percent. While these countries have their economic issues—as does every economy—there's no denying their standards of living are quite high by world standards. And as the size of unions diminishes in the United States, we have to wonder whether a potentially valuable voice for labor interests isn't being muted or lost.

One labor market issue even more likely to provoke high emotion than unions is discrimination. In economic terms, labor market discrimination occurs when a person is turned down for a job or paid less than an equally qualified worker because of that person's gender, race, age, religion, or some similar factor. In our supply-and-demand framework, we might say that because of discrimination, demand is lower for the labor of specific demographic groups in certain labor markets. However, economists have long pointed out that in some cases, discrimination has a variety of possible sources, and in some cases, markets will fight against discrimination.

For argument's sake, let's say a group of workers is paid less because its members are actually less productive. Perhaps this group of workers had inadequate schooling, or perhaps society discouraged people in this group from taking certain career paths early on. Paying these less qualified workers lower wages may seem like discrimination, but in this case the relevant discrimination isn't happening in the labor market; it happened earlier in these workers' lives.

Now let's consider two groups of workers who are equally productive, but some employers wish to discriminate against one of the groups and pay its members less well. On the flip side, workers who are paid less than they produce are attractive to a nondiscriminatory employer, who can offer these talented workers a more attractive wage. In this case, markets tend to fight against discrimination, and the worker and the new alternative employer both benefit from the employer's nondiscriminatory practices.

In some scenarios, however, markets can reinforce discrimination. If customers of a certain firm are bigoted and don't want to deal with workers from a certain ethnic group or don't think workers of a certain gender should perform a certain job, they might take their business to a firm that shares their prejudice. Or perhaps some workers are bigoted, and if forced to work with members of the undesired group, they will have low morale and productivity. In these cases, a profit-maximizing firm—even if management is not personally bigoted—will have an economic incentive to perpetuate discrimination in hiring to keep both productivity and sales high.

Finally, consider the form of discrimination in which workers have the same skills but work in different jobs with different pay. This is often the scenario with gender discrimination, sometimes called the "pink-collar ghetto." Women were traditionally often funneled into certain kinds of jobs with less chance for advancement or high earnings, whereas men were funneled into jobs requiring similar skills but with more potential for advancement and higher earnings. In such cases, discriminatory practices need to be addressed at the levels of training and entry-level hiring, to make sure all groups have equal access to whichever paths suit their talents.

In short, labor discrimination isn't a single phenomenon. It can happen at different points; it can stem from different actors in different markets; it can respond to differing sorts of incentives. Discrimination clearly continues to exist in American society, but at this stage in American history it's neither accurate nor helpful to place most of the blame on employers. You have to discover and target the sources of discrimination, wherever they may occur.

Finally, we've been talking about the price of labor in terms of wages—meaning money—but in the modern labor market, compensation for labor is often a combination of wages and benefits. Employees like benefits; they shift part of the financial responsibility for things such as health care, retirement savings, and so forth onto their employers. But an employer doesn't really care whether your wage is in the form of cash or insurance premiums; what we've been calling the equilibrium wage is, from an employer's point of view, just the total cost of an employee's compensation. This is why, when unions are negotiating contracts with employers, the union is often asked to choose between higher salaries and better benefits; it's all the same cost to the employer.

For private industry workers, on average about 70 percent of their total compensation comes in the form of wages, with the rest in the form of benefits. For example, about 10 percent of total compensation is retirement benefits, including Social Security, Medicare, pensions, and retirement savings accounts. Another 6 percent or so is vacation leave, and 6–7 percent is health insurance. But for any worker, when your employer offers you those "generous" benefits, you're still the one who's paying for them, in the form of lower take-home pay.

To many of us, a job feels like a social relationship between us and our employer. That's part of the relationship, of course; social interaction happens everywhere. But your pay and benefits are not determined by whether your boss likes you as a person or by the generosity of your employer. They're not determined by some standard of fairness, either. When it comes right down to it, labor is a market, and your wage or salary and benefits are the price on what you produce.

CHAPTER 7

Financial Markets and Rates of Return

There's a long-standing prejudice against financial capital markets. In the Middle Ages, the Roman Catholic Church considered charging interest on loans to be the sin of "usury." In some Islamic countries today, there is still a prohibition against charging interest, which, as you can imagine, can make running a bank a more complicated business. People may feel that the price in a goods market or the wage in a labor market isn't fair, but rarely do they feel that such payments should be treated as illegitimate. However, many people do have a nagging sense that the payment of interest—which is the price in a financial capital market—is somehow wrong. Why might this be?

One likely reason is that the essence of what is being exchanged in a financial capital market can be hard to grasp. Goods and services are tangible and visible. The old economic planners in the Soviet Union, about thirty years ago, had a list of 20 million goods (!) that were involved in the economy. Jobs are something we experience directly as part of our day-to-day lives. But interest payments and returns on financial capital are more abstract, and the workings of the financial market can seem invisible. The term "investment" also causes some confusion, because it's used in different ways. Sometimes "investment" refers to purchasing financial instruments such as stocks and bonds. Other times it refers to businesses buying physical capital, such as machinery or a factory. When you talk about the former, you're talking about investors as suppliers of financial capital seeking a maximum return for minimum risk. When you talk about the latter, you're actually discussing firms as demanders of financial capital, which they turn into physical investment assets. So "investment" can refer to either supply or demand—no wonder it's confusing! To sidestep this confusion, I will refer to "financial investment" when I mean supply of financial capital and "physical capital investment" when I mean the demand for financial capital that is used to build assets.

Financial capital markets can be interpreted using the same supply-and-demand framework as markets for goods and markets for labor. The supply of financial capital comes from those who save financial capital. We typically think of this supply of financial capital as coming from households. Firms save money, too, but since firms are owned by shareholders—and thus ultimately by households—you can think of firms who save as doing so on behalf of households.

Economists think of the supply of financial capital as a relationship between the quantity of capital supplied from households—that is, the savings of households—and the price they are paid for that capital, which is the rate of return on their investment. I'll often use the interest rate as a concrete example of a rate of return on capital, but returns on investments in corporate stock, or in buying a share of a small business, are also returns on capital. You might expect that the quantity of financial capital supplied should rise with the rate of return—that is, quantity supplied rises when price rises. In practice, however, the quantity that people save doesn't seem to rise a heck of a lot with rising rates of return. Instead, the amount that people save seems to depend more on habit, cultural patterns, and employer incentives such as matching contributions to retirement funds.

From an economist's perspective, demand for financial capital is also a relationship—in this case, between the quantity of capital demanded by borrowers and the rate of return they need to pay. Demand for financial capital comes from people who want funds now and are willing to pay a rate of return in exchange. With lower interest rates, a higher quantity of financial capital is demanded; for example, if someone wants to buy a car, they are more likely to buy when the interest rate on their car loan is low than when it is high. Similarly, firms are more likely to undertake physical capital investment in plants and equipment when they can borrow the money at a low rate of interest.

If you put together the demand and supply of financial capital, you get an equilibrium quantity of money saved and invested, at an equilibrium rate of return. There are many different markets for financial capital, just as there are many different labor and goods markets. One key difference lies in who is receiving the financial investment—a large firm, or a small firm, or an individual, or a government. A related factor is the financial history of whoever is receiving the funds: Do they have a good history of repayment, or a poor one, or no history at all? In addition, is the financial investment simply a loan, eventually to be repaid, or is the supplier buying a share of a business? All these factors play a role in determining the supply, demand, and rate of return in each financial capital market.

In thinking about how financial capital markets work, the key trade-off occurs across time. When you're buying and selling goods, it's happening at a point in time. Labor is performed at a point in time. But when you borrow money—that is, when you receive financial capital—you're buying the use of the funds in the present and paying for it later. This is what individuals do with a college loan or mortgage, and it's what firms do with loans for new equipment. On the supply side, when you save, you're agreeing to give someone your money now and be paid for it later. You're handing off the money on the expectation that you will receive repayment and a rate of return in the future.

So how do you calculate the worth of a loan in the present compared with what it costs to repay the loan in the future? Economists use the concept of present discounted value, which is a way of taking costs or benefits that occur at different points in time and comparing them directly. Present discounted value is the amount that a future payment is worth in the present, if it were to be received immediately.

To put it in practical terms, what is $100 to be received a year from now worth in the present? Assume, for the sake of the argument, that the interest rate in your bank account is 10 percent. So you pull out your handy-dandy calculator and determine that if you were given $90.91 right now and invested it for a year at 10 percent, you would have $100 a year from now. Thus, the present value of $100 a year from now would be $90.91.

What's $100 two years from now worth in the present? If the interest rate is 10 percent, you pull out your handy-dandy calculator again and find that $82.64 invested right now would equal $100 at the end of two years. So the present value of $100 two years in the future is $82.64 in the present. The formal version of this calculation is the present discounted value equals the future value divided by a quantity equal to one plus the interest rate raised to the power of t years. Or writing this as an equation: $PDV = FV/(1 + r)^t$. When there is a series of payments at different times in the future, a present discounted value calculation can be done for each future payment—and then summed up for an overall present value.

This concept of present discounted value is heavily used in business and finance. Businesses have to think about investment expenses they incur in the present when they build new plants and equipment and compare the returns they would get in the future after they produced stuff with that equipment. For example, let's say a firm wants to build a factory that costs $2 million, and it calculates that five years from now it will earn $3 million. That $3 million five years in the future would need to be discounted back to the present to compare it directly with the $2 million the firm is thinking about spending in the present.

If you have a home mortgage, present discounted value is a key concept, too. If you have a thirty-year mortgage and you look at your total payments, you will see that you are paying a huge amount of interest over time. But the idea of present value explains why this is so: the total value of all your loan payments, including interest, is exactly equal to the present discounted value of your house, which is the purchase price. After all, you could either pay cash for your house—that's paying the purchase price in the present—or you could borrow money and pay over time. Those ways of paying have the same economic value. It's much easier for me to pay off my house slowly, rather than all at once. But the present discounted value is the same in both cases.

When it comes to social policy, lots of government programs involve buying something now or building something now in return for a later payoff. Lots of environmental policies have a cost now and a benefit in the future. Traffic safety might involve building a highway now for saving lives in the future. Educating children now pays off as a more skilled workforce in the future. When a government plans its policies, it needs to analyze the costs and benefits using this idea of present discounted value.

Here's one odd application of present discounted value. When most state lotteries announce their big jackpots, they add up all the payments you would receive over thirty years. They don't tell you the present value of these payments; they just add up the checks that you would get over thirty years. Some years back, the New Jersey state legislature proposed a law that if an older person won the lottery, that person could request a lump payment, rather than distribution over thirty years. As a result, the lottery commission had to explain that their announced jackpot paid over thirty years was not the present discounted value; the present value was only about two-thirds that amount. Now, that smaller figure wasn't chopped liver; it was still a huge payout, but it was not quite as large as advertised. The lotteries use the sum of payments over time, not present discounted value, to make their prizes look bigger than they actually are.

Now that you've got the basics of how the financial capital market works, let's focus on the firms that demand financial capital. Firms that want to make capital investments can turn to several sources for funding. One is retained earnings, which are more commonly known as profits. "Retained" means the firm decided to hold on to that money and reinvest it in the business rather than pay it out to shareholders as dividends. You can think of this as a firm doing its own saving and reinvesting in itself on behalf of outside investors. For long-established firms, retained earnings are the primary source of capital to fund physical investment.

Firms can also borrow money in one of two ways. They can borrow money from a bank or they can issue bonds. Bank lending is familiar to most people; bonds, somewhat less so. A bond has a face value, an interest rate, and a time. For example, a basic bond with a face value of $1,000 and an 8 percent interest rate for ten years will pay 8 percent interest each year for ten years, and at the end of ten years, it will repay that face value of $1,000. A bond is just a way for firms to borrow money; but instead of borrowing from a bank, they borrow from buyers, who may be individuals or organizations such as pension funds or investment companies. If a firm doesn't repay its bonds, it can be legally declared bankrupt and taken over. Of course, a company will borrow financial capital only if it believes the return on its capital investment will be high enough so that it can make the interest payments and still have some funds left over as profit.

The interest rates paid on bonds vary depending on risk. A highly profitable firm such as Walmart could issue bonds at a relatively low rate of interest because people know it is likely to repay. Likewise, governments—at least stable ones—issue bonds at low rates of return. On the other hand, a less stable firm might issue a high-interest-rate, high-risk bond, which is sometimes called a "junk bond."

The final way for a firm to raise money is through equities, more commonly known as corporate stock. Corporate stock essentially gives its owners part ownership of the firm. So if a firm has a total of one hundred shares of stock, and you own twenty of them, you own 20 percent of the firm. If the firm pays out its profits as dividends, then you receive those dividends in proportion to your ownership of the firm's stock. If the firm were sold, then 20 percent of the sales price of the firm should come to you. However, unlike bonds, which have predetermined interest rates, there's no guarantee that the owner of a stock will receive anything like regular payments—or any return at all. The return when buying and selling stocks can be higher than bonds, or lower—or even negative.

Selling stock is often a way for younger and smaller companies to raise money. Smaller firms will often sell some of their stock to specialized investors such as venture capital firms or "angel investors" who want to put their money into small companies. As the small firms grow larger, at some point they often need a big infusion of capital to sustain that growth, and that's when they sell stock on the open market in a public offering. Once the firm is fully established, it is more likely to use its own profits and, in some cases, bonds or borrowing for capital investment. It will issue more stock only for huge expansions, such as buying out another firm. A firm can't issue stock indefinitely, because stock is part ownership of a firm, and more stock means that the pie of the firm is sliced up more ways. If a company has one hundred shares of stock, then next year issues one hundred more shares, the original investors' ownership is diluted, and the company is likely to be seen as a poor investment.

Raising capital and investing are extraordinarily important because the physical capital and innovations that come from investment contribute mightily to expanding productivity and raising the standard of living over time. The United States has historically lagged behind much of the industrialized world in the proportion of its economy that is devoted to savings and investment. The ability of an economy to gain the benefits of capital investment is built on the willingness of households to save and invest.

CHAPTER 8

Personal Investing

One of the most important sets of economic decisions any household faces is how to save for retirement. It can be intimidating, because the sums that are desired by retirement age are so large. No one gets to live their life over dozens of times, trying out a different retirement strategy each time. When it comes to planning for retirement, you get just one try. From our supply-and-demand perspective, decisions about retirement savings involve the supply side of the financial capital market. People who save and invest supply financial capital to this market with the goal of increasing their wealth without taking on too much risk.

The key to accumulating wealth over a lifetime lies in the power of compound interest, which works in this way. Let's say that you start with $100 and an interest rate of 10 percent. At the end of the first year, you'll have $110 in that account—the original deposit plus the interest. In year two, you're earning 10 percent on $110, making a total of $121; in year three, 10 percent on $121; in year four, 10 percent on $133.10; and so on. Notice that the amount of interest increases a bit each year, or compounds, because the base on which it is calculated is growing each year. Over time, the power of compound interest can lead to gratifyingly large returns on saving.

Here's the formula for calculating how much a financial investment will grow over a period of time at a certain rate of return. Take the amount you start with (the present value), multiply it by one plus the interest rate, raised to the power of however many years that money is saved. That will give you the future value. Grab a calculator and try plugging in different values for present value and interest rate, and watch how much the value rises over ten, twenty-five, and forty years of saving. You might be amazed.

Total Accumulated on Original Savings of $1,000 over Ten, Twenty-Five, and Forty Years

TIME	ANNUAL INTEREST RATE		
	5 percent	10 percent	15 percent
Ten years	$1,629	$2,594	$4,046
Twenty-five years	$3,386	$10,835	$32,918
Forty years	$7,039	$45,259	$267,863

Note: Compound interest is calculated using the formula $PV(1 + r)^t = FV$, where PV is the present value (in this example, $1,000), *r* is the annual interest rate, t is time, and FV is the future value.

When thinking about retirement saving, the time horizons are quite long, which gives compound interest time to do its work. If a person took $1,000 at age twenty-five and invested it at 5 percent a year, when that person reached age sixty-five, that $1,000 would have increased to a little over $7,000. In a more aggressive investment, with a 10 percent return—roughly speaking, what the U.S. stock market has delivered on average over the decades—after ten years, you're up to about $2,600. After twenty-five years, it would be almost $11,000. Finally, $1,000 at a 10 percent annual return over forty years works out to $45,000. Want to get even more aggressive? At a 15 percent annual rate of return—which would require some luck!—over ten years, your original $1,000 would have reached $4,000. Over twenty-five years, your original $1,000 would have built up to $33,000. And the big number: $1,000 at 15 percent over forty years works out to $267,863—an almost unbelievable multiple.

To be honest, a 15 percent rate of return is a stretch. But the forty-year time frame makes sense because it is roughly the length of a working life—from age twenty-five to sixty-five. It's not at all implausible that if you can put aside $5,000 each year starting at around age twenty-five or thirty and let it accumulate, you will have more than a million dollars accumulated at retirement. This isn't a get-rich-quick scheme, but the results are nonetheless impressive—and more important, realistic.

All that said, when you look at a financial investment, you need to think about not just the rate of return—not just the expected or hoped-for rate of 5, 10, or 15 percent per year—but also three other characteristics: risk, liquidity, and tax treatment. Choosing which characteristics matter most for you will involve trade-offs among these factors and the rate of return.

The risk of an investment is defined as how much higher or lower the rate of return might be versus the investment's average expected value. It's the financial capital market's way of saying "your mileage may vary." A U.S. Treasury bond is a very low-risk investment; you're virtually certain to get the promised rate of return. Investing in a firm producing a new technology is a much higher risk. You have no idea if the firm will succeed, but it might succeed beyond all expectations. All other things being equal, risk is undesirable. That is, if two investments promise the same average rate of return, you should prefer the one for which the rate has varied less over time—the one with lower risk. As a result, higher-risk investments such as buying stock in new small companies typically have to offer a higher average expected rate of return to attract investors and compensate for the fluctuations they're asking you to endure.

The risk of investing in any specific company or any specific bond can be reduced by diversifying your investments. "Diversification" means buying a large number of different investments, to reduce the overall risk. Diversification works because those investments that do unexpectedly badly will be offset to some extent by other investments that do unexpectedly well. So, as the old saying goes, don't put all your eggs in one basket. Perhaps the easiest way for an individual investor to diversify is by investing in a mutual fund, a fund that combines a group of stocks or a group of bonds in a single investment. We'll talk more about mutual funds in just a bit.

"Liquidity" refers to how easy it is to turn your investment into cash. A bank account is quite liquid; it's easy to get your money out. A house is not very liquid, because it takes some time and energy to sell it. Financial investments such as stocks and bonds lie between these extremes. In general, other things such as return and risk being equal, you'll prefer to have a liquid investment.

A final characteristic to consider is how the investment is favored by the tax code. Certain investment opportunities are exempt from federal income tax—interest from bonds issued by state and municipal governments, for example. Other returns on your investment are taxable, but you don't pay the tax until you sell the investment; this applies to capital gains from the value of stocks and capital gains in the value of your home, and payments from certain retirement accounts.

Tax breaks can obviously benefit an investor, but in a world of trade-offs, a higher tax break means less of something else. For example, a tax-free bond issued by a state or local government tends to pay a lower rate of return than a taxable bond. You avoid the tax, but your rate of return isn't as good. As a general rule, people with high incomes and high tax bills should care more about tax breaks and choose their investments accordingly. Those with lower incomes and lower tax bills don't need to worry as much about the tax advantages of their investments.

Your age—or, more specifically, how far you are from retirement—should figure into your financial investment choices as well. After retirement, most people aren't earning much income; therefore, they don't pay a lot of taxes, and the tax break doesn't matter as much to them. But during their main earning years, say ages thirty to fifty-five, most people will have higher income and tax bills, and so tax breaks will matter more.

Now let's consider a variety of possible financial investments, how they measure up on four key characteristics—rate of return, risk, liquidity, and tax status—and how trade-offs work among the characteristics. We're going to focus in particular on the trade-off between return and risk, judging levels of risk by using what Burton Malkiel, the Yale economics professor who wrote the classic *A Random Walk Down Wall Street* (1973 [2003]), has called the sleeping scale: If your money were in this financial investment, how well would you sleep at night?

Let's start with bank accounts. Bank accounts offer a very low rate of return and no tax breaks on interest, but they're extremely safe and very liquid. In the United States, the government guarantees the safety of your money in typical bank accounts through the Federal Deposit Insurance Corporation (FDIC). On Burton Malkiel's sleeping scale of risk, if all your money is in a bank account, you could be comatose. The level of risk is very close to zero.

The next step up from bank accounts might be a money market fund. A money market fund invests in a lot of very low-risk bonds. They might be bonds issued by the federal government or by very large companies. You'll get a slightly better return from a money market than from a bank account. The funds are still pretty liquid, although not quite as liquid as in a bank account; such funds are pretty safe, although not quite as safe as a bank account. On Malkiel's sleeping scale of risk, with your money in a money market fund, you can take long afternoon naps and get a sound night's sleep.

A next category of investment is certificates of deposit, or CDs. A CD is an agreement to deposit funds with a bank or financial institution for a set period of time. It might be six months, or a year, or several years, but whatever the period, you can't touch those funds during that time. In exchange, you get a higher rate of return than you would in a regular bank account. Clearly, funds in a CD aren't very liquid; in a pinch, you could retrieve your money, but you'd pay a penalty. But the rate of return is better than that of a bank account and more or less guaranteed. On Malkiel's scale, you're still sleeping soundly at night.

What about a diversified portfolio of corporate bonds or a mutual fund that invests in these kinds of bonds? Remember what a bond is: a bond is an investment with a predetermined rate of return over a fixed time period. Typically, a portfolio of diverse corporate bonds will get you a better rate of return than a certificate of deposit. If you buy those bonds through a mutual fund, usually it's fairly easy to turn your investment back into cash, if you wish. However, the risk is somewhat higher; in most cases, the rate of return on a bond is a fixed nominal rate of interest. That means that if inflation and nominal interest rates rise, you're locked into that lower rate of interest, and you'll suffer financially as a result. So you're bearing a little more risk if you're in a bond fund. The sleeping scale might say that you're still sleeping all night, but now you're having the occasional bad dream or two.

The next option along the line would be a diversified portfolio of corporate blue chip stocks. By blue chip stocks, I mean stocks in big, well-known companies: General Electric, Walmart, ExxonMobil, and so forth. A mutual fund that buys a lot of these well-established and historically profitable firms will need to provide a better return than a bond portfolio over time, because stocks—even blue chip stocks—are riskier than bonds. There is a tax advantage to stocks, however, because you don't usually have to pay taxes on your capital gains until you sell. Thus, if you hold on to stock for a long time, you can defer paying taxes until you receive the capital gains. Also, the diversity in your portfolio mitigates risk. A drop in the value of any one company's stock is not likely to hurt you too much. If you bought these stocks through a mutual fund, the investment would be fairly liquid, too.

However, your investment in a stock portfolio is not only unguaranteed, but it can *lose* value. In the stock market crash of 1987, for example, the stock market lost 20 percent of its value in a day. In the slower crash of 2000–2001, the average of the stocks traded on the New York Stock Exchange fell 18 percent over the unlucky thirteen months between August 2000 and September 2001. During the recession of 2007–2009, the average of stocks traded on the New York Stock Exchange fell by more than half from October 2007 to March

2009. So if you're investing in a mutual fund that buys a lot of stocks, according to the sleeping scale of risk, you would do some tossing and turning before you dozed and maybe would experience some vivid dreams before awakening.

Want more risk? How about a diversified portfolio of growth stocks? Growth stocks are investments in less-established companies that tend, on average, to pay a higher return than a portfolio of blue chips. With luck, you might do better than that historical market average of 10 percent for a few years. Once again, if the stock is purchased through a mutual fund, your money will be fairly liquid. Diversifying across these stocks mitigates your risk a bit, but the companies themselves are riskier. For example, from August 2000 to September 2001, when blue chips lost 18 percent of their value on the New York Stock Exchange, the smaller growth companies, which tend to be listed on the NASDAQ stock exchange, lost an average of *60 percent* of their value. That's not just a loss; that's a meltdown. So in terms of the sleeping scale, if you're in a mutual fund that's all growth companies, you're going to have nightmares from time to time. But if you can hold on for the long run, through all the ups and downs and ups again, you'll wind up pretty well-rested.

When you buy a home, it's not just a place to live; it's also an investment in real estate. For most people, their primary residence is by far the biggest single investment they'll ever make. Historically, the rate of return on owning a home has been solidly positive on average, but for individual homeowners in a depressed market, waiting for their homes' values to rise can take a long time. In other words, the risk is fairly low in the long term, measured in decades, but much higher in the short term, measured in months and years. Liquidity is low for houses, but on the positive side, tax breaks are available for buying a home. Mortgage interest, for example, is tax deductible, and any capital gain from the value of your house is not taxed if you roll it over into the purchase of a new house. It's hard to place investment in a home on the sleeping scale because, on a personal level, a home is far more than an investment. At least a house gives you a place to live and to sleep! But housing may also cause you some sleepless nights, as millions of households experienced in the aftermath of the drop in housing prices that started in 2006.

A final set of investments available to individuals is precious metals—gold, platinum, and so on. These are among the riskiest investments an individual can make. Prices move sharply in precious metals markets. If you time the buying and selling just right, you can make a lot of money, but if you time it wrong, you can take a spectacular loss. On the sleeping scale, we're talking bouts of insomnia. Personally, I leave these investments to the professionals.

With this menu of choices in mind, what's the best strategy for personal investing? The truth is there's no one-size-fits-all approach. A useful starting point is to consider your time horizon. Risk in the stock market can be high in the short term, but if you're saving for the far future—say, a retirement that is several decades away—the ups and downs of the stock market will tend to cancel one another out, and over the long run you are likely to be compensated for your patience. However, if you're looking at the money for this week's groceries, for next month's mortgage, for next semester's tuition, you probably can't tolerate much risk. You need your money safe and liquid, and to heck with the rate of return. If your horizon is in between—say, you're planning on buying a new car or a bigger house a few years down the road—you might not be risk-tolerant enough for stocks, but you can take bigger risks than a basic bank account. Bonds and CDs might be your best bet. Your time horizon is a critical determinant of your tolerance for risk.

Perhaps the biggest mistake most people make with their retirement money is not taking enough risk, especially early in life. They're so concerned about safety that they put too much of their money in bonds, bank accounts, and money market funds. Even people who are in their fifties and sixties can often expect to live twenty or thirty or more years. That's a long time for compound interest to accumulate.

Why not just pick the stock that has the highest rate of return and put all your money in that stock? Why mess around with all this risk and liquidity and diversification stuff? The problem, of course, is that nobody actually knows which stock will offer the highest rate of return in the future. The price of a stock is based on the market's estimate of that company's future profits. What makes a stock price rise is new information suggesting that the company will be more profitable than previously believed. But the arrival of such new information is, by its nature, unpredictable. Since you can't predict what new information will arrive, whether a stock price moves up or down next will be unpredictable—what statisticians and economists call a "random walk."

The stock you really want to buy is the one that, right now, everyone else thinks will do poorly (low quantity demanded, thus low price) but that, in the future, everyone will think will do great (high quantity demanded, thus a high price). Maybe—*maybe*—a sophisticated professional investor who works sixty or eighty hours a week can pick those kinds of stocks on a regular basis. But if you're sitting at home looking at the *Wall Street Journal*, which was written yesterday about news that happened the day before that, you need to understand that professionals in the stock market knew much of that information weeks ago. You're not going to outguess the market that way. Financial journalists at places such as the *Wall Street Journal* and *Forbes* magazine sometimes put together a "dartboard fund," in which someone literally throws darts across the room at the Financial section of a newspaper pinned to the wall and buys whatever stocks they hit. Then they compare that dartboard fund to results from professional investors. The results? The dartboard comes out pretty much average—and so do the professional investors as a group.

All personal investment advice is ultimately based on one fact: you need to save some money, and the sooner you begin the better. There are always a million reasons not to save when you're in your twenties, and in your thirties, and in your forties, and in your fifties, but if you don't steadily put money aside, there is no clever strategy you can deploy at age sixty or sixty-five to suddenly enjoy a high level of income after retirement.

CHAPTER 9

From Perfect Competition to Monopoly

Up to this point, we have discussed how economists see the economy from a microeconomic perspective. You might summarize this perspective by saying that it involves the forces of supply and demand interacting in markets for goods, labor, and financial capital. With this chapter, we start our discussion of how these market forces can go astray. For example, profit seeking by firms is a double-edged sword for society as a whole. The desire for profit pressures firms to produce innovative products with high quality and low cost, which benefits consumers. But profit seeking can also encourage conspiring to raise prices, skimping on quality, misleading consumers, producing pollution, and other undesirable behaviors. One of the government's roles in the economy is to set up a framework of law and regulation that encourages the positive outcomes of profit seeking, but discourages the darker manifestations of this economic force. This chapter offers a discussion of how monopoly and other less-than-competitive markets work, and the subsequent chapter, a discussion of government policy responding to anticompetitive behavior. The chapters that follow then look at other problems that are likely to arise with unregulated markets, including pollution, poverty, inequality, dysfunctional insurance markets, and a lack of incentives for innovation or building infrastructure.

I've been using the word "firm" casually thus far to refer to businesses, so before talking about how firms compete, we should take a moment to unpack just what is meant by a "firm." In the U.S. economy, firm size ranges from single-person operations to megacorporations. There are three broad types of firm ownership. Proprietorships are owned by a single individual. Partnerships are owned by a group of individuals. Corporations are organizations that have a legal existence independent of their owners; they may be owned by an individual or a group of stockholders. In the early 2000s, there were about 18 million proprietorships, 2 million partnerships, and 5 million corporations in the U.S. economy. But corporations, although not the biggest group numerically, dominate in size. Those 5 million corporations had about $20 trillion in sales, whereas the 2 million partnerships had only about $2.5 trillion in sales. The 18 million proprietorships combined had a total of about $1 trillion in sales.

The range of industries across the U.S. economy is truly extraordinary. If you page through government statistics, some of the main categories include agriculture, mining, utilities, construction, manufacturing (which, of course, includes a lot of different products), retail (a lot of variety there as well), transportation, telecommunications, broadcasting, finance, real estate, professional and technical services, waste management, education, health care, arts, entertainment, accommodations, food service, auto repair, laundry services—the list goes on and on. You may think that almost everybody works at a really big company. That's actually not quite true; firms that have 500 or more employees employ roughly half the labor force, but firms with 500 or fewer employees employ the other half. In particular, firms with twenty or fewer employees employ about one-fifth of all workers. In an average economic year, about half a million businesses start and about half a million businesses die in the United States. As you might expect, most of these are small firms, but several hundred of these startups begin with more than 500 employees.

Any type of firm, of any size, in any industry, might engage in one of four different types of competition. You can think of these four types as lying along a spectrum. At one end is "perfect competition," in which many small firms are making nearly identical products. At the opposite extreme there is "monopoly," in which a single producer has all or nearly all the sales in a given market. In between, "monopolistic competition" refers to a situation in which many firms compete to sell somewhat different products; all restaurants serve food, for example, but what they serve varies in style and quality. Finally, the case of "oligopoly" is a bit closer to monopoly, except instead of one firm having all the sales, a few firms have most or all the sales in a given market. Let's discuss each of these in more detail.

The key characteristic of a perfectly competitive industry is price taking—that is, perfectly competitive firms must take the market price as given. Firms in these industries have no choice but to be price takers because, from the consumer's point of view, substitution is easy. If a perfectly competitive firm raises the price of its widgets by a dollar, the consumer will simply buy someone else's identical, cheaper widgets. Firms can enter and exit a perfectly competitive industry easily because the products tend to be straightforward to make; they're usually well-understood objects such as socks, wood screws, and so forth. In this competitive environment, prices will closely reflect the cost of production, because competition drives the price down to the bare minimum above production cost. As a result, firms in a perfectly competitive market tend to make similar rates of low profits.

Truly perfect competition, in the textbook sense, is like pure gas in a laboratory: It's a theoretical extreme. Products are rarely identical. People will prefer one style and color of socks to another, or prefer the way their screwdrivers fit with the head of one wood screw or another. There are also many intangibles to consider, such as the reliability of the supply or the quality of the product. But the idea of perfect competition, with identical products and price competition, serves as a useful benchmark. A number of everyday products, such as gasoline, television sets, and farm products, operate in markets that are very close to perfect competition, in the sense that many products are nearly identical and price competition is intense.

Monopoly, at the opposite extreme, is the situation in which a single seller has all or most of the sales in a given market. For example, Microsoft dominated the market for computer operating systems in the late 1990s and the early 2000s. About two or three decades earlier,

IBM dominated the market for mainframe computers. Xerox once dominated the market for photocopying machines. The U.S. Postal Service dominates daily letter delivery. Most people have no choice about who provides their garbage pickup or their electricity. Those are usually monopolies as well, although at a local or regional level.

How do monopolies come to exist? Usually some barrier prevents other firms from entering the market. For example, let's say the barrier to entry is a patent on a technology, such as on a new drug invented by a pharmaceutical company. The company that owns such a patent is the only one that can make that drug, at least for a certain period of time, and so it may be the only drug company in the industry that sells the drug, creating a monopoly. In fact, the economic argument in favor of patents is that they promote innovation with the promise of a monopoly for a limited time. The trade-off for this limited monopoly is that the public benefits from the incentive for new inventions.

Some monopolies are created by law. For example, the U.S. Postal Service has a monopoly on mail, and in most cities the local government has a monopoly on garbage pickup. Yet another barrier to entry can be what's called a natural monopoly. A natural monopoly occurs when the industry has economies of scale that give a large, established firm an advantage over any new entrants. Imagine, for example, that electricity can be produced at a lower average cost in a large hydroelectric dam than in a small solar plant. Once you've built the dam, small producers of electricity will find it very difficult to enter the market—even if they might possibly be cost-competitive if they could produce at a much larger scale. Theoretically, a monopoly can also arise if all the large firms in an industry merge, or at least agree to act in coordination—although this would be illegal conduct under the U.S. antitrust laws that will be discussed in the next chapter.

Unlike industries with perfect competition, monopolies have some power to set prices in their markets above production costs, and therefore to earn higher profits. A monopoly will set the price for a product according to the elasticity of demand for that product. If demand for the product is highly inelastic, then the monopoly can raise the price with only a small decline in the quantity demanded. Again, consider a pharmaceutical company with a monopoly on a certain drug. People are going to pay a lot of money for that drug if it's the only one that works for them.

Monopolies don't have to take their profits in only monetary form, however. The economist Sir John Hicks (1935, p. 8) once wrote, "The best of all monopoly profits is a quiet life." With no competitors, you can relax a bit. In a perfectly competitive market, you can't relax for a minute. The nineteenth-century economist and philosopher John Stuart Mill (1848 [1878], p. 376) wrote, "Wherever competition is not, monopoly is, and monopoly in all its forms is the taxation of the industrious for the support of indolence, if not plunder." At their worst, monopolies have a choice between lazy inefficiency and the ability to suck consumers dry through higher prices.

Monopolistic competition lies closer to perfect competition than to monopoly. Monopolistic competition occurs when many firms compete by selling "differentiated" products, meaning products that are similar but not identical to one another. When you go to shop for pants, for example, you could buy jeans, or you could buy chinos, or you could buy wool dress pants, and you might go to a different store for each. These stores are competing to sell pants, but not with identical products. Another way for firms to differentiate themselves is location; you might fill up at the gas station that's along your way home from work every week and never visit the one that's two blocks out of your way. Or firms might offer incentives to buyers: Should I buy this book at online retailer A, which offers me 20 percent off list, or retailer B, which offers me free shipping?

Like a monopoly, a monopolistically competitive firm does have some power to set its price based on the elasticity of demand, but it doesn't have as much power as an actual monopoly to raise price. It still has to consider its competitors' prices. Also there are no barriers to entry for monopolistic competitors. You can have more restaurants; you can have more clothing stores; you can have more gas stations. So if restaurants selling barbecue are really popular in your neighborhood, more will open over time. As a result of this process of entry and exit, monopolistically competitive firms can make higher-than-usual profits for the short run but not in the long run. The higher their profits, the more attractive the industry is for competitors to enter, and additional competition will drive prices and profits back down.

The nice thing about monopolistic competition from a consumer's point of view is it gives firms a strong incentive for spotting trends, making innovations, and offering variety. A big unanswered question for economists is whether a free market provides an appropriate amount of variety. Most of us like a world with some variety; we wouldn't choose to live in a world where everyone wore blue jeans and white T-shirts and ate American cheese sandwiches on white bread every single day, even if the economy were more efficient producing only one kind of jeans and T-shirt and cheese and bread. On the other hand, are we really living better lives because we have hundreds of styles of basketball shoes or scented soaps to choose from? The answer is not at all clear.

Finally, an oligopoly is closer to monopoly than to perfect competition. It's a situation in which a small number of firms have most or all the revenues in a given market. For example, Coke and Pepsi dominate sales in the soft drink market. For any oligopoly, the key question is whether the firms compete hard against one another, in which case they're acting like perfect competitors and driving down profits, or whether they (perhaps implicitly) collude to hold prices high, like a monopoly.

Business leaders are often not particularly in favor of competition. After all, would you rather try to run a perfectly competitive firm (scrabbling and scratching against many competitors for a tiny profit) or a monopoly (with great freedom to set your own price, change your own production methods, and receive high profits for your firm)? Competition makes businesspeople's lives extremely difficult. Consumers, on the other hand, should favor competition, because competition provides innovative products at a lower cost. Competitive markets are the ultimate way of favoring consumers.

CHAPTER 10

Antitrust and Competition Policy

It may seem as if economists are perpetually singing the praises of competitive markets. But for centuries, economists have been well aware that firms often seek to avoid competition. As Adam Smith (1776 [1994]), the founding father of economics, famously wrote in *The Wealth of Nations*, "People of the same trade seldom meet together, even for merriment and diversion, but the conversation ends in a conspiracy against the public, or in some contrivance to raise prices." How can firms be prevented from conspiring and encouraged to compete?

In the United States the primary federal agencies that carry out antitrust and competition policy are the Federal Trade Commission (FTC) and the U.S. Department of Justice. The FTC is an independent agency that reports to Congress. It's headed by five commissioners who are nominated by the president and subject to confirmation by the Senate. They serve seven-year terms, and no more than three of them may be members of the same political party. The U.S. Department of Justice has an antitrust division dedicated to investigating and prosecuting antitrust cases.

One of the main tasks of these authorities is to ensure that firms aren't merging their way into monopoly. Under law, the federal government has the power to review mergers before they happen. The U.S. government is far from hostile to mergers; the FTC's Web site even says, "Most mergers actually benefit competition and consumers, by allowing firms to operate more efficiently." But it also warns, "Some mergers are likely to lessen competition. That, in turn, can lead to higher prices, reduced availability of goods or services, lower quality of products, and less innovation." The underlying philosophy is a balanced one; the United States has a fundamentally free market economy, and firms are allowed to make their own choices. But if firms seek to make choices that will limit competition and impose costs on consumers, we want the government to have the ability to step in.

Any merger involving a firm that does more than $100 million in sales annually must be reported to the government before it happens. In the mid-2000s, about two thousand mergers each year crossed this threshold. About half of those were deals in which the price paid for the merger was $200 million or less; about 10 percent of the deals were $1 billion or more. Of this group, about two hundred mergers each year trigger a government request for more information. Such a request leads to three possible outcomes: the government might block the merger; it might set conditions on the merger (often requiring that part of the business be sold off at the time of the merger); or it might let the merger go through as planned.

But the issue of firms avoiding competition doesn't end there. Firms can engage in anticompetitive behavior without actually merging—for example, if they agree to act together to raise prices. While outright agreements to raise prices are clearly illegal and thus unusual, the FTC has the task of deciding if industries are concentrated in a way that makes it possible for businesses to pursue more subtle strategies that lead to higher prices without an explicit agreement.

One task of antitrust enforcement is defining how much competition exists in a market, then determining whether it's sufficient. The simplest way to measure the extent of competition in a market is called the four-firm concentration ratio. You calculate the market share of the four largest firms in the industry and add them up. The extreme case would be a market with only four firms; those four would make up 100 percent of the market share, and so the four-firm ration would be 100. A higher number for the four-firm concentration ratio implies that competition is somewhat limited. But while the four-firm ratio is a good quick-and-dirty measure of competition, it's not always subtle enough. Consider an industry with eight firms, and say that four of the eight each has 20 percent of the market, and the other four have 5 percent each. Here, the four-firm ratio would be 80 percent. But what if among an industry with eight firms, one had 65 percent of the market and all the rest had 5 percent each? You'd still get a four-firm ratio of 80 percent, but in real-world terms, you would be a lot closer to monopoly in this market.

The Herfindahl-Hirschman Index (HHI) is a more sophisticated way of measuring the extent of competition. This formula takes the market share of every firm in the market—that is, the percentage of total sales going to each firm—squares it, and adds up the sum of the squares. For example, if a monopoly firm has 100 percent of the market, its HHI would be 100 squared, or 10,000. A market with 1,000 small firms, each with 0.1 percent of the market, would have an HHI of 10. Thus, low numbers indicate high competition in a market, and vice versa.

A couple of decades ago, it used to be that if the HHI of a market after a proposed merger was less than 1,000, the Federal Trade Commission would usually approve the merger. If the HHI was between 1,000 and 1,800, the FTC would scrutinize the deal and make case-by-case decisions. When the HHI was greater than 1,800, the FTC tended to challenge the merger, either by tacking on conditions or blocking it entirely. However, in the past twenty years or so, the FTC and the Department of Justice have moved away from mechanical measuring of market shares, in part because it can be hard to figure out just where an individual market begins and ends.

A classic legal case for the problem of defining the size of a "market" was decided in 1956. The DuPont company was accused of monopolizing cellophane production. DuPont readily admitted that it produced, at that time, about 70 percent of all cellophane. However, the company said that the right way to define the market was as all "flexible packaging materials," which included all sorts of other products, such as waxed paper. With the market defined this way, DuPont held less than 20 percent of the market. Ultimately, the U.S. Supreme Court agreed with DuPont's argument, and thus found that although it made almost all the cellophane, it wasn't a monopoly in the relevant market for flexible wrapping paper.

A similar problem arose in the 1990s. Microsoft had 80 percent or more of the market for computer operating systems, but was "operating systems" the right category for this market? Should you include the entire software market? If you included computer games, for example, Microsoft's share of the overall software market would be much smaller. Microsoft argued that it was a small fish in a big software pond; the government held that Microsoft was a huge fish in a tiny operating system pond. In this case, the courts agreed with the prosecution and defined "operating systems" as the narrower market. The government lawsuit against Microsoft was eventually settled out of court, with Microsoft agreeing to make it easier for outside competitors to link their software to the Microsoft operating system, so that the competitors could compete more effectively with other Microsoft software products.

Imagine the complications you'd encounter when judging competition in the global marketplace. There are, as of this writing, three large U.S.-based automobile manufacturers—General Motors, Ford, and Chrysler—in varying states of financial health. That sounds like a highly concentrated market. But of course, these companies also have to compete in the U.S. market with automakers from around the world. It would be absurd to say that the three U.S.-based companies form an oligopoly that dominates the U.S. auto market.

The global perspective goes a long way toward explaining how, late in 1998, the Exxon Corporation and Mobil Oil were allowed to merge. At that time, Exxon had 80,000 employees and total revenues of something like $137 billion per year, and Mobil had 42,000 employees and revenues of $66 billion a year. In fact, Exxon was the fourth largest company in the United States and Mobil was the thirteenth. So why did the FTC and Department of Justice allow this merger of giant firms to proceed? Because the two firms competed on a global energy market, and when you compared even a merged ExxonMobil with the nationalized oil operations in countries such as Saudi Arabia, Nigeria, and Venezuela, they didn't even come close to dominating their market.

When judging the level of competition in a market, the alternative to looking at market shares is to look carefully at patterns of prices in the market. A classic example occurred in 1997, when Staples and Office Depot announced their intention to merge. Defining their market broadly to include superstores and grocery stores and drugstores—basically, anywhere you could buy a pencil—the two firms showed that their combined share of the office supply market was only about 6 percent, nowhere near a monopoly. Rather than argue about the appropriate size of the market, the FTC and the Department of Justice took another tack. Using each company's sales data from individual stores, they found that prices at Staples were higher in towns that didn't have an Office Depot than they were in towns with both stores. This evidence suggested that the firms were competitors and that the proposed merger could lead to higher prices for consumers, and so the government disallowed it.

Not only does the U.S. government have the power to block or constrain mergers, but it can also break up large firms if they are found to be monopolies. Standard Oil was famously broken up in the early 1910s. In the 1980s, AT&T was broken up into the so-called Baby Bell local phone companies, the Bell Labs research company, and one long-distance carrier. The government tried and failed to break up IBM many times over the years, until IBM sold off parts of its company voluntarily. More recently, some have suggested that Microsoft be broken up. But in recent years, courts have been quite hesitant to break up companies, based on a belief that the economic costs of chopping up a well-functioning company are likely to exceed the benefits.

Firms can conspire to eliminate competition in their markets in other ways. A price-fixing cartel is a group of independent firms in the same market that agree to set their output levels and prices together, which is clearly illegal under U.S. and European law. In the late 1990s and early 2000s an international cartel of vitamin manufacturers, including the Swiss firm Hoffman–La Roche, the German firm BASF, and the French firm Rhône-Poulenc, were investigated for conspiring to drive up worldwide vitamin prices. The manufacturers were fined hundreds of millions of dollars, and one top executive served four months of jail time. In the early 2000s the U.S. government was actively investigating about thirty different possible cartels. You may not have heard of lysine, a food additive made by about five big producers worldwide, but to antitrust economists, it is associated with an infamous case. Top leaders from these five companies were getting together in hotel rooms and agreeing on how much of it to sell and what to charge. The Department of Justice obtained surveillance tapes in which one company president, from Archer Daniels Midland, claimed that his company's slogan was "Our competitors are our friends; our customers are the enemy." That statement could be a watchword for cartels everywhere.

As with other crimes that cross national borders, it can be difficult to determine who has the authority to prosecute a cartel. For example, members of the Organization of Petroleum Exporting Countries (OPEC) get together to set oil prices, but under whose law are their acts illegal, and who can prosecute them?

Besides forming cartels, would-be competitors may engage in a variety of other restrictive business practices.

- In a price maintenance agreement, a product manufacturer who sells to a group of dealers insists on a certain minimum price, which prevents the dealers from competing with one another past a certain point. Under law, the manufacturer is legally allowed to *suggest* a minimum price and to stop selling to dealers who regularly undercut the suggested price, but they're not allowed to *require* a minimum price—a subtle distinction.
- Exclusive dealing occurs when a manufacturer requires that the dealer sell only its products and none of its competitors' products. These deals are legal if their purpose is to encourage competition,

the way Ford dealerships compete with General Motors dealerships. But if the manufacturer is too powerful, these deals can stifle competition from other manufacturers and may be judged illegal.

- In a tie-in sale, or bundling, a customer is allowed to buy a product only if the customer also buys another product. Again, this may be legal, like a season ticket package to a sports team or a bundled package of software, but if similar items are unavailable individually, this practice may be illegal.
- Predatory pricing is when an existing firm slashes its price just low enough for just long enough to drive a new competitor out of the market, then raises its price again to the monopoly level. In practice, it's often hard to define the line between predatory pricing and good old tough price competition.

These definitions of exclusive dealing, predatory pricing, and so forth may seem squishy and uncertain, and the truth is, they are. The rules regarding anticompetitive behavior will always have some gray areas. There's also a lively ongoing debate over the extent to which government intervention is necessary to encourage more competition. Skeptics who typically oppose government antitrust action argue that cartels will usually break apart and that monopolies will soon come under pressure from competition. They point out that government regulators may be influenced by political pressures and may not be acting in the best interest of consumers.

In theory, most people say that they favor strong enforcement of antitrust laws and believe the government should go after big companies blocking competition in the market. But in specific cases, the commitment to competition becomes uncertain. For example, the U.S. Postal Service is a monopoly. All around the world, other high-income countries are breaking up their mail monopolies and allowing competition in the mail delivery market. If you're in favor of breaking up monopolies but flinch at the thought of increasing competition for the U.S. Postal Service, you might have some soul-searching to do.

CHAPTER 11

Regulation and Deregulation

In some industries, market competition isn't likely to work well. Instead, it leads to a situation in which all firms can suffer enormous and unsustainable losses. Back in the late nineteenth century, the U.S. railroad industry seemed to be booming. The biggest outlay that firms had was the cost of laying track; once that was done, the cost of moving goods along those tracks was low. If a company had the only tracks in a given area, it could charge high prices for shipping goods and use the profits to pay high dividends, which attracted more investors, which gave that company the money to lay more track, and so on. By 1882 almost 90,000 miles of track had been laid by competing railroads. But then competition drove shipping prices way down, and firms were unable to pay the bills incurred from building those tracks. By 1900, half the railroad tracks built by private firms were being operated by the bankruptcy courts. As a result, for most of the twentieth century, the U.S. government regulated the railroads—and, later, for similar reasons, the airlines.

Competition doesn't work very well among public utilities, either. Why not? Try to imagine a city with four separate water companies; that's four sets of pipes, one for each company, under every building in the city. It's not viable. Imagine four times the number of electrical lines running down your street, or four times the number of railroad lines crisscrossing a city. Many water and electrical companies are technically privately owned, but they are closely regulated by the government.

These regulated industries share a common underlying characteristic: they rely upon networks of some kind. The cost of building the overall network tends to be high, whereas the cost of running it tends to be low. If you leave these big companies alone, you'll tend to end up with a monopoly. Alternatively, two or more such firms in competition, once their infrastructure is in place, may compete each other into ruin—or to a merger, in which case there's a monopoly again. This situation is referred to as "natural monopoly," because the way in which the good is produced, with high fixed costs of building the network and low costs of delivering services afterward, can so easily lead to a monopoly outcome.

No option for regulating these kinds of industries is perfect, but some are better than others. Historically, the most common method of setting prices for public utilities was cost-plus regulation: calculating the firm's cost of production, allowing for a low level of profit (often based on what an average firm would make in a competitive market), and fixing the price so that this level of profit was earned. This was also the method by which prices were set for the airlines and railroads in the United States for most of the twentieth century. Cost-plus regulation sounds reasonable, but it provides some unattractive incentives. Firms under cost-plus regulation don't have to seek ways to trim costs or become more efficient, and they have little incentive to innovate. Indeed, firms under cost-plus regulation have an incentive to generate high costs, to build huge new plants, or to hire lots and lots of staff, because prices are set to cover costs.

An alternative to cost-plus regulation is called price-cap regulation. Under this system, the regulator (that is, the government) sets a price that the regulated firm can charge, extending several years into the future. For example, a regulator for an electrical company might set the rates that can be charged to consumers for the next three years. If the electrical company can cut costs, its profits rise, because it doesn't have to lower its prices for several years to come. When the price cap expires, the regulator resets it according to the new costs, and the cycle starts again. Both the firm and the consumers can benefit.

Any method of regulation faces the danger of what economists call "regulatory capture," when regulators start believing their job is to protect industry profits and industry workers, rather than protect competition and consumers. Regulators often seem to develop a form of Stockholm syndrome, sympathizing with the firms they are regulating until it impedes their judgment about protecting consumers.

Thus, in some cases the answer to the best form of regulation has been to deregulate. The U.S. economy experienced a wave of deregulation in a number of industries in the late 1970s and early 1980s. Deregulated industries included airlines, banking, trucking, oil, intercity bus travel, phone equipment, long-distance phone service, and railroads. When these industries were deregulated, they stopped being nice, neat, orderly markets with a predictably high level of profit year in and year out. Yet by the end of the 1990s, America's great deregulation experiment of the 1970s was saving consumers about $50 billion a year in lower prices. Consumers' choices mushroomed. The airlines reorganized themselves into hub-and-spoke systems, creating more connections between cities. Trucks set up similar hub-and-spoke delivery systems, improving their reach. Deregulation in banking brought in automatic teller machines and flexible financial services. Deregulation of telecommunications led to an explosion in new technology.

After the fact, it's easy to argue that many of these changes would have happened anyway. After all, science marches on. Aren't new services such as smartphones and automatic teller machines technologically inevitable, regardless of market competition? Don't be too sure. Telephones, for example, changed relatively little over the decades from when they were invented until the telecom industry was deregulated, despite huge technological changes over that time. Today's toddlers may not even recognize a phone with a cord by the time they become teenagers. It's not a foregone conclusion that all this change would have happened in a regulated market—at least, not this rapidly.

Of course, deregulation has trade-offs, too. When these industries were opened to competition, their labor markets, which had been artificially protected, came under competitive pressure. Salaries for some of the preexisting jobs fell, because as certain industries such as trucking and telecommunications expanded dramatically in the aftermath of deregulation, the number of jobs in those industries increased. Some workers did suffer from reduced wages or layoffs after deregulation; after all, their former wages had been based on government regulations that limited competition and, in that way, required consumers to pay higher prices.

Even in cases where some regulation is needed, regulated industries might have one or more parts that could be carved off and left to competitive market forces. Maybe the best example of this process is the breakup of the former telephone monopolist AT&T. AT&T's long-distance, equipment, and research arms certainly became more innovative in the aftermath of competition. The local phone companies left in the wake of the breakup proved a bit slower to compete, but with the spread of smarter cell phones and Web-based technology, competition is rising. Other settings in which some level of competition might help include garbage collection, in which independent firms could bid for neighborhood contracts; and the service industries that support city and county governments, such as cleaning services, maintenance and repair services, cafeteria services, and building management.

Electricity has long been thought of as a natural monopoly and has been regulated as a public utility, thanks to the physical network of the grid. But arguments about the grid don't focus on how the electrical power is generated. The grid might be publicly owned and regulated, but firms could compete to supply energy—including energy from alternative sources such as solar and wind farms. The United Kingdom has been experimenting with energy markets since 1989, and a number of U.S. states tried electricity deregulation in the 1990s, with some successes (Pennsylvania) and some disasters (California). There are as many lessons to be learned from what didn't work as from what did.

Broadband Internet access has some of the traits of a natural monopoly. Again, it can be provided by setting up a network that has high fixed costs—running cable to everybody's home. Therefore, some jurisdictions have argued that it should be provided by a regulated monopoly. But the broadband Internet industry also has potential for competition through the various delivery methods that have become viable over the past decade: cable, fiber optics, even wireless. With a rapidly evolving technology, it's often better to encourage a multiplicity of technologies than for government to anoint one technology and then regulate it.

The forces of competition can encourage innovation and efficiency and benefit consumers. But in certain well-defined circumstances, when competition can't or won't work well, government has a useful role as a referee of economic competition. Government is also a logical arbiter of safety standards, financial honesty, and information disclosure. The real challenge when the outcomes of market forces seem undesirable is to identify the specific underlying problem and design the policy response accordingly. Is the problem a monopoly, a cartel, a restrictive business practice, a natural monopoly, a regulated industry that doesn't need regulation anymore, or low-income people needing access to a certain service? Rather than locking yourself into a mental box—either vehemently for or against regulation—it's often wise to take a case-by-case approach. Regulation works poorly when it assumes that government can simply dictate the outcome; regulation is more likely to work well when it respects the power of incentives and market forces.

CHAPTER 12

Negative Externalities and the Environment

Environmentalists sometimes see the free market as the enemy of a clean environment, but free markets are often not the worst enemies of the environment. In fact, low-income countries with weak markets often have environmental problems that are much worse than high-income, market-oriented countries. Countries that have tried to eliminate free market forces—such as China and the former Soviet Union—have had severe pollution problems. Meanwhile, in recent decades, U.S. air and water quality has improved on average, even as the economy has grown. Perhaps a government that makes a free market possible is also well suited to providing a background of law and regulation to ensure clean air and water. Let's investigate the economics of pollution and see how this could work.

The central economic concept here is an "externality," which occurs when a party other than the immediate buyer and seller is directly affected by a transaction. The idea of a free market is based in part on the notion that buyers and sellers will act in their own best interests. However, when a market transaction adversely affects a third party—one who didn't choose to be involved in the transaction—the argument that free markets will benefit all parties does not hold as well.

Externalities can be positive or negative. As an example, imagine your next-door neighbor is throwing a party and hires a really loud band. Your neighbor is happy to have music; the band is happy to be hired. You, as the external party, could go either way. If you like the music, great! Free concert! If you don't like the music, not so great. You'll have to suffer through it (or call the police). Either way, the deal between your neighbor and the band didn't take you into account.

Pollution is the most important example of a negative externality. In an unfettered market transaction, the firm looks only at the private costs of production of a good. Social costs, the costs of production that the firm doesn't pay for, don't figure into the calculation. If a firm doesn't have to pay anything to dump its garbage, it's likely to generate a lot of garbage. But if firms have to pay for garbage disposal, you can be sure they'll find ways to reduce their waste. Similarly, public policies concerning pollution seek to make those who create pollution face its costs and take them into account.

"Command and control" is the name economists give to the kind of regulatory policies that specify a maximum amount of pollution that can legally be emitted. Early environmental regulation in the United States in the 1970s took this approach with the passage of the original Clean Air Act and Clean Water Act, and they were effective. According to U.S. Environmental Protection Agency statistics, between 1970 and 2001, the level of particulates in the air fell by 76 percent, sulfur dioxide by 44 percent, volatile organic compounds by 38 percent, and carbon monoxide by 19 percent. The level of lead in the air—which is particularly harmful to growing children—fell by 98 percent, mainly from the use of unleaded gasoline. It's harder to measure water quality consistently, but the widespread construction of better sewage treatment plants and better provisions for disposing of wastewater has made a huge difference over the past four decades.

Despite this good news, command-and-control environmental regulations have some prominent weaknesses. One obvious weakness of any regulatory system is that the regulators may start acting in the interests of industry—the regulatory capture scenario discussed earlier. In addition, command-and-control regulatory standards are typically inflexible. They often specify exactly what technology must be used to reduce a certain kind of pollution. Command-and-control regulation doesn't reward innovative ways of avoiding pollution in the first place or reducing pollution below the legal standard.

The alternative to command-and-control regulation marches under the broad heading of market-oriented environmental policies. These policies seek to work with market incentives, rather than ordering firms to take certain actions. These policies come in several flavors. One is a pollution tax imposed on producers per unit of pollution. For those allergic to the word "tax," it can instead be called a pollution "charge." Such a charge creates an obvious incentive to reduce pollution, and unlike in a command-and-control system, it encourages firms to keep seeking ways to reduce pollution—rather than cutting pollution to just a hair below the legal limit. A pollution charge is also highly flexible, allowing producers to determine the best way to clean up their act.

Another market-oriented environmental policy is a marketable permit system. Marketable permits give polluters the legal right to emit a certain amount of pollution; often the permissible levels are set to decline over time. If the polluter can reduce pollution by more than the amount of the permit, then the permit can be sold to someone else—hence the word "marketable." If a new producer wants to enter the market, it has to purchase a pollution permit from some existing firm. The United States has had some success with marketable permits—to reduce lead in gasoline, for example. Permits provide the same reason to reduce pollution and create cleaner technology as the pollution tax, but instead of reducing a tax, cleaning up their act enables producers to make a profit. In recent years, the European Union has sought to use marketable permits as a way of reducing carbon emissions into the atmosphere, and the U.S. Congress has debated similar measures.

Yet another alternative for reducing market-oriented environmentalism is the use of property rights as an incentive. Think about the problem of protecting elephants or rhinoceroses in Africa. If no one owns the animals, they are vulnerable to poachers and a shrinking habitat. But if you declare their habitat a protected park, and everyone who lives around the park has an economic incentive from tourism to protect the park, then the people surrounding the animals have a sound economic reason to protect them.

Over the past twenty to thirty years, environmental policy has moved away from pure command and control and toward market-oriented mechanisms. In general, economists have tended to favor these mechanisms.

One of the biggest environmental issues of our time is the threat of global warming due to emissions of carbon dioxide and other gasses. It's a controversial topic, to say the least, from both economic and policy standpoints. Here's my take, as an economist who has no claim to any specialized knowledge about climate science. A number of prominent climate scientists clearly believe that our present level of carbon emissions raises a risk of severe worldwide environmental damage. The probability and size of this risk is hard to measure, but when faced with a real possibility of a severe risk, it's often worth taking out some insurance. In this case, one form of "insurance" would mean finding ways to limit the amount of carbon in the atmosphere. We could have command-and-control rules, for example, about maximum carbon emissions and minimum gas mileages for all cars. We could pass rules about carbon emissions from factories and other pollution sources. We could, alternatively or in addition, institute a carbon tax. We could issue marketable permits for carbon emissions to factories, refineries, automobile manufacturers, and the like. We could invest in research and development for technologies that remove carbon from the air or to spur development of energy sources that don't emit carbon. It's no challenge to come up with ways to reduce carbon emissions; the real trick is to do it in a market-oriented and flexible way that limits carbon emissions at the lowest possible economic cost.

For many environmentalists, all these ways to address pollution miss the point because they don't lead to zero pollution. Wearing my hardheaded economist hat, I have to declare that zero pollution is not a realistic or a useful policy goal. Zero pollution would mean shutting down most industry and most of the economy. All our policy options—both command-and-control and market-oriented environmental policies—involve allowing some pollution. The argument for absolutely zero pollution is neither viable nor intellectually serious. The reasonable policy goal is to balance the benefits of production with the costs of pollution, or, to put it another way, bring the social costs and social benefits of production into line with each other.

CHAPTER 13

Positive Externalities and Technology

Thomas Edison's first invention was a vote-counting machine. It worked just fine, but no one bought it and Edison vowed from then on to make only inventions people would actually buy. More recently, Gordon Gould put off patenting the laser, an idea he came up with in 1957. He had his working notebooks notarized to be sure he could prove when he had developed the idea, but he mistakenly believed he needed a working prototype before he could apply for a patent. By the time he did apply, other scientists were putting his ideas into action. It took twenty years and $100,000 in legal fees for him to earn some money from the invention.

These examples help to illustrate the reason why a free market may produce too little scientific research and innovation: there is no guarantee that an unfettered market will reward the inventor. Imagine a company that's planning to invest a lot of money in research and development on a new invention. If the project fails, the company will have lower net profits than its competitors, and maybe it will even suffer losses and be driven out of business. The other possibility is the project succeeds; in that case, in a completely unregulated free market, competitors can just steal the idea. The innovating company will incur the development expenses but no special gain in revenues. It will still have lower net profits than all its competitors and may still be driven out of business. Heads, I lose; tails, you win.

In conceptual terms, new technology is the opposite of pollution.

In the case of pollution, parties external to the transaction between producer and consumer suffered the environmental costs. With new inventions, parties external to the transaction between producer and consumer reap the benefits of these new innovations without needing to compensate the inventor. Thus, innovation is an example of a positive externality.

The key element driving innovation is the ability of an innovator to receive a substantial share of the economic gains from an investment in research and development. Economists call this "appropriability." If inventors, and the firms that employ them, are not being sufficiently compensated for their efforts, they will provide less innovation. The appropriate policy response to negative externalities such as pollution is to find a way to make the producers face the social costs; conversely, the appropriate policy response to positive externalities such as innovation is to help compensate the producers for their firm's costs of innovating. Granting and protecting intellectual property rights is one mechanism for accomplishing this goal. Such rights help firms avoid market competition for a set period of time, so that the firm can earn higher-than-normal profits for a while as a return on their investment in innovation.

In the United States, the notion of intellectual property rights goes all the way back to the Constitution. Article 1, Section 8 reads, "The Congress shall have the power to promote the progress of science and useful arts by securing for limited times, to authors and inventors, the exclusive right to their writings and discoveries." Congress used that power to create the U.S. Patent and Trademark Office and the U.S. Copyright Office to help inventors secure these rights. Over time, the protection of intellectual property has taken on four forms:

- A *patent* is an exclusive legal right, granted by the government, to make, sell, or use an invention for a specific and limited time—in the United States, typically twenty years.
- A *trademark* is a word, name, or symbol that indicates the source of a good and helps the seller establish a reputation. Common

examples of trademarks would be a name such as Chiquita bananas or a symbol such as the Nike "swoosh." There are more than 800,000 trademarks registered with the U.S. government. A firm is allowed to renew its trademark over and over again for an unlimited period of time as long as the trademark remains in active use. If the product stops being used, then the trademark eventually expires.

- A *copyright* is legal protection against others who might copy or use an original work of authorship (including literary, musical, and artistic) without the permission of the author. Copyright protection now lasts the lifetime of the author, plus seventy years. Roughly speaking, patent law covers inventions and copyright protects books, songs, and art. In certain areas, such as software, the law has gone back and forth over whether to apply the protections for inventions or works of authorship.
- A *trade secret* is a formula, process, device, or item of information that gives a business an advantage over its competitors that is not generally known or easily discovered and that the business makes reasonable efforts to keep secret. Probably the most famous trade secret is the formula for Coca-Cola, which is protected under neither copyright law nor patent law but is guarded by the company. Theft of trade secrets can come in various forms. In one famous 1969 case, two photographers were found guilty of theft of trade secrets for flying over a DuPont chemical plant and taking pictures of the company's new methanol production process. The courts ruled that DuPont had gone to reasonable lengths to keep the process secret, both on paper and physically by using fences and security guards and the like, and that taking photos from the airplane was an improper method of discovering the trade secrets.

Even with patents, trademarks, copyrights, and trade secret laws in place, an innovating company typically manages to get only 30–40 percent of the new value of what it creates. The rest of that value is captured by consumers or by other firms who buy its products. Perhaps the most famous example of an inventor who was unable to gain from his invention is Eli Whitney and his cotton gin. Whitney obtained one of the first-ever U.S. patents for his invention, but the cotton gin was so important to the Southern economy that society—or, rather, the courts in Southern states—just wouldn't enforce his patent rights. As Whitney wryly observed, "An invention can be so valuable as to be worthless to the inventor."

The U.S. government uses a range of policies to subsidize innovation. It directly funds scientific research through grants to universities, private research organizations, and businesses. According to the National Science Foundation, in 2008 some $397 billion was spent on research and development in the United States; 65 percent of that was spent by industry, 25 percent by the federal government, and the rest by the nonprofit and educational sector—including state universities. Most of the R&D in the United States is paid for by private industry, with the government's share shrinking since the aerospace- and defense-related research boom of the 1960s and '70s. One advantage of industry-funded R&D is that it is likely to focus on applied technology with near-term payoffs. Government-funded research, on the other hand, focuses on big-picture discoveries that might stretch across multiple industries with payoffs that might not appear for decades, such as breakthroughs in how we think about physics or biology. Government-funded research is more often released directly into the public domain, meaning the results are available to anyone who wants to build on them. Firm-financed research is typically subject to patent and trade secret law, so in many cases government-funded research disseminates more quickly through the economy.

Another approach to supporting research and development is to provide tax credits for businesses for research and development. The nice thing about tax credits is that they are relatively flexible. Direct government spending on R&D means the government calling the shots, giving a thumbs-up or thumbs-down to certain areas of research, perhaps favoring certain kinds of clean energy or health care technologies over others. But there's no reason to believe that even the most savvy and best-intentioned outsider can be aware of all the most promising research projects. An R&D tax credit lets firms follow their own leads. In the United States, there's been an R&D tax credit since 1981, but it has often been allowed to expire before being reinstated—an approach that doesn't help in providing industry with incentives for long-term R&D planning.

There is some controversy over whether inventors might be receiving too much protection and too large a benefit from this combination of tax breaks, government spending, and intellectual property law. After all, the ultimate goal of subsidizing innovation is to benefit consumers, not to make it easier for firms to earn huge profits for a long time. Is it possible for at least some inventors to receive too much protection? Let's look at some numbers.

The U.S. Patent Office grants about 200,000 patents a year, many after relatively brief consideration. It takes on average about three years to get a patent, but the patent examiner on each case spends about eighteen hours deciding whether to grant the patent. Still, in the mid-2000s, there was a backlog of about 750,000 patent applications. Something like 85 percent of all patent applications eventually result in a patent, although some have to be revised along the way to be approved. Meanwhile, only about 0.1 percent of all patents are ever actually litigated. The overwhelming majority of patents end up having almost no economic value, but a very small number of them end up having extremely large economic value. And some patents seem downright silly, if not outrageous. One firm received a patent that seemed to cover peanut butter and jelly sandwiches with the crusts cut off, going so far as to sue other sandwich makers—ultimately without success.

Patents are intended to forestall competition, but they can become large—and in some cases permanent—blockades to other competitors wishing to enter the market, and a hindrance to additional innovation. In the early 1970s, for example, Xerox received more than 1,700 patents on various elements of the photocopying machine. Every time Xerox improved the photocopier, it would patent that tiny little improvement. The company was continually improving the machine, and continually getting new patents. Consequently, no other firms could enter the photocopy market because no one could get through this so-called "patent thicket." In the early 1970s the U.S. antitrust authorities told Xerox that it was abusing the patent process to create a monopoly. Xerox, without admitting guilt, agreed to drop its outstanding patent infringement lawsuits and allow others to use its patents. Unsurprisingly, the floodgates of competition opened, and Xerox's share of the photocopier market dropped from 95 percent to less than 50 percent by 1980.

Patent thickets remain a problem in certain industries, especially in high-tech industries such as pharmaceuticals and complex electronics, in which a given product may rely on many different patents. Consider, too, that new innovations often build on old ones. If you give current inventors a lot of power to protect their inventions, you may block development of ideas that build on those inventions. This problem can be especially severe if groups of innovators work together; any one of the current patent holders can block the new invention.

Copyright extensions can also be granted in a way that doesn't make a lot of sense from the standpoint of helping innovators. In 1998 the Sonny Bono Copyright Term Extension Act increased the length of U.S. copyright terms from fifty years after the creator's death to seventy years after the creator's death. It's hard to believe that extra twenty years matters much to an individual creator, but it mattered a lot to the media empires whose oldest creations were about to enter the public domain. Disney, for example, was about to lose exclusive rights to Mickey Mouse.

The ultimate goal of economic innovation is not to be nice to innovators; it's to encourage a steady stream of innovation that will increase the broad standard of living in a society. Invention transformed the United States from a technological backwater into a world economic power over the course of the nineteenth century, and has kept America at the forefront of the world economy since. It will be just as important to America's future economic success.

CHAPTER 14

Public Goods

Do you drive on a highway to get to work? If your home catches fire, do you expect someone to answer when you dial 911? You might not think of roads and fire departments as goods, but economists do. There are some goods that many of us rely on every day, but it is difficult to imagine buying the quantities we desire from a group of private firms competing in the market. Some classic examples are national defense, funding basic research and development, roads and highways, and police and fire protection. These fall into the category of what economists call "public goods."

Public goods share two key characteristics: they are nonrivalrous and nonexcludable. "Nonrivalrous" means that the good itself is not diminished as more people use it. When you have a private good, such as a slice of pizza, if Max eats the pizza, Michelle can't. Compare that to, say, national defense. Max being protected by the armed forces doesn't diminish the amount of protection Michelle receives. "Nonexcludable" means a seller cannot exclude those who did not pay from using the good. That slice of pizza is excludable; you don't buy it, you don't get to eat it. But if someone doesn't wish to be protected by the armed forces, there's no realistic way to exclude them.

It's important to remember that this term "public good" has a very specific meaning to economists. It does not refer to everything that is both provided by government and (arguably) good. It's also important to recognize that categorizing something as *not* a public good does not mean that there is no economic argument for public policy in that area. Many of the things we call public goods aren't perfectly nonrivalrous or perfectly nonexcludable, but they are close enough to make it difficult for a private market to provide them. For example:

- Public health measures, such as vaccinations, are nonrivalrous because a rise in population doesn't diminish the benefit of reducing infectious disease, and they are nonexcludable because the benefit extends to the whole population.
- A good road system offers society all sorts of benefits. Barring toll roads, it's hard to exclude people from using it. Barring extremes of traffic congestion, my use of a highway doesn't stop you from using it, too.
- Scientific research—in fact, ideas in general—are nonrivalrous. As Thomas Jefferson (1813) put it, "He who receives an idea from me, receives instruction himself without lessening mine; as he who lights his taper at mine, receives light without darkening me."
- Many of the benefits of education aren't just to the person who is educated; there are benefits to all of us from living in a society in which the overwhelming majority of adults can read and understand basic mathematical calculations.

When some people receive the benefits from public goods without paying their fair share of the costs, economists call it a free-rider problem. Imagine the difficulties that could arise if you told people you wanted them to pay for their roads the same way they pay for their groceries. People know that, in the industrialized world at least, odds are the road will be built whether they agree to pay for it or not, and that the government can't or won't stop them from using the road once it's built. Guided by self-interest, most people would prefer that everyone else living nearby chip in for road construction, but that they themselves take a free ride. Since roads are mostly nonexcludable and nonrivalrous (with the exception of toll roads and congested roads), people may decide to be free riders. But if everyone makes this self-interested decision, no road gets built and no one benefits.

The free-rider problem is important to economic analysis. For the most part, economics argues that producers and consumers following their own self-interest offer many benefits for society. But in a situation of public goods, if everyone follows individual narrow self-interest, the result is actually worse for everyone.

How can public goods be provided if a self-interested market works against them? A variety of social mechanisms can help solve the problem. For example, how do public radio and public television survive? They typically use a combination of social pressure (pledge drives, mass mailings) and incentives (thank-you gifts for your pledge, member benefits and events, special programming) to persuade you to contribute. They're trying to overcome the free-rider problem with a mixture of public recognition for contributors and mild shaming for those who don't contribute.

The government uses taxes to require citizens to pay for a public good—whether each individual citizen would want that quantity of that good or not. This applies to goods the government provides directly (such as a standing army or a court system) or indirectly, via private contractors (as with road and building construction). When we say that government supplies a public good, we're actually saying that the government collects the money to pay for the good; it's an open question whether public workers or the private sector provides the good.

Taxes overcome the free-rider problem by force: if you don't pay your taxes for the public good, you go to jail. These benefits and costs are part of an implicit social contract. If members of society don't find a way to come together to provide public goods—through either political or social mechanisms—they all lose out.

CHAPTER 15

Poverty and Welfare Programs

A market can easily create high incomes for some while leaving others in poverty. In a market economy, there will be some people who are lucky, advantaged, talented, or just extremely hardworking who will end up with high levels of income. There will also be some people who are unlucky, disadvantaged, disabled, or just plain lazy who end up in poverty.

But what do economists mean by "poverty"? How is the poverty line or the poverty rate determined? Back in the early 1960s, no official U.S. government definition of poverty existed. The working definition of a household in poverty in 1963 was any household with less than $3,000 in annual income, but there were no adjustments for, say, the number of children or whether it was a one-parent or two-parent family, and there was really no strong justification for that $3,000 figure, except that it was a nice round number. At that time, Mollie Orshansky, a statistician and economist, was working for the Social Security Administration, which is concerned with whether benefits are providing sufficient income. She had previously worked in the Department of Agriculture, where they kept statistics on how much it cost to feed families of different sizes. Orshansky's innovation was to combine these two concepts—to use the cost of food to determine the cost of living and thus poverty.

Orshansky's definition of poverty started by determining how much it cost to provide a basic diet for all members of the household.

(An advantage of using this number was that it adjusted automatically for the size of the household.) Starting with the Department of Agriculture's "economy" food plan—that is, the cost of basic sustenance, no frills—Orshansky determined a food budget for sixty-two different family types, which varied by age, number of children, number of parents, and so forth, and made separate calculations for farm families, who could grow part of their own food.

Orshansky then argued that food expenditures should be about one-third of the family budget. This figure was based on a study from 1955 that found one-third to be the national average across households. She took each family type, multiplied its food budget by three, and came up with a definition of poverty for each of the sixty-two family types. She later pointed out the rationale behind this system—namely, that providing for a family involved weighing trade-offs. She said, "It's not just that the poor had less money; they didn't have enough. I knew you couldn't spend for one necessity without taking away from another." If whether you could feed your family involved trade-offs between necessities, you were properly defined as poor.

Orshansky asked the Census Bureau to calculate how many U.S. citizens fell below her poverty line. The Census Bureau had published breakdowns of income by family size, but they had never before split up the data by number of parents, or gender of head of household, or age of the children. They eventually determined that, at that time, about 20 million American children were living in households that were below the poverty line.

Orshansky's definition of poverty spread very quickly. It was being used in prominent government reports as early as 1964, and by 1969 it was the official government definition. It remains so to this day, with a few minor tweaks. The separate poverty lines for farm households and for female-headed households were abolished in 1981, and categories for families of eight and nine children have been added.

As Orshansky liked to emphasize, the actual incomes defined by the poverty line are not a lot of money. In 2010, for example, the poverty line for a family of four—two parents and two children—was $22,162. Now, let's say that that family spends one-third of its income on food—$7,387 a year, or about $20 per day. With three meals per day and four people at each meal, that's an average of $1.66 per meal per person for the entire year. That's not an exorbitant standard of living.

Any measure of poverty will be subject to a range of potential criticisms. For example, Orshansky's formula is based on the assumption that families spend one-third of their income on food, but the average household spending on food has actually dropped over the decades; at present, it's about one-fifth of income. Yet we haven't raised the multiplier; we don't calculate poverty based on food budget times five. Also, the economy food plan Orshansky used was never meant to be an everyday standard. It was what a family could scrape by on for a limited time. It's a rare family that routinely eats the most basic possible diet made up of items such as oatmeal, beans, and cabbage.

The poverty line that Orshansky set is adjusted each year for inflation, so it has risen over time. But should the poverty line also be increased to reflect economic growth and the fact that we're living in a richer society? Poverty is relative to other members of society: Shouldn't we be defining a "have-not" in part by comparison to the "haves"? What about the effect of changing technology? Are cell phones and home access to the Internet part of a poverty-level standard of living in the twenty-first century? And what about geographic disparity? Shouldn't the poverty level be a higher number in a high-income, high-cost-of-living state such as California or New York and a lower number in a lower-income, lower-cost-of-living state such as Arkansas or South Dakota?

Another set of complexities lies in how to define "income." Should we consider government benefits, such as Medicaid and food stamps, a form of income? What about tax credits, such as the Earned Income Credit, which provides additional income to the working poor? If a working poor family doesn't have employer-sponsored health insurance, does that family have less income than a family that does get this benefit, even though on paper their take-home incomes are the same?

The deeper you go, the more questions that pop up. Many alternative systems for measuring poverty have been suggested. In the mid-1990s, for example, the National Academy of Sciences suggested setting the poverty line by looking at what the average household spends on a combination of food, clothing, and shelter, and then setting the poverty line as a percentage of that. The U.S. Census Bureau publishes multiple sets of poverty rate statistics based on multiple definitions. But the official poverty line, used by programs in which eligibility is linked to the poverty line, such as Medicaid, remains essentially the same as Orshansky's original approach, adjusted upward over time according to the rate of inflation.

The U.S. government calculates the poverty rate as the share of population with income below the poverty line. In 1960 the share of the U.S. population below the poverty line was about 22.2 percent. That number dropped dramatically during the rapid economic growth of the 1960s, down to 12.1 percent in 1969 and 11.1 percent in 1973. But the 1970s brought deep recessions and high inflation; by 1982 the poverty rate had risen to about 15 percent, and it stayed in that vicinity, with a little fluctuation, through 1993. During the strong economic growth of the late 1990s, poverty sagged, and by 2004, it was 12.4 percent. However, when recession hit again, the poverty rate rose to 13.2 percent in 2008 and 14.3 percent in 2009. In short, little progress has been made in reducing poverty in any substantial way since the 1970s.

What *has* changed is the demographics of the poor. Back in the 1960s and '70s, if you had to describe the poor in a single word, the word "elderly" would have been a reasonable choice. That's no longer the case today, thanks to help from Social Security, Medicare, and similar programs. The poverty rate among the elderly is now no higher than among other age groups. For some years now the group that is disproportionately poor has been best described as single-parent households headed by a woman.

What is the best way to help the poor? There's an old saying, "Give a man a fish and he'll eat for a day, but teach him how to fish and he'll eat forever." When you're thinking about the problem of poverty, that statement contains both a great truth and a great dilemma. It's clearly better to make people self-sufficient than to make them dependent, but there's a tension between giving people immediate assistance and helping them learn how to help themselves. What is the man supposed to eat while you're teaching him to fish? Is the plan that you're going to need to give the man fish while he's learning, and then stop? Isn't there a danger the man will just take the fish and not bother learning the skill?

Every method of trying to help those with low incomes runs into this fundamental tension. If a wealthy society doesn't help the poor, it seems cruel and immoral. But if society does help the poor, it reduces, at least to some extent, the incentive of the poor to support themselves. The social safety net shouldn't be a hammock. It shouldn't be something that is hard to climb into and hard to climb out of. It should be more like the safety net for a trapeze artist. It breaks your fall, but it also helps you bounce up and out again.

To understand these trade-offs, and how to minimize them, let's start with a stripped-down basic proposal to help the poor: Say the U.S. government guarantees that all its citizens will, at a minimum, receive the poverty level of income. Thus, a two-parent family of four would be guaranteed no less than $22,162. If it earned less, the government would make up the balance. What could be wrong with this proposal—other than maybe not being generous enough?

The problem involves incentives. If no one in the family works, its total income is $22,162, all from the government. Now imagine that one parent gets a full-time job and works 2,000 hours per year, but it's a low-wage job earning $8 an hour. That's a $16,000 annual income. Their reward for the effort of earning that $16,000 is that total family income is brought up to—you got it—$22,162, exactly the same as if that person had not worked at all. Now let's say the second parent gets a part-time job and earns an additional $8,000 a year. This takes total family earnings to $24,000—so that they are now above the poverty line. Now the parents are working a total of 3,000 hours a year, and their total gain in income is only about $1,800 over what it would be if neither of them worked at all. And if they're both working, they probably have extra expenses for child-care and transportation—and they're going to owe taxes, too. It's quite possible they won't come out ahead at all compared with if they had not worked at all.

Economists call this problem a "negative income tax." A negative income tax arises when the government reduces welfare benefits as a person earns additional income. Contrast this with the familiar positive income tax, in which you earn money and the government takes part of that money. Both kinds of taxes reduce the incentive to work. In this example, the negative income tax is set at 100 percent; that is, every time that family earned one dollar (up to the poverty line), they lost one dollar in government benefits. For that family, there is no incentive to take a low-paying job. There is no incentive to take the first step onto the employment ladder, because they literally get zero gain from working. When the negative income tax is high, it creates a poverty trap.

You might be thinking that this is interesting in a hypothetical sort of way, but that no moron would ever set up a welfare system that offered no reward at all for working. Actually, the U.S. government did just that. The main welfare program in the United States, Aid to Families with Dependent Children (AFDC), offered a 100 percent negative income tax throughout the 1960s, '70s, and '80s. In fact, it was even worse than that. A working family would not only lose one dollar of AFDC for every dollar earned, but they would also lose benefits such as food stamps and Medicaid. On top of that, wage earners paid positive income taxes on money they earned from work, reducing their take-home pay even further. In other words, the negative income tax was for many years typically greater than 100 percent!

How do we disarm the poverty trap? Several approaches are

available. One is to phase out a newly employed family's benefits more slowly. This was the idea behind the 1996 replacement of AFDC with Temporary Assistance for Needy Families, often known as TANF. Under that program—although this varies by state—there's often a 50 percent reduction in TANF benefits for each dollar earned, rather than 100 percent. The negative income tax is still rather steep at 50 percent, but there's at least some incentive to work.

Another policy used in the United States is the Earned Income Credit, which gives low-income families additional income when they earn money, in a way that helps to offset the withdrawal of other government benefits. Here's how this worked in 2010 for a single earner with no children: When you earned an income up to $12,590, you got an extra 40 percent back in a tax credit, or up to $5,036. Between $12,590 and $16,450, you still received a $5,036 tax credit—no more than you received at $12,590, but no less, either. Above $16,450, benefits were reduced; every additional dollar you earned lost twenty-one cents of the tax credit money. This pattern results in a negative income tax at and above this income level—but you have to phase out the benefits at some point! It's interesting to note that that the amount of money paid through the Earned Income Tax Credit in 2006 was about $41 billion, substantially greater than the amount of welfare paid that year.

Another way the United States has tried to get around the problem of negative incentives to work is through work requirements. From the late 1980s through the mid-1990s a series of welfare reforms passed by individual states required welfare recipients to go back to work (or in some cases be in job training programs), often within two years of registering for benefits. These reforms also capped lifetime welfare benefits, usually at five years. In 1996, welfare-to-work requirements were integrated into the new TANF program. In 1994 there were about 14 million recipients of the old AFDC welfare program. After the 2001 recession, fewer than 6 million people were receiving TANF.

Another way to avoid the poverty trap is to provide in-kind help, meaning help in the form not of cash but of some service. Medicaid and food stamps both fall into this category. Such approaches are often politically popular because they seem to promise that the poor won't use public assistance unwisely. But economists have pointed out that in-kind help has incentive issues, too. For example, Medicaid can create a "job lock," in which you're worried about moving to a job that pays more but that doesn't have health insurance, because you might lose eligibility for some or all your Medicaid benefits.

TANF, the Earned Income Tax Credit, Medicaid, and food stamps aren't the whole of the U.S. government's assistance to the needy. There are dozens of other federal programs in which eligibility is based on income level, from housing subsidies to school lunches to home energy assistance. All these programs create potential trade-offs between assistance and incentives. With some of them, we're not too worried about the trade-offs; we don't expect the elderly or school-age children to go to work, for example. But we still need to be aware of the tension between assistance and incentives in most of these programs. Ultimately, of course, our goal should be not just distributing money so that people have more than a poverty level of income, but helping people to develop the skills they need to earn a living in a dynamic and growing economy.

CHAPTER 16

Inequality

The subjects of poverty and inequality are often scrambled together, but they aren't the same thing at all. Poverty, as we've just discussed, refers to falling below a certain level of income. Inequality, on the other hand, describes the gap between those with low and high incomes. It's quite possible for the poverty rate to fall while the amount of inequality in a society rises. For example, this happens when a strong economy helps the poor get a little bit richer but helps the rich get *much* richer. Similarly, in a down economy when the stock market declines substantially, it's possible that the poor could be a bit worse off, but many of the rich could lose their proverbial shirts; in that case, poverty rises, but inequality falls.

At a fundamental level, we care about poverty and inequality for different reasons. Poverty cuts into a person's ability to consume the basic necessities of life. Inequality concerns us more out of a sense of fairness, a feeling that in a just society the rewards and disparities should not be primarily distributed by birth or family connections or even luck, but should have some reasonable relationship to people's efforts and skills.

To measure inequality, we need some way of describing the entire distribution of income, not just the low end of it. A standard approach is to split the income distribution into parts such as fifths, tenths, or even single percents and then determine what share of overall income is being received by the people in each division. For simplicity, we're going to stick with fifths, with some mention of the top 5 percent. If each fifth of the income distribution got exactly 20 percent of total income in a given year, then income is equally distributed.

Looking at the U.S. economy, the bottom fifth gets a lot less than 20 percent of total income and the top fifth gets a lot more. In 2009 the bottom fifth of the income distribution got 3.9 percent of total income. The second fifth got 9.4 percent of total income. The middle fifth got 15.3 percent of total income. The fourth fifth got 23.2 percent of total income. The top fifth, which represents those households with an income of $100,000 or more, got 48.2 percent of the income. If you look inside that top fifth at the top 5 percent of the income distribution, which starts with those households with $180,000 or more in income in 2009, that group received 20.7 percent of the total income in the economy.

Since the 1970s there's been a trend toward those with high incomes having a larger proportion of all total income. In 1975 the top fifth of the income distribution was getting 40.7 percent of total income; in 1985, 43.1 percent of total income; in 1995, 46.5 percent of total income; in 2000, 47.7 percent of total income; and a bit higher, at 48.2 percent, in 2009. That shift in which the top fifth gets seven percentage points more of total income is quite large, and if you look at that top 20 percent in more detail, almost all of that seven percentage point increase went to the top 5 percent of the income distribution.

Should this level of inequality be a public policy concern? Realistically, some degree of inequality at any point in time is inevitable. For example, people typically earn less in their twenties than they do in their fifties, and then income drops again after retirement. So, across the population, there will be some income variation by age. From one year to the next, you'll see shifts occur. People might have an especially good year or an especially bad one. Whole industries—construction, farming, investment, electronics—can have good or bad years. And people often have some choices about their earning power—which career path to choose, how many hours (or jobs) to work, and so forth. To some extent, inequality in incomes will result from these kinds of preferences. Perfect equality isn't a plausible goal. A better question might be, how reasonable is the level of inequality we have now?

One way to start addressing that question is by looking at mobility across the income distribution. The income distribution at any given time is a snapshot. It tells you where people are located at a certain time, but not whether they are on their way up, or down, or on an even keel. Evidence of movement over time would indicate that people aren't trapped at certain levels. To determine movement across the income distribution, you need to track the same people for a sustained time. Most government surveys don't do this. They focus on the whole population, not individuals. However, the University of Michigan's Panel Study of Income Dynamics (PSID) has been tracking a representative sample of the U.S. population since 1968.

The patterns in the PSID data show a fair amount of movement between the quintiles of the income distribution, but that movement tends to be happening between maybe one or two quintiles. People who are the very bottom of the income distribution move up a little bit, but rarely do they move all the way to the top. Similarly, people at the very top of the income distribution might drop, but rarely do they fall all the way to the bottom. The rate of mobility hasn't changed much over time. Finally, international comparisons have demonstrated that, over the past thirty years or so, people in the United States have not shown more intergenerational mobility (that is, they tend to remain in or near the same economic bracket as their parents) than many other high-income nations. Thus, although the level of inequality has been rising, and there's some mobility, the higher level of inequality is not being counterbalanced by a greater level of mobility.

What has been driving the rise in inequality in the United States over the past thirty or so years? Most of the world's high-income economies have seen some increase in inequality during this same period. The single biggest reason appears to be changes in information and communications technology and their effect on the labor market.

As we've already discussed, the labor market isn't a monolith, but it is made up of many different markets—the market for construction workers, the market for doctors, and so on. The supply of skilled workers has expanded over time; today's students are more likely to complete high school and go on to at least some college than their parents or grandparents. But the phenomenal developments in technology have also dramatically increased the demand for skilled workers. For example, information technology has dramatically increased the productivity of skilled workers, as anyone who, say, kept accounting records before and after the invention of spreadsheet software can tell you. Conversely, at the other end of the wage scale, many lower-skilled jobs have disappeared because the technology has reduced the demand for them.

Technology is not the only cause of the rise in inequality. The increase in foreign trade, or globalization, means American workers have to compete more directly with workers in countries where wages are much lower, which drives down both wages and the demand for low-skilled labor in the United States. By some estimates, approximately one-fifth of the growth in inequality is due to the pressure of globalization on wages.

A drop in unionization has altered the distribution of income and led to greater income inequality in the United States. Unions have historically tended to encourage a more equal distribution of income. In the early 1950s about one-third of the U.S. workforce belonged to a union. By the mid-2000s, union membership had dropped to about 13 percent; if you leave out public-sector unions such as the teachers' unions, only about 8 percent of private-sector workers are in a union.

What public policies are available to reduce inequality? One obvious choice would be high taxes on those with high incomes. Interestingly, the share of federal taxes paid by those with high incomes has risen significantly even as inequality has risen. According to the Congressional Budget Office, in 1980 the top 20 percent of earners paid 56.3 percent of all federal taxes collected—which includes not only income tax, but Social Security and Medicare, excise taxes, and the share they ended up paying indirectly through the corporate income tax. By 1990 that number was up to 57.9 percent; by 1995, 61.9 percent; by 2000, 66.7 percent of all federal taxes; by 2007, 68.9 percent of all federal taxes. If you look at just the top 5 percent of households, they were paying 44.3 percent of all federal taxes as of 2007. In short, those with higher incomes are receiving more income, but also paying a higher share of taxes.

Distributing more money to the poor, in whatever form, will reduce inequality, but as we discussed in the previous section, such policies must be carefully designed to maintain incentives to work. Redistributions also may not address the underlying social problems that add to income inequity, such as varying degrees of access to quality education.

Some have proposed dramatically expanding the Earned Income Tax Credit, a policy discussed in the previous chapter; the idea is if someone is working full time, then we should make sure they earn a decent wage. An aggressive plan to reduce inequality with this policy tool could be extremely costly—$100 billion or more each year. But it might also pay large social dividends in terms of family stability and reductions in related social problems.

Government spending to reduce inequality doesn't have to be a direct cash payment to poor families. It might take the form of expanded spending on public schools or school lunch programs. Where geography favors it, it could take the form of expanding mass transit, which tends to be used more by families with lower incomes. Government could spend more on public safety protection, such as more police in low-income areas. The government could commit more resources to public spaces such as libraries, parks, schools—especially after-school programs—community centers, and so on. These kinds of steps wouldn't distribute income directly to low- and middle-income families, but they would increase the safety and security of public spaces and public resources on which low-income people often rely. Personally, while I am bothered by the rise in income inequality over time, the high incomes of the rich worry me less than the conditions of life that the poor face every day.

CHAPTER 17

Imperfect Information and Insurance

Imagine you're shopping for a used car, but you're basically clueless about what happens inside a car's engine. You know that you have imperfect information, so you read *Consumer Reports,* you visit some Web sites, maybe you even hire a mechanic to check out the car you're thinking about buying, but you still can't be sure. Now imagine that you're out shopping for cars and you find two used cars that are the make and model you wanted. These two cars look about the same to you, but one costs about what you expected to pay; the other one costs one-third as much. Which car do you buy? Do you buy the one that costs what you were expecting to pay, or do you buy the really cheap one?

In a world of perfect information, your information says the two cars are equal. Buy the cheaper car—you're getting a great deal! In a world of imperfect information, you have to worry that maybe the very low price is telling you something. Maybe that low price means that someone else, better informed than you, believes that the low-priced car is a lemon. Because of imperfect information, your choice is not a simple one.

The standard example of a market, with a willing buyer and a willing seller, presumes that when each party makes a voluntary trade, they know what they're getting. You give the butcher ten dollars and the butcher gives you a nice piece of meat. However, the real world is full of situations of imperfect information that can create real problems for how markets function.

Imagine you're in charge of hiring at your company. Somebody applies for a job, and a line on the job application asks for "expected salary." That person names a salary that is half the salary you expected to pay. What a bargain! You collect more information about this worker: résumé, references, and so on. But at the end of the day, you're still uncertain. You have imperfect information about what sort of worker this person would be. Should you go ahead and hire that worker, who's offering to work for half of what you expected to pay? Is that worker a disaster waiting to happen? You just can't know for sure. Again, an element of risk and uncertainty has entered the picture because of imperfect information.

Now imagine you're in charge of making loans at a bank, and an applicant says, "I really, really want this loan. I want it so much I'll pay you ten percent a year more interest than you usually charge." Of course you can collect financial information and business information about this borrower, but how would you feel about lending to someone who offers to pay a really high interest rate? Maybe you'd say, "That sounds great for the bank. Here's the loan." But you might also reason, "This person sounds pretty desperate, as if he's high risk and he knows it. The high interest rate doesn't do me or the bank any good if he defaults on the loan."

Markets have a variety of methods for attempting to mitigate imperfect information. Warranties, guarantees, and service contracts help defray the consumer's risk should the product not work as advertised. Trademarks and brand names can reassure consumers about the quality of what they are getting. In the labor market, résumés and references help lessen the problem of imperfect information, as do licenses and professional certifications held by teachers, nurses, accountants, lawyers, massage therapists, and real estate brokers, to name a few. In the financial capital market, there are mechanisms such as credit checks, loan cosigners, and collateral.

In many markets these kinds of mechanisms provide enough information for the market to work well. In other cases there's an argument for the government entering the picture to make rules about what information should be available. For example, the government requires ingredient and nutrition labels on packaged foods so we're able to make more informed choices. Companies owned by shareholders are required to disclose certain financial records and to be audited. But in one highly important set of markets, imperfect information creates extraordinary problems that are difficult to resolve: markets for insurance.

Insurance markets include private insurance such as health insurance, auto insurance, property insurance, life insurance, and social insurance such as Social Security, unemployment insurance, workers' compensation, and government-provided flood insurance. Insurance providers have to estimate the risk that buyers will be involved in an event that requires compensation. But the information about who will suffer what event is quite imperfect, and as a result, insurance markets can break down.

To understand the difficulty, let's look first at how insurance works. Statistically speaking, we know that an undesirable event is likely to happen to a certain percentage of the members of a group, but we don't know exactly which members of the group will suffer. When people buy insurance, they are paying into a common pool of funds, and then that pool is used to compensate those who actually experience the negative event.

To make this concrete, consider a simple hypothetical example of auto insurance. Suppose there's a group of 1,000 drivers whom an insurance company can divide into four groups. Nine hundred of the 1,000 don't have any accidents in a year. Fifty of the people have only a few door dings or chipped paint, tiny little accidents that cost $100 each. Thirty of the drivers have medium-size accidents that cost an average of $1,000 each. The remaining twenty drivers have big accidents that cost an average of $15,000 apiece in damages. The insurance firm knows these numbers, but it doesn't know which drivers will end up in which group by the end of the year.

Given these statistics, what's the total payout this company will need to make to this pool of drivers in a year? If you calculate all the costs that will be incurred, it comes to $335,000. So if each of the 1,000 drivers paid an insurance premium of $335 each year, then the insurance company would collect the $335,000 it needed to cover the cost of all the accidents that were going to happen. Of course, this calculation ignores two key issues. First, insurance companies need to pay their employees and overhead—and ideally earn a bit of profit—for providing this service. Second, between the time an insurance company collects premiums and the time it pays claims, it can invest that money in the financial capital market and earn some rate of return. But for many insurance companies, in an average year, the costs of running the company and the returns on their investments will more or less balance each other out, so it is fair to compare the premiums paid into the company with the insurance claims paid out.

Indeed, this description of insurance markets implies a fundamental rule: What an average person pays into insurance over time must be very similar to what the average person gets out of insurance over time.

Insurance companies' payouts typically go to a relatively small share of their customers who have large claims. In the example just given, $300,000 of that $335,000 was paid out to twenty people out of 1,000—that's 0.2 percent. So at the end of a given year, those twenty people will feel as if their insurance paid off, but the vast majority in any given year may feel that they paid money into the system and didn't get much back. The same could be said of the health insurance or property insurance or any insurance market.

Up until this point, we've been implicitly assuming that the chance of the bad event happening to any one of the people in our group is random and equal. But what if it's not? The risk of bad things happening, such as an automobile accident, may be affected to some extent by people's own actions. No matter how thoroughly the insurance company goes about collecting information, that information will be imperfect. Several problems arise as a result.

The first big problem is called moral hazard, which means that having insurance leads people to take fewer steps to avoid or prevent the bad event from happening in the first place. The insured have a little bit less incentive to change the habits or improve the conditions that make them more vulnerable to a negative event. For example, a company with good fire insurance might worry less about preventing fires at an older factory. Someone with insurance against theft might be less likely to buy a security system. Someone with health insurance is more likely to head for the doctor for every sniffle and cough than someone without health insurance. As a result of this disincentive, the existence of insurance makes the payouts from insurance higher than they would otherwise be.

The other big issue with every insurance market is the problem of adverse selection. Those who are especially likely to experience the bad event are more likely to purchase insurance, while those who are very low risks are less likely to purchase it. If the company merely sets the price of the insurance at the average loss, then everyone who knows they're safer than average will tend to drop out of the market, or at least purchase the minimal coverage. On the flip side, those who have greater risk will load up on insurance at this price. When an insurance company attracts high-risk customers, it will need to raise premiums, but as premiums rise, the low-risk and medium-risk customers drop or reduce their coverage. Because of adverse selection, insurance turns into a game that isn't about spreading risk across an entire population; it starts to focus on how an insurance company can select low-risk customers and exclude the high-risk ones.

Insurance plans have a variety of ways of addressing moral hazard and adverse selection. Deductibles, copayments, and coinsurance shift some of the financial risk back onto the customers and can encourage them to minimize their moral hazard behavior. One classic study of health insurance found that when one group of patients had modest copayments and another group didn't, those who had the copayments used one-third less health care. However, the health status of the two groups was essentially the same.

Another thing insurance companies can do to mitigate risk is to draw upon a larger pool of customers. The larger the customer pool, the more likely it is to contain a good percentage of low-risk participants to offset the high-risk ones. Thus, health insurance can be less expensive if purchased through your employer than for you as an individual, and health insurance is often less expensive per person for a large company than a small one. In the car insurance market, almost every state requires every car owner to get insurance, so low-risk drivers can't drop out of the market, which again moderates the whole pool's risk.

In most of the industrialized world, the imperfect information problems inherent to the health insurance market have been addressed by a nationalized health care system. Countries have structured their national programs in a variety of ways, but they share a belief that the problem of imperfect information is so great in health care that a free market cannot cope with it. Governments around the world—except in the United States—address the moral hazard problem by controlling the amount of care provided, when care should be delivered, and how much it should cost. They address the adverse selection problem by bringing the whole country into the insurance pool.

As you may know, the United States spends much more on health care than any industrialized nation in the world. According to the World Health Organization, in 2007 U.S. health care spending (both privately and publicly funded) was about $7,300 per person. In comparison, Canada, France, Germany, Japan, and the United Kingdom spent between $2,700 and $3,900 per person. As a share of gross domestic product, health care spending in the United States was 15.7 percent; in Canada, France, and Germany it was between 10 and 11 percent of GDP; and in Japan and the United Kingdom it was roughly 8 percent of GDP. In short, the United States is spending twice as much per person on health care as do other nations with comparable economies.

A standard explanation for this pattern is the extraordinary quality of both health care and health care research in the United States.

Innovation—whether in pharmaceuticals or equipment—is better rewarded, and doctors and nurses are better compensated for their hard work and long years of schooling. Yet it doesn't appear that the quality of U.S. health care is twice as good as in these other nations. The United States doesn't seem to be seeing a big enough payoff in terms of health for this high level of spending, especially given that through the mid-2000s, 40 million people in the country had no health insurance at all.

There is no simple answer to the conundrum of imperfect information. In the United States the government has for some decades been the primary payer for health care under programs such as Medicare (for the elderly), Medicaid (for the poor), veterans' benefits, and insurance for government employees. In 2010, President Obama signed the Patient Protection and Affordable Care Act into law, with the goals of expanding health insurance coverage and holding down costs. The implementation of the law seems sure to be controversial, which is really no surprise. The 2010 legislation would inject the U.S. government more deeply into health care markets. Meanwhile, many countries around the world that have far heavier government intervention into health care markets than the United States are trying to find ways to insert a greater degree of competition and cost-awareness into their health care systems. No country seems fully happy with its health care system; no country has found the magic institutional structure that combines breadth of coverage with holding down rising health care costs.

CHAPTER 18

Corporate and Political Governance

Some people trust corporations but distrust the government. Some people trust political leaders but distrust private-sector firms. Economists don't trust anyone. After all, business leaders are capable of providing high-quality goods and services at a great price and great jobs for employees, and politicians are capable of passing farsighted legislation in the greatest public interest. But we also know that some business leaders make themselves rich by running their companies into the ground, and some politicians are more interested in keeping their jobs and lining their pockets than in serving the public good. This raises the issue of governance. How are corporate and public organizations governed? To what set of incentives are their leaders responding?

We can analyze the issues of governance by using an analytical structure economists call the principal-agent problem. In a principal-agent problem, one party, the principal, wants to motivate another party, the agent, to exert effort to act in a certain way. In a political context, citizens are the principals and politicians are the agents, who, in theory, act in the interest of the citizens. In a corporate context, the company's shareholders are the principals and its executives are the agents, who are supposed to act on behalf of the company's shareholders. The relationship between an employer and an employee is a common example of a principal-agent problem.

Principal-agent problems typically involve imperfect information.

The principal has a hard time knowing whether the agent is working hard, or efficiently, or acting in the principal's best interest. In the employment context, for example, when an agent's output is highly observable by both principal and agent—perhaps the employee is installing automobile windshields, or selling office supplies, or picking farm products—the principal and the agent can agree on pay for what's produced. But most of the time, output is not perfectly observable. What's the output of a research scientist? What's the output of a fast-food cashier? What are the outputs of these individuals versus the other members of their teams? How do you account for circumstances beyond the employees' control, such as faulty equipment or snowstorms that keep customers away? In most cases, it's hard to put together a pay package without an element of subjectivity.

In the case of corporate and political leaders, evaluating their output can be especially difficult. It's possible to observe whether a company or a country is experiencing good times or bad times. But perhaps great leadership means preventing the bad times from being even worse, or bad leadership means blocking the good times from being even better. How can a corporate shareholder or a voter tell? Another problem that arises in both corporate and political principal-agent problems is that there are a vast number of principals, which raises a variation on the free-rider problem. For any individual principal, the effort to monitor the agent may be too much effort. After all, among thousands of shareholders or millions of voters, why should *you* be the one spending the time, cost, and energy to monitor the performance of the leader? Add to this the fact that a lone shareholder or voter's opinions might not hold much sway with the agent unless that shareholder or voter has support from many other principals. To put it another way, if individual principals lack power to control the agents, then the agents will lack an incentive to act in a way that will benefit the principals.

One classic case of the principal-agent problem in recent years is the Enron Corporation. On December 31, 2000, stock in Enron—a company that bought and sold natural gas and electricity, among other goods—was selling for eighty-three dollars a share. That stock price had risen 87 percent in 2000, 56 percent in 1999, and 37 percent in 1998. It was on a roll. Enron was rated the most innovative large company in America by *Fortune* magazine's survey of the most admired companies, for its Internet-based markets and long-term contract strategies. But by December 2, 2001, less than one year later, Enron had filed for bankruptcy and was under investigation for fraud.

How does a company go from being a role model to having its top executives threatened with jail in less than a year? What safeguards were supposed to be in place that failed to work? For starters, the individual shareholders lacked power and the incentive to monitor top executives. In most companies, shareholders elect a board of directors, who are directly responsible for the hiring and monitoring of top executives. But quite often those same executives are the ones who decide who can run for membership on the board. The independence and neutrality of the corporate board of directors can be questionable. Being a board member is also a part-time job. It consists of a few big meetings a year, where the information and the agenda are provided by—you guessed it—those same top executives. So an aggressive board of directors can provide some oversight, but there are limits to what it can do.

Publicly owned firms, by law, must also be audited and must publicly report their financials. However, in the aftermath of the Enron debacle, it became clear that some auditors had not been as aggressive in questioning financial arrangements as the shareholders might have liked. After all, an auditor works for the firm and is paid by the firm. Somehow, at the same time, it's supposed to be monitoring the firm. Some accountants may develop what I think of as the tax lawyer mentality. A tax lawyer's job is to think up ways to beat the tax code. It seems that some accountants felt they needed to deliver certain profit numbers for a company, regardless of the underlying reality. Enron's auditors, the Arthur Andersen Company, earned $52 million in fees from Enron in 2000, which was certainly an incentive to help out Enron's upper management.

Another possible monitor for top executives would be large outside investors, such as mutual funds or pension funds that own large blocks of stock. The bigger their investment in the company, the more incentive they have to keep an eye on its inner workings. But in Enron's case, the large investors didn't seem to do much, either. About 60 percent of total Enron stock was owned by large investors late in 2000. In October 2001, many months after it had become clear that something was deeply wrong with this firm, large investors still owned about 60 percent of Enron's stock. The large investors did not react quickly, and they didn't seem to monitor very aggressively.

Who else could monitor the executives at a large company? The broader financial community—the stock market analysts who give advice to financial investors; the banks that make loans to firms; the journalists who write for the business press—are all employed for the purpose of assessing a company's health, and all have some power to monitor top executives. For example, in March 2001 *Fortune* magazine ran a prominent story questioning what was going on at Enron, but few other watchdogs barked. After all, stock market analysts' pay and, to some extent, their access to information is determined by whether they are viewed as good team players. The same is true of business journalists and bankers. No one wants to be the skunk at the garden party, because they won't get invited back.

Stock options for top executives were once touted as a way to make those executives act in the shareholders' interests. The idea was that if top executives owned a lot of stock, they would be more interested in raising the stock price. Stock options for top executives became far more popular in the 1990s, but they did not always improve performance. Some executives did whatever it took to pump up the firm's short-term stock price—in some cases up to and, unfortunately, including fraud—and sold their stock before the price fell again, leaving the other shareholders holding a significantly lighter bag.

In 2002, in the aftermath of Enron and other similar disasters, Congress passed the Sarbanes-Oxley Act. It imposed new rules on the institutions of corporate governance concerning how to choose boards of directors, the rules for auditors and stock market analysts, and a new government accounting oversight board. These rules may help modestly, at some cost. But they are far from eliminating the principal-agent problem in corporate governance. Top executives still have strong incentives to report high profits and to take high salaries. Many of the people who are supposed to be monitoring the top executives still have strong incentives not to upset or anger the people who are ultimately supporting their career, in one way or another. After watching a number of banks and financial firms make unwise lending and financial decisions in the lead-up to the recession of 2007–2009, it's clear that the problems of corporate governance remain substantial.

Let's shift to the problem of governance in government. People who are most distrustful of corporate management are often among those most likely to trust the government to monitor corporations and to enforce good behavior. But economists point out that conceptually similar governance problems can arise in both corporate and political settings.

We've looked at many roles the government might play in the market, intervening in various ways to improve social welfare: fighting monopolies, blocking anticompetitive behavior by firms, reducing pollution, supporting technology, organizing for the provision of public goods, addressing poverty and inequality, and dealing with information problems. Democratic governments are supposed to be—as Abraham Lincoln famously said in the Gettysburg Address—"of the people, by the people, for the people." In a simple theory of democracy, voters choose and monitor elected officials; but in fact, many people don't vote at all. In recent U.S. presidential elections, more than half of voting-age citizens actually voted—but not a lot more than half, just 57 percent in the 2008 election, 55 percent in 2004, and 51 percent in 2000. In city elections, voter turnout is often as low as one-third or one-quarter of registered voters.

Why don't people vote? In most elections of any size, the margin of victory is measured in hundreds, or thousands, or even millions of votes. A rational voter will recognize that one vote is not likely to make a difference, and thus many of them will not bother to become informed or vote. In *An Economic Theory of Democracy*, economist Anthony Downs (1957) put the problem this way:

> It seems probable that for a great many citizens in a democracy, rational behavior excludes any investment whatever in political information per se. No matter how significant a difference between parties is revealed to the rational citizen by free information, or how uncertain he is about which party to support, he realizes his vote has almost no chance of influencing the outcome.

Even in some of the harrowingly close elections of the past decade or so, the decisions have come down to hundreds or thousands of votes, not one vote.

Common proposals to increase voter turnout have included keeping the polls open longer, moving Election Day to a weekend, and loosening the rules for absentee voting. Yet the United States has been moving in that general direction for decades, making it easier and easier to vote, without seeing any upsurge in the voter turnout rate.

If the majority isn't always going to make its wishes felt, who will? Special interest groups, which are numerically small but well organized, could pressure legislators to enact public policies that benefit the group at the expense of the broader population. Among themselves, politicians can use the power of their own votes to enact pork-barrel legislation—spending that benefits mainly a single political district. Pork-barrel spending can be thought of as yet another case in which democracy is challenged by the problem that benefits are concentrated and costs are widely dispersed. The benefits of pork-barrel spending are obvious and direct to local voters; the costs are spread out over the country. There have been times when groups of legislators passed a bill that included a pork-barrel project for every one of their districts. Big transportation bills often work this way, with something for every political district. Support for the U.S. government's defense budget is encouraged by spreading out military bases and spending on weapons programs to congressional districts across the country.

In addition to the problems of low voter turnout and special interests, when multiple choices exist, the outcome of a race might not reflect the majority's preferences. Consider the situation of a state where 60 percent of the population is liberal and 40 percent is conservative, so if a single liberal candidate runs against a conservative, the liberal is going to win. But in a three-way race, with two liberal candidates and only one conservative candidate, it's possible that the liberal vote will be split and victory will go to the minority party.

A final difficulty in public governance is that government finds it hard to exit. When a firm produces a product nobody wants to buy or produces at a higher cost than its competitors, the firm will suffer losses. If it can't change its ways, it goes out of business. This puts a lot of pressure on firms. But what if a government program isn't working? Who puts the government program out of business? What if a government agency provides bad service? Who provides competition to counteract the bad service? With few exceptions, there's no mechanism within government to allow exit and entry of better producers.

Of course, it would be an overreaction to conclude from this litany of woe that we should abandon democratic government. But a practical student of economic policy needs to recognize that democratic government is not ruled by all-wise and public-minded paragons. Hot-breaking news here: Government is political. It's a set of agents, with voters and citizens trying to exercise direction and control but not always succeeding. Even the best-intended government actions could make problems worse, rather than better.

At this point, we've covered the basics of microeconomics, so let's pause to pull together some of the big ideas. Economic wisdom requires an understanding of several potentially contradictory lessons at the same time:

- Markets are extraordinarily useful institutions through which society can allocate its scarce resources. They provide incentives for efficient production, innovation, wise use of resources, the meeting of consumer needs and desires, and an increase in the standard of living over time.
- Markets may sometimes produce unwanted results: monopolies, imperfect competition, negative externalities such as pollution, failure to support technology or to build public goods, poverty, inequality, failure related to imperfect information, and mismanagement.
- Governments can have a useful role to play in addressing the problems of markets, but government action is also imperfect, and can even in some cases create larger or additional problems of its own.

The challenge in thinking about economic policy is to stay pragmatic. Be specific about the problem that the market is having. Be specific about the solution. Be realistic about what government is actually doing. Face the trade-offs and the risks openly. When you take that approach—whatever policy conclusions you eventually reach—you're thinking like an economist.

CHAPTER 19

Macroeconomics and Gross Domestic Product

Macroeconomics is the aggregated top-down view of the whole economy as one large organism: growth, unemployment, inflation, the trade balance, and more. A macroeconomic perspective is not just a scaled-up version of microeconomics, which has been the main focus of the earlier chapters. Microeconomics focuses on individual markets for goods, labor, and capital, and on issues that arise including monopoly, competition, pollution, technology, poverty, inequality, insurance, and governance. But microeconomics has no real language for talking about overall macroeconomic problems in the economy, such as growth and trade deficits. Microeconomics can explain why the price of one good might rise, or why one firm might hire or fire workers, but it cannot come to grips with macroeconomic issues such as inflation or unemployment for the entire economy. Moreover, microeconomics has no structure for talking about macroeconomic policies such as the federal budget and budget deficits or the actions of the Federal Reserve in affecting interest rates and credit.

In fact, behavior that is rational for individuals at the microeconomic level can lead to unexpected results when everyone in a group acts that way. Imagine you're in a stadium among a big crowd watching a concert. You want a better view of the antics onstage, so you stand up. Then some others stand up for a better view, and eventually everyone is standing up. Everyone acted rationally from a microeconomic, individual point of view, but the end, macroeconomic result was that no one saw any better than they did before.

To provide a broad framework for thinking about macroeconomic policy, we will look at four broad goals of macroeconomic policy, then at an analytical framework for thinking about the relationships between these goals, and then at two sets of tools for accomplishing those goals. The four goals of macroeconomic policy are: (1) economic growth, (2) low unemployment, (3) low inflation, and (4) a sustainable balance of trade. The framework for discussing policy is called the aggregate supply/aggregate demand model. This framework helps to organize macroeconomic analysis and should allow us to analyze the trade-offs among growth, unemployment, inflation, and the balance of trade. The two main sets of tools for macroeconomic policy are fiscal policy and monetary policy. Fiscal policy is government tax and spending policy, including the federal budget and budget deficits. Monetary policy refers to the policies of the Federal Reserve, which affect interest rates, credit, and how much money is being loaned and borrowed in the economy.

Before embarking on the topic of macroeconomics, it's important to have a firm grasp of the concept of gross domestic product (GDP), which is the standard measure for the size of a nation's economy. GDP is defined as the total value of final goods and services produced in an economy in a year. GDP can be measured according to the value of either what is produced and sold or what is demanded and bought. Because the total quantities of what is bought and what is sold need to be equal, by definition, these two ways of measuring GDP will lead to the same answer.

For example, in 2009 the total GDP of the United States was $14.2 trillion. In terms of what was produced, this was 13.4 percent durable goods—things such as refrigerators and cars; another 13.4 percent nondurable goods, such as food and clothing; 66.2 percent services; and 7.7 percent structures. (This adds up to slightly more than 100 percent because about 1.1 percent of what was produced was added to inventories, and since it was not yet sold, it was not counted as output.) When many people think about the economy, the first thing that leaps to mind is durable goods, hard stuff that comes out of factories. But the nondurable goods and services—such as health care, education, financial services, legal consulting, haircuts, car repair, lawn-mowing or home-cleaning services, and childcare—are well over half of all U.S. output. When people say we live in a service economy, that's what they mean. The share of services in the U.S. economy has been expanding for decades.

You can also measure GDP from the demand side. Demand from household consumption accounted for about 70 percent of GDP in 2009. Investment spending by businesses was running about 11 percent in 2009, but it varies considerably from year to year. Government spending is about 21 percent of GDP. That may seem a bit low when you recognize that federal, state, and local governments together collect about one-third of GDP in taxes in a typical year, but this figure represents only what government buys directly; government programs that pass money along to citizens, such as Social Security and welfare, show up as part of consumption. The final categories are exports and imports. Exports are demand from other countries for what is produced in the United States. Exports are added to total demand, but imports—U.S. demand going to products made abroad—are then subtracted from total demand. In recent years in the United States, imports have been a lot bigger than exports. That means the United States has a trade deficit, a subject we'll look at later on. Some quick shorthand is useful here. If you ask an economist what GDP is, sometimes the economist will answer that it is $C + I + G + X - M$: consumption plus investment plus government spending plus exports minus imports.

Who actually measures this stuff across the fourteen-figure U.S. gross domestic product? A branch of the U.S. Department of Commerce called the Bureau of Economic Analysis (BEA) collects data from all sorts of surveys and sources—some monthly, some quarterly, some annually. Sometimes the government statisticians need to extrapolate. Right after each quarter, they make a preliminary estimate;

they issue a final estimate later when all the data is in. Every five years, the BEA reviews all the results it has issued over that period and corrects them—sometimes substantially.

Economists often look next at per capita GDP, or GDP per person. This is a simple but rough way of estimating the standard of living at any given place and time. In 2009 that $14.2 trillion in GDP would be divided by the population of 307 million, which equals about $46,000 per person. Per capita GDP is useful as a comparison tool because it automatically adjusts for differences in population, either between countries or over time.

The next important calculation is called real GDP, meaning GDP adjusted for inflation. Say that in a given year, GDP increased 5 percent over the previous year. When the statisticians look at the change in prices, it turns out that 3 percent of the overall 5 percent rise in GDP is attributable to inflation—that is, to prices being higher. As a result, the other 2 percent is the real increase in goods and services being produced. Adjusting for inflation is important for short-run comparisons, and indispensable for long-run comparisons.

GDP has its share of conceptual imperfections. Indeed, *all* economic statistics have conceptual imperfections. Because GDP is a measure of what is bought and sold, things that affect the quality of life but aren't bought or sold aren't directly included in GDP. A classic example is home production. Around the late 1960s and the early 1970s, there was an enormous surge of women into the paid workforce. As a result, many goods and services that had previously been produced at home—meals, house cleaning, and childcare—were now more likely to be bought and sold in the market, and are now included in GDP. That's a significant change in GDP that does not reflect an actual change in the amount of those goods and services being produced in the economy—it only reflects whether these goods were produced at home or purchased in markets.

Many other things affect people's standard of living and their happiness but cannot be measured as things that are bought and sold. For example, if everyone worked ten hours a week less or had an extra two weeks of vacation every year, but output remained the same, GDP would not show any overall gain. Greater or lesser pollution levels don't show up directly in GDP measures. Traffic congestion or length of commute doesn't show up as something bought and sold, except indirectly, such as in gasoline or cups of takeout coffee consumed. Negative events, such as a natural disaster, can lead to the rebuilding of a large part of a city, which makes short-term GDP look positive, but the locals have clearly suffered a lower standard of living. The costs of preventing crime count as part of GDP, but the costs of the actual crimes in terms of loss and violence are not part of GDP. The fact that people have longer life expectancies and are living healthier for longer doesn't show up in any direct way in GDP, although their spending on health care services is counted.

Even within GDP, you might ask—if you were in a skeptical frame of mind—if things that are priced the same really have the same value. For example, is a bag of potato chips the same value as an organic fresh apple? Does *Fortune* have the same value as a pornographic magazine? Is a ticket for admission to a shoot-'em-up movie the same value as a ticket for admission to an art museum? GDP is just about adding up what's bought and sold. It's not about value judgments.

One final note: GDP includes only finished goods, not the intermediate parts that go into making those goods—the steel that goes into the car, the lumber that goes into the chair, and so forth. If you added up the production of all the parts that go into making your car at each stage of production, you'd be counting the same steel or plastic over and over at each stage. Also, transfers of ownership do not show up in GDP; so, for example, it registers the new car you bought, but it doesn't register the used car you sold to your neighbor's son. It registers a new home you constructed or the costs of renovating an old home, but not an old home you bought. When you buy and sell shares of stock in a company, that doesn't register on the GDP, either, since nothing has been created, just exchanged. Only the stockbroker's fee, as a service, is included. When the stock market rises or falls substantially, it has no direct effect on GDP at all.

Despite these limits, the GDP is a worthwhile measure of the state of an economy. Societies with higher per capita GDP tend to be better off in lots of ways. They have more personal consumption—not just what we think of as luxuries but also things such as health care and education. Societies with high per capita GDP also tend to have cleaner air and water. They tend to have a greater degree of personal security. As a wise Nobel laureate named Robert Solow (1986) once said, "If you have to be obsessed by something, maximizing real national income is not a bad choice."

Historically GDP shows a long-term upward trend. After adjusting for inflation, GDP in the mid-2000s was about 5.5 times as large as it was in 1950. The average growth of real GDP from 1950 through 2010 was about 3 percent per year. That's not to say that GDP rose in every single year. A significant and lasting downturn in GDP is called a recession. Some economists consider six months—two economic quarters—to be a lasting downturn, but there's nothing official about that span of time. The starting and ending points of recessions are not defined by any U.S. government agency; rather, they're defined by a committee of academic economists at a nonprofit research institution called the National Bureau of Economic Research (NBER).

The U.S. economy, according to NBER data, had twenty-three recessions from 1900 to 2010. Thus, there was a recession, on average, about every five years. In the aftermath of the 2001 recession, it was common for economists to note that the most recent recessions—in 2001 and in 1990–1991—had been relatively far apart and relatively mild. But the recession of 2007–2009 was brutally long and deep. Thus, a one-sentence summary of the U.S. macroeconomy, as captured by GDP, would report that the long-term trend is up, but this trend is sometimes interrupted, often once or twice a decade, by shorter periods of negative growth. Clearly, the policy goal in this setting should be to discourage or limit these downturns, while nourishing the roots of long-term growth.

CHAPTER 20

Economic Growth

Here's a question for you: Would you rather be a person with an average standard of living in the modern U.S. economy whose household earns about $60,000 per year, or would you rather earn that same $60,000 per year in 1925, which is the dollar equivalent of nearly $800,000 in 2010? Before you choose too quickly, think about this: That $60,000 income would make you extremely rich in 1925. You'd live in luxury, in a big house, with servants and the best of everything that was available. However, you'd also be living with the technological standards of 1925. No modern telecommunications. No modern transit. No modern health care.

Which would you prefer? When I pose this question to various groups, they tend to answer about two to one in favor of the present. Of course, this question has no right or wrong answer, but it illustrates some of the reasons why people value economic growth even over being relatively wealthy compared with others at a certain point in time.

Economic growth compounds over time. Small differences in annual growth rates work out to enormous differences in the standard of living over a generation or two. The formula for predicting the future value of an economy is to take its present value and multiply it by one plus the growth rate of the economy, raised to the power of the number of years into the future. Actually, it's essentially the same formula we used to calculate rates of return when people are saving for retirement. The process of compounding economic growth rates is exactly the same as the process of compounding growth in interest rates.

Let's plug in some numbers to see how this works. Imagine you've got an economy that is growing at 1 percent a year. It starts off—just to keep the calculation simple—with a GDP of 100, measured in the imaginary currency of this hypothetical economy. After ten years, it would be just a bit over 110; the compounding doesn't do much over those ten years. After twenty-five years, 1 percent growth a year would give you a GDP of 128. After forty years, GDP would reach 149. Not bad, but not overwhelming, either.

Now let's run the numbers for a growth rate of 3 percent a year, which is more or less the average for the U.S. economy over the past few decades. After ten years of growth at 3 percent, GDP would go from 100 to 134; after twenty-five years, to 209; after forty years, to 326. In other words, over forty years of growth at 3 percent a year, an economy would more than triple in size. The power of compounding starts to make a real difference.

An Economy Starting with GDP of 100 and Growing for Ten, Twenty-five, and Forty Years

		ANNUAL RATE OF REAL ECONOMIC GROWTH		
		3 percent	5 percent	8 percent
TIME	Ten years	134	163	216
	Twenty-five years	209	339	685
	Forty years	326	704	2,172

Note: The table is calculated using the formula $PV(1 + r)^t = FV$, where PV is the present value of the size of the economy (in this example, a GDP of 100), r is the annual growth rate of the economy, t is time, and FV is the future value.

What if you had a growth rate of 5 percent a year? That's the rate the U.S. economy might have in a really good year, and many countries, including Brazil and Mexico, have had growth rates like that on an ongoing basis for sustained periods of time. At 5 percent a year, an economy that starts out at 100 GDP reaches 163 after ten years. It reaches 339 after twenty-five years; it more than triples. And if you could sustain that growth rate for forty years, the GDP would be 704; it would increase more than sevenfold over forty years.

Finally, let's try an 8 percent rate of economic growth. To be honest, 8 percent is the far upper end of what's possible, at least over long periods. We're talking about the fastest periods of Japanese economic growth, back in the 1960s and '70s; we're talking about the growth rate of China in more recent decades. But let's look at the numbers anyway. With an 8 percent rate of economic growth, in just ten years, GDP would go from 100 to 216, so it would more than double in size in a single decade. After twenty-five years, the economy would go from 100 to 685—almost sevenfold in a time period well within the life span of a person; it's even within the working life of a person. If you could sustain that 8 percent rate of growth for forty years—which no country has done, but just for illustration's sake—then the GDP would grow from 100 to 2,172. In other words, over the course of a person's working life, from age twenty-five to sixty-five, they could see the economy expand by a multiple of 22. That's an extraordinary change in standard of living.

The lesson here is that seemingly small differences of a few percentage points in the annual growth rate have a huge effect. In the long run, you can argue that economic growth is the only thing that matters to the standard of living.

When a country starts off behind other nations in terms of the size of its economy, can it catch up? Definitely, if it can sustain a high rate of growth over time. In fact, some economists believe that countries that start off at lower levels of productivity might be able to take advantage of a period of so-called "catch-up growth." The country that is behind can copy and use technologies that have been invented in other places; they don't have to invent it all themselves. It seems as if the lower-income nations of the world should be able to diminish the gap in per capita GDP with higher-income nations gradually over time.

However, this didn't happen much in the twentieth century. The world economy, from about 1870 up to the early 2000s, has actually seen a divergence between the richest and poorest economies of the world, not a convergence. In 1870 the per capita GDP of the richest countries in the world was about nine times the size of the GDP of the poorest countries in the world. By 1960 the GDP of the richest countries in the world was about thirty-eight times greater. In 1990 it was forty-five times greater. Essentially what happened is that the poorest countries in the world were near a subsistence standard of living in 1870 and remained at a subsistence standard of living, while economic growth in the rest of the world has been compounding all that time.

The lowest-income countries are not poor because of globalization; they're poor because they are almost completely detached from the rest of the world economy. In fact, globalization and the international economy have been extraordinarily helpful in lifting countries such as Japan, China, and India out of poverty. Saying that globalization creates poverty is kind of like saying that exercise makes you overweight because you don't do it. If you're not participating, then the activity in which you are not participating is probably not causing the problem, either.

However, even though the twentieth century was a time of divergence between the high-income and the low-income countries, might the twenty-first century be a time of convergence? Economies of countries such as China and India, who were among the poorest in the world in the 1970s, have surged forward in recent decades. If their example can continue, and be followed, over the course of the next century the gap between rich and poor nations will diminish.

Predictions about catch-up growth are controversial. Some argue that we should expect continued divergence. We can't be sure, for example, when Africa will experience a productivity takeoff, if ever. There are several countries, particularly in Latin America, that seem to take a few leaps forward and then a few steps back. Also, if an economy is far behind, it can take an extraordinarily long time to catch up. We can demonstrate this by using our formula for the effects of long-term growth. Let's say nation A has a real GDP of $500 per year and nation B has a real GDP of $30,000 per year. If nation A somehow sustained a remarkable 8 percent growth for forty years, its real GDP would reach $10,862. Meanwhile, if nation B sustained a mediocre 2 percent growth over that same forty years, its real GDP would be up a little over $66,000. So after forty years of explosive growth in one country and modest growth in the other, per capita GDP in nation B is only six or seven times higher than that in nation A, instead of being sixty times higher. Even under the most optimistic conditions, the world's poorest nations will remain behind in standard of living half a century from now.

The underlying cause of long-term economic growth is a rise in productivity growth—that is, higher output per hour worked or higher output per worker. The three big drivers of productivity growth are an increase in physical capital, that is, more capital equipment for workers to use on the job; more human capital, meaning workers who have more experience or better education; and better technology, that is, more efficient ways of producing things. In practice, these work together in the context of the incentives in a market-oriented economy. However, a standard approach is to calculate how much education and experience per worker have increased and how much physical capital equipment per worker has increased. Then, any remaining growth that cannot be explained by these factors is commonly attributed to improved technology—where "technology" is a broad term referring to all the large and small innovations that change what is produced.

When economists break down the determinants of economic growth for an economy such as the United States, a common finding is that about one-fourth of long-term economic growth can be explained by growth in human capital, such as more education and more experience. Another one-fourth of economic growth can be explained by physical capital: more machinery to work with, more places producing goods. But about one-half of all growth is new technology. If you do a similar breakdown of the reasons for growth in low-income countries, where education levels and physical capital are being updated more rapidly, more of their productivity growth tends to come from gains in physical and human capital and less from new technology.

In the 1950s and '60s, U.S. productivity growth—as measured by the increase in output per hour worked—hovered near 3 percent a year. But starting in the 1970s, productivity growth sank to about 1.5 or 2.0 percent per year, where it stayed for approximately twenty-five years, rising again in the late 1990s. This twenty-five-year period suffered a lot of difficult economic adjustments: periods of high inflation and high unemployment; spikes in oil prices; a big defense spending drop and then a big defense spending buildup; a buildup of budget deficits. But of all those issues, the productivity slowdown was the most significant from a long-run perspective. Let's say the economy lost 1.5 percent productivity growth per year for thirty years. In rough terms, not worrying about compound growth rates, real GDP would be, as a result, 45 percent smaller at the end of that time than it would otherwise have been. Thus, in an alternate universe where that growth slowdown didn't happen, GDP would be nearly 50 percent larger. People would have had nearly 50 percent more money in their paychecks. Whether your goal for government is tax cuts or spending increases, having per capita GDP be almost 50 percent larger would make your goal a lot easier to achieve.

Starting in the late 1990s, the U.S. economy began to see a boost in productivity amid a lot of talk about a "new economy," one built on the dramatic advances in information and communications technology. Productivity growth bounces up and down from year to year, depending on recessions and recoveries, but from 1996 to 2010, productivity growth averaged about 2.6 percent per year. The single most important factor for the long-term prospects of the U.S. economy is whether productivity growth falls back to the quarter century of slow growth from the 1970s into the early 1990s, or whether this higher level of productivity growth can be sustained for the long term.

CHAPTER 21

Unemployment

What is unemployment? That question may seem too obvious to need an answer. But should a homemaker not looking for work be counted as unemployed? What about a worker who has an unrealistic idea of how much pay he or she is going to receive and is waiting for a job offer that is never going to come? A specific definition of unemployment can clarify these sorts of issues.

The official government unemployment rate, calculated by the U.S. Bureau of Labor Statistics, is based on a monthly survey that records how many people do not have work *and* are presently looking for work. A person who does not meet both of those conditions is counted as "out of the labor force." About one-third of all U.S. adults are considered to be out of the labor force.

Defining unemployment in this way offers a consistent definition over time, but the underlying meaning can be controversial. For example, what about a discouraged worker—a person who has been looking for a long time but can't find work and has finally given up? If that person answered the survey by saying, "I'm not looking," that person is not counted as unemployed. What about someone who's working part time and answered, "I am working," even if that person would much rather have full-time work? That person is not counted as unemployed. What about the people who, as occurs in any survey, don't answer truthfully, who claim they're looking for work when they're really not? They are counted as unemployed, even though they may be out of the labor force altogether.

Economists view unemployment in a slightly different way than do government statisticians. In a standard example of a market for, say, bananas, a fall in demand would result in a lower price for that product. When the economy falls into recession, and demand for labor declines, wages and salaries rarely fall in any substantial way. Instead, the quantity of labor demanded falls, and unemployment results. Thus, to economists, unemployment occurs when someone is willing to work at the going wage for that person's skills and experience level, but can't find a job. From this perspective, unemployment is a situation in which wages are, for some reason, stuck above the equilibrium level, so that the quantity of labor supplied at that wage rate exceeds the quantity demanded.

Economists have devoted considerable effort to determining why wages might be "sticky downward" and to the policy implications of this insight. For example, one reason why wages might not decline much when the economy turns down is that for some employees, minimum wage law or explicit union contracts might block the wage from falling. But minimum wages and union contracts don't affect most workers in the U.S. economy.

Thus, economists have turned their attention to the so-called implicit contracts that workers have with their employers. For most employees, wages are fairly fixed over a given year; that is, your salary is the same in a month when business is bad as it is when business is good. Most employees prefer it this way: they don't get an immediate boost in wages if the firm does better, but neither do they risk an immediate drop in wages if the firm does poorly. Firms also prefer not to cut wages, because they fear what it might do to the morale of their existing workers—and perhaps especially the morale of the better workers in a firm. After all, if a firm reduces wages, it must be aware that its best workers will be the ones who find it easiest to get jobs somewhere else. Thus, when the economy falls into recession and the demand for labor drops, firms are highly reluctant to cut wages; instead, they stop hiring or even lay off existing workers.

We now arrive at one of those questions that only an economist could ask: Why is unemployment bad? Or, if you prefer, what are the costs of unemployment?

On the individual level, unemployment harms those who are unemployed. The costs to individuals start with lack of income, but they go well beyond that. Unemployment also causes social pathologies, from strain on the family to poor health to crime in the community. On a social level, unemployment reduces the size of the economy. When people are unemployed, the economy loses the potential output of those workers. For example, in 2010 the U.S. economy as measured by gross domestic product was about $14.6 trillion. If the U.S. economy had had 1 percent more employment and therefore produced roughly 1 percent more output, that increase would have been worth $146 billion. With the unemployment rate hovering near 10 percent through 2010, the unemployment rate represents hundreds of billions of dollars' worth of missing output. On top of this, unemployment raises the demand for government spending on welfare and social services.

Economists commonly divide unemployment into two categories: the natural rate of unemployment and cyclical unemployment. The natural rate of unemployment results from the dynamic ebb and flow of workers and industries. In any economy at any given time, some workers are moving between jobs, some new workers are entering the labor force, some are retiring, and some are moving temporarily into or out of the labor force for any number of reasons. These natural patterns of employment in an evolving market-oriented economy will happen in a context of laws and regulations that affect the incentives of employers and workers. For example, employers will be less eager to hire if they face rules that make it hard or impossible to start or expand a business in some way, such as zoning laws that prevent building a new factory. If firms are required to offer certain benefits to all employees, those firms will be less likely to hire. The generosity (or lack thereof) of unemployment insurance benefits will affect how diligent workers are in looking for jobs. In short, the natural rate of unemployment isn't a natural law, such as the freezing point of water. It's an expected outcome in the labor market given the existing social institutions. The natural rate of unemployment will prevail even when the economy is doing well. If you want to change the natural rate of unemployment through public policy, you need to make it easier for workers to find out about new jobs, to be trained for new jobs, or to move to alternative jobs, or you need to revise laws that may be creating unintended disincentives for hiring or unintended incentives for firing.

The other main category of unemployment is called cyclical unemployment, where "cyclical" refers to the business cycle in which the economy moves in and out of recessions. During a recession, lots of businesses, all at once, are unable to sell as much as they had expected. The overwhelming majority of them decide to not trim wages in an attempt to preserve jobs, but instead they cut back on hiring or reduce their workforce.

The obvious policy for reducing cyclical unemployment would be to fight recessions by raising demand for goods and services, so that a firm in turn would have a greater incentive to hire. The government has two main tools for encouraging spending, which will be discussed in more detail in later chapters. One approach is fiscal policy, which uses tax cuts to encourage households and firms to spend more or an increase in direct government spending. The other is monetary policy: the Federal Reserve can lower interest rates to encourage borrowing for things such as cars and houses, which will encourage firms producing those kinds of things to hire more people. Again, the strengths and weaknesses of these approaches will be discussed in more detail in later chapters. But it's important to remember that when the economy is confronted by a severe shock—such as the much higher oil prices of the 1970s, or the meltdown of dot-com stocks at the end of the 1990s, or the financial crisis during the recession of 2007–2009—these policies can't erase the hard times: at best, they can only help cushion the blow.

If you look at the pattern of U.S. unemployment rates over time, you'll see that these rates were relatively low from the 1950s up through the early 1970s—typically between 4 and 6 percent. In the 1970s and '80s, they were generally higher: the good years had unemployment rates of about 6 percent and the bad years of about 8 percent. In 1982, unemployment reached nearly 10 percent for the entire year. In the 1990s, unemployment rates declined into the range of 4 or 5 percent; in bad years, such as right after the 2001 recession, they reached about 6 percent. The unemployment rate hovered around 5 percent from 2006 through early 2008, before spiking up to the 9 to 10 percent range by late 2009, where it remained into early 2011. The cyclical fluctuations are large, but there is also an underlying natural rate of unemployment that doesn't seem to change a lot over time. For the United States, it's very roughly in the range of 5 or 6 percent.

European unemployment rates rose dramatically in the 1970s and early 1980s, like unemployment rates in the United States. But in much of Europe, unemployment rates remained high through the 1990s and even into the 2000s. Why is that? Economists argued that the natural rate of unemployment was higher in Europe for a number of reasons. Minimum wages are often much higher in European countries. Unions are much stronger, and the prohibitions against firing workers are much stronger as well. Many European governments required firms to offer their employees a lot of benefits, which raised the costs of hiring. Many European governments had limits on when, say, retail businesses could be open. All those factors make the incentives to hire and to work somewhat less, generating a higher natural rate of unemployment. European countries that made an effort to reform these kinds of policies—such as the United Kingdom and the Netherlands—saw a substantial fall in their unemployment rates.

Of course, the issue in labor markets is not only the number of jobs, but also how to have good jobs that pay decent wages. Over time the labor market will tend to push wages toward underlying levels of productivity. After all, if a worker is receiving more than that worker produces, then the business will have an incentive either to fire that worker or at least not adjust wages upward until productivity rises. If a worker is producing more than that worker's wage, then a competitive alternative employer should be willing to bid for that worker, and one way or another, the worker will end up with a bigger paycheck. Thus, in the long run, the basis for strong wage growth over time is to increase average worker productivity. That means investing in better education, encouraging investment in better physical capital equipment, and discovering and adopting new technology. When an economy can bring those factors together, the ideal of good jobs at good wages becomes achievable.

CHAPTER 22

Inflation

Inflation eats away at what your paycheck can buy. At any given time in a market economy, some prices will rise and others fall. But in a situation of inflation, as the prices of many necessities such as gasoline and food all spike higher at the same time, many households must make difficult adjustments.

Inflation is an overall increase in price measured over some combination of goods and services. A thirty-cent rise in the price of gas or a two-dollar hike in the price of a movie ticket, by itself, is not inflation. To measure an overall rise in price level, it's necessary to gather data on price changes for many different goods and find some way to calculate an average rise in the price level. The basic approach is to define a "basket" of goods in which the quantity of each good in the basket represents typical consumption for a household over a certain period of time. Then you can calculate how the total cost of buying that overall basket of goods—not each individual good—has changed over time.

This idea of using a basket of goods as a way to measure inflation goes back a long time. One of the first examples occurred during the U.S. Revolutionary War, when Massachusetts was trying to determine how to pay its soldiers. The Continental Congress was issuing dollars, but it was hard to say what those dollars were actually worth. So Massachusetts said it would pay its soldiers the value of 5 bushels of corn; $68\frac{4}{7}$ pounds of beef, 10 pounds of wood, and 16 pounds of leather, whatever that amount was, when they returned from war.

There are a variety of different measures of inflation, depending on what basket of goods is used. The Consumer Price Index (CPI), for example, is a common measure of inflation calculated by the U.S. Bureau of Labor Statistics on the basis of the Consumer Expenditure Survey, a very detailed survey of what households are actually buying. Another common measure of inflation is the Producer Price Index (PPI). This index is based on the basket of goods that producers buy, such as steel, oil, and other raw materials or equipment. There's also something called the Wholesale Price Index (WPI), which looks at wholesale prices that retailers pay. Finally, there's something called the GDP deflator, which includes everything in the GDP. Remember, the GDP includes not only consumption but also investment, government spending, and exports, minus imports. The CPI and the GDP deflator are probably the measures you'll encounter most. Depending on the question you are studying, you can make up a price index for any group: for example, what the elderly buy, or what the poor buy, or what people in a certain state buy.

The problem with using a fixed basket to calculate inflation is that the basket of goods in the real world doesn't stay fixed. People aren't buying identical goods one year and the next and the next. One reason for this involves the concept of substitution—that is, how people shift away from a good when the price of that good rises. If the price of coffee goes sky-high, people will buy tea or soda instead. If the cost of gasoline rises, more people may choose public transit for their commute. The actual contents of the basket vary in each time period. So when trying to measure inflation, should I use the basket that reflects the quantity of coffee sold at the higher price, or the one that reflects a quantity of coffee sold at the lower price, or some average of the two? Either way, no single basket can account for a constant pattern of shifting demand in the real world.

Another problem with a fixed basket of goods arises from changes in technology. Imagine, for example, you have phone service as one item in your basket of goods, but then cell phones come into the market. The price of cell phones might look high, but it's more flexible than the price for a landline, so it has some appeal. Then smartphones arrive, and voice-over IP services, and videophone services. If you just keep looking at the price of a traditional landline, your basket won't be taking the changes in technology into account. As a result, you'll miss a way in which people are actually doing better in terms of cost of living, in the sense that they have more options than before.

In 1996 a prominent group of economists headed by Michael Boskin, of Stanford University, published a report on measuring inflation. By their estimate, the Consumer Price Index at that time was overstating the true rate of inflation by about one percentage point per year, by not appropriately taking substitution and new technologies into account in its basket of consumer goods. One percent may not seem like much, but the implications are huge. Let's say in a given year the nominal GDP grows 5 percent and inflation is 3 percent, so the real growth is 2 percent. But if inflation was overstated by 1 percent, real growth would actually be 3 percent that year. Of course, an additional one percentage point of real growth per year, compounded over several decades, will have an enormous impact on the standard of living. In the aftermath of the Boskin report, the Bureau of Labor Statistics adjusted its statistical methods to allow for some substitution among goods, and rotated old goods out of and new goods into the baskets over time to help adjust for technology. Also, when the quality-of-life adjustments caused by these factors are large—say, in computers and information processing—the Bureau of Labor Statistics tries to estimate the change directly, and plug that estimate right into its inflation formula. The overstatement of inflation has surely diminished as a result of these changes, but some overstatement persists.

From 1900 until about 1965, inflation averaged about 1 percent a year in the United States. However, the inflation rate did have some periods of extreme fluctuation. In the years right after World War I and again right after World War II, inflation went into double digits for a few years. The standard explanation for this phenomenon is that inflation, at some fundamental level, occurs when there's a lot of buying power in the economy and not quite enough goods. Right after a war, for example, a lot of soldiers return home with back pay in their pockets and a desire for goods all at once. The Great Depression was the one period of the twentieth century during which the United States experienced substantial deflation. The average level of prices fell by about one-third between 1929 and 1933 because the economy was exactly the opposite of the postwar economy: nobody had any money and banks were broke and not lending, so instead of too much money chasing too few goods, there was hardly any money chasing goods—and the price level dropped.

Aside from these instances, inflation in the United States was generally low up through the mid-1960s. Then, in the late 1960s, inflation began to climb. In 1971 it hit 4.4 percent. Back then, 4.4 percent was considered such a terrifying, destructive rate of inflation that a conservative and generally free market president, Richard Nixon, felt it necessary to impose national wage and price controls. They didn't work any better than you'd expect, leading to confusing patterns of shortages and surpluses and arguments over attempts to evade the controls. By 1974, when the wage and price controls were removed, inflation took off. It was 11 percent by 1974; it hit double digits again in the late 1970s.

In the early 1980s inflation came way back down, for reasons we'll discuss later. It was typically in the range of about 2 to 5 percent. In the 1990s it fell to around 1 to 4 percent. For most of the 2000s it has been in the range of 2 to 3 percent, although it fell to nearly zero during the depths of the 2007–2009 recession, when consumers weren't spending, banks weren't lending, and therefore not much money was chasing goods.

Why is inflation bad? This may seem like another of those questions only an economist would ask. Isn't it obvious that we don't want to pay higher prices? Well, not exactly. Here's a thought: inflation isn't necessarily bad—if it happens everywhere at once. Imagine that one night, magic money elves sneak into every wallet, every purse, every bank account, every cash drawer, every paycheck, every place where money is, and they double the money everywhere in the economy. What happens the next morning? In the morning, everyone counts their cash and says, "Yippee!" and goes out shopping. But all the storekeepers know what's happened, so they double all the prices on everything. So even though everyone has twice as much money, they're no better off (or worse off) than they were the day before.

The point of this little parable is that if all prices and wages and interest rates and bank accounts rise at the same rate, and that rate is known to everybody, then nobody will care. In the real world, however, inflation is not evenly distributed, and it's not fully predictable. As a result, it will benefit some groups and impose costs on others. For example, if your pay doesn't rise with inflation, the purchasing power of your money will fall behind. If you borrowed money to buy a house at a fixed 5 percent interest and inflation rises to 10 percent, you come out way ahead, because you can repay your loan in inflated dollars that are worth less than expected. (It's worth remembering, incidentally, that the biggest single borrower at a fixed rate in the U.S. economy is, by far, the U.S. government. Therefore, a big burst of inflation would reduce the real value of all the government debt that's been accumulating.) On the other hand, if you borrowed money to buy a house at a fixed 5 percent and the inflation rate falls to 1 or 2 percent, then the bank is going to come out ahead. If you're the sort of person who holds a lot of cash—maybe buried in a jelly jar in the backyard—inflation will cause you to fall somewhat behind. Even relatively low rates of inflation can make a big difference over the long term.

The process of automatic adjustments for inflation is called "indexing." For example, if you have an adjustable-rate mortgage on your house, your interest rate will go up and down with inflation. The U.S. Treasury issues indexed bonds for which the payout changes automatically with the rate of inflation. Some union contracts specify that union wages will rise automatically with inflation; this is sometimes called a cost-of-living adjustment (COLA). Social Security payments have a COLA, too; they are indexed to the Consumer Price Index. In a sense, indexing is protection against inflation.

When inflation rates get high, they can make it difficult for markets to work well, because firms will find it difficult to focus on long-term productivity growth. When inflation reaches 20 or 40 percent a month or more, it's called hyperinflation. Hyperinflation occurred most famously, perhaps, in Germany in the 1920s, but it also happened in Argentina, Israel, and Bolivia in the 1980s, and in Zimbabwe in the 2000s. These countries offer some examples of the costs of letting inflation get completely out of control. Imagine trying to run a business in a situation in which the buying power of the money you earn at the beginning of the month is worth 40 percent less at the end of that same month. In that situation, trying to minimize your possible losses from inflation becomes more important than any efforts to serve your customers better or to improve long-run productivity.

It is likely no coincidence that the great productivity slowdown of the early 1970s coincided with a burst of inflation, or that after inflation had been under control for about a decade, productivity growth recovered. Prominent economists such as John Taylor, of Stanford University (no relation), have argued that there is a connection between the two, and that one of the causes of the period of low productivity was inflation getting out of control.

During hyperinflation, consumers face problems, too. Ordinarily, when people shop, they compare current prices to their memory of current prices and react according to whether current prices seem higher or lower than expected; but when prices change continuously, people find themselves in the dark, uncertain of their spending decisions. Sticking to a personal or household budget becomes a near impossibility. The government budget process becomes useless for similar reasons. An economy with high and volatile inflation becomes a truly dysfunctional economy.

To understand the policy tools for fighting inflation fully, you need to understand fiscal and monetary policy, which we'll discuss in later chapters. But we can talk about policy in general terms for now. Higher inflation can have many different starting points, but it is always a matter of too much money chasing too few goods in the economy as a whole. Thus the policy tools for fighting inflation all involve holding down the overall level of demand, so that there are fewer dollars chasing goods. Policies to fight inflation are never popular. For example, it's possible to hold down demand by raising taxes, cutting government spending, or raising interest rates to discourage borrowing. When inflation is 400 percent a year, it's fairly easy to get agreement that something must be done. But if inflation is 5 percent, then there will be controversy over whether fighting inflation is worthwhile.

Inflation hawks—those who want to keep inflation extremely low all the time—tend to argue that you need to nip inflation in the bud. You want the actors in an economy—including people who are making current buying decisions and planning for retirement, and firms making current production decisions and long-term investment decisions—to be able to make thoughtful plans. You don't want people playing games to make money off inflation, by borrowing at a fixed rate and repaying in inflated dollars. You don't want firms obsessing over how to avoid the costs of inflation, and ignoring actual productivity growth.

Inflation doves, on the other hand, argue that fairly low inflation, at, say, 2 to 5 percent, isn't such a terrible thing. For one thing, it helps keep wages from getting stuck above equilibrium; if inflation is at 4 percent, giving employees a 2 percent raise is actually a cut in real pay, yet because it looks like a raise, it won't hurt morale in the same way. Allowing a little bit of inflation, they argue, is also better than overcompensating and causing deflation. Deflation can bring economic growth to a screeching halt by making all existing loans more expensive to repay, which in turn can cause widespread defaults. Finally, inflation doves would also say that there's no strong evidence that a country with 2, 3, 4, or even 5 percent inflation is likely to zoom up to 20 percent or 30 percent inflation per year. Low rates of inflation are comparatively easy to cope with.

The empirical evidence—at least as I read it—shows that there's not much effect on an economy with an annual inflation rate between 5 percent and 3 percent. In fact, some economists argue that a lot of middle-income economies around the world have fared pretty well, in the sense of having rapid economic growth, with inflation rates as high as 10, 20, or even 30 percent a year. Once you get above about 40 percent a year, even most of the inflation doves would say there's a real problem. A common goal in high-income countries is to keep inflation steady at around 2 percent. This rate of inflation is low enough to provide a steady basis for long-term economic growth, but it also gives a bit of a cushion to avoid the risks of deflation.

CHAPTER 23

The Balance of Trade

A lot of economic statistics are deeply misunderstood, but none more so, in my opinion, than the balance of trade. For one thing, most people think about balance of trade in terms of goods: cars and computers, imports and exports. If exports are bigger than imports, a country has a trade surplus. If imports are bigger than exports, a country has a trade deficit. That's a good starting point, and economists call it the "merchandise trade balance," but it's not the end of the story. About twenty or thirty years ago international trade really was all about ships and planes filled with cargo. But international trade involves everything of value that is produced in one country and sold in another, and in the modern world, services such as telephone call centers and software design can be in India or Ireland, and American workers can interact with these employees just as if they were in the next building, or in the next town. In this world, merchandise trade balance alone is a pretty limited description of the overall balance of international trade.

The current account balance is the single statistic that captures the most comprehensive picture of a nation's balance of trade. This number includes merchandise trade, but it also includes international services, international investments, and so-called "unilateral transfers," which are payments that are sent without a purchase of goods or services, such as foreign aid. Using data collected by the U.S. Bureau of Economic Analysis for the year 2009, these four categories of the current account balance looked like this:

- In terms of merchandise, the United States exported $1,046 billion in goods and imported $1,562 billion in goods, resulting in a merchandise trade deficit of $516 billion.
- In terms of services, the United States exported $509 billion in services and imported $371 billion in services, resulting in a services trade surplus of $138 billion.
- In terms of international investment income, the United States paid $472 billion to other nations and brought $561 billion back into the country, resulting in an $89 billion investment income surplus.
- In terms of unilateral transfers—including everything from government foreign aid to individuals sending money to family in their home nations—the United States ran a deficit of about $130 billion.

Add up these numbers, and the current account balance for the U.S. economy in 2009 was a deficit of $419 billion.

From the 1940s through the 1960s the current account balance was typically a surplus; during the 1970s it was typically a deficit. Either way, the numbers were small, typically less than 1 percent of GDP. But starting in the early 1980s the U.S. trade deficit became substantial, reaching 3 percent of GDP. After a little sag in the late 1980s and early 1990s, the trade deficit began rising again in the late 1990s and 2000s. By the mid-2000s, trade deficits were running at around 4 or 5 percent of GDP—really very large numbers for an economy the size of the United States. Keep this information in the back of your mind for now; later we're going explore why these two surges in the trade deficit happened.

To understand the categories of the current account balance, think of it this way: Everything on the surplus side of the trade balance involves money flowing into a country. Everything on the deficit side of the trade balance involves money flowing out of the U.S. economy. When the money flowing out equals the money flowing in, the current account balance, the balance of trade, is zero.

When there's a trade deficit—such as the one the United States has mostly had for about forty years—money flows out of the economy and to other nations. But where do those dollars go? They're certainly not being used to buy U.S. goods and services. They're not being paid to U.S. investors in foreign firms. They're not coming back as unilateral transfers. If any of these were true, there wouldn't be a current account trade deficit!

One important twist to remember is that, while the United States pays for its imports in U.S. dollars, the producer in, say, Japan doesn't want U.S. dollars; it wants Japanese yen. After all, the Japanese supplier needs yen, not dollars, to pay for wages and supplies related to production in Japan. Thus, a Japanese firm that exports to the United States and receives U.S. dollars wants to trade the U.S. dollars for yen with someone in the foreign exchange market. Once the Japanese exporting firm trades its dollars for yen, where do the dollars go? One way or another, the dollars end up invested in U.S. assets. Maybe they go to someone who buys stocks, bonds, or property, or maybe that someone puts the money in a bank account; then the firm that issued the stock or bond expands its operations in the United States, or the bank lends out the money to someone who wishes to buy or build or invest in the United States, and so on. The dollars that flow overseas and don't come back as goods or services represent a flow of financial investment back into the U.S. economy.

To economists, a trade deficit literally means that a nation, on net, is borrowing from abroad and receiving an inflow of investment from abroad. For exactly the same reasons, a trade surplus literally means that a nation, on balance, is lending money abroad and having an outflow of foreign investment. A trade surplus and a trade deficit aren't just about the flow of goods. In fact, to most economists, trade imbalances aren't even *primarily* about the flow of goods. They're about this flow of money, and whether the flow is bigger in one direction or another.

How can we put this flow of money into an overall macroeconomic context? Economists use a tool—one that's useful in a lot of macroeconomic contexts—called an identity. An identity, mathematically speaking, is a statement that is true by definition. The national savings and investment identity starts with a basic idea: the total quantity supplied of financial capital has to equal the total quantity demanded of financial capital. There are two main sources of supply for financial capital: domestic savings of financial capital plus all the inflows of foreign financial capital. There are also two main sources of demand for financial capital: domestic physical capital investment and government borrowing. Thus, the national savings and investment identity is telling us that the U.S. macroeconomy has two big sources of capital, and they have to equal the two big demands for capital. From this perspective, a trade deficit is an extra source of money flowing into the economy that can, in turn, be borrowed by firms or by the U.S. government.

Because quantity of financial capital supplied must equal the quantity demanded by definition, a change in one component of this relationship *must* lead to changes in another part or parts of the equation. For example, if the U.S. government borrows more money, the quantity of financial capital demanded goes up. Where does the extra money come from? The national savings and investment identity says that, in theory, the extra supply of financial capital for the government could come from one of three sources. It could be that the U.S. government borrows more, and domestic firms have less financial capital available for private investment. It could be that government borrows more, and people react by increasing savings. Or it could be that as the U.S. government borrows more, there's more inflow of capital from other countries. To determine which of these three changes actually happens, one must go beyond the theory and look at the evidence.

For the United States, one main result of an annual inflow of financial capital is that the U.S. economy has become a net debtor to the rest of the world. At the end of 2008, for example, U.S. individuals, firms, and government combined owned $19.9 trillion in foreign assets. But foreign firms, foreign investors, and foreign governments owned $23.3 trillion in U.S. assets. To put it another way, the U.S. economy owned $3.4 trillion less of the rest of the world than the rest of the world owned of the U.S. economy.

Borrowing from abroad is not always bad. For example, the U.S. economy ran a trade deficit year after year after year in the nineteenth century. In fact, international financial capital financed the growth of railroads and industry that spurred the U.S. economy at that time. Similarly, South Korea ran big trade deficits in the 1960s and '70s, as a result of an inflow of foreign investment funds that spurred Korea's rapid economic growth. Indeed, borrowing from abroad makes economic sense, as long as there's sufficient economic growth in the future to pay back the loan. But if there isn't sufficient growth, borrowing from abroad can turn out badly. Throughout the 1990s and into the 2000s, countries such as Argentina and Russia found themselves running large trade deficits that represented capital inflows that they eventually couldn't repay.

With any borrowing, whether at the national or the individual level, the challenge is to make that borrowed capital generate sufficient benefits or returns over time so you can pay back the loan. For example, when an individual borrows for education, the underlying economic justification is that the degree will pay off over time—in part through higher wages, which allows the individual to pay the loan back over time and come out ahead. If a firm borrows money to build a factory, it's hoping the increased output will allow it to pay back the loan over time and come out ahead. However, if you borrow a large sum of money to go on vacation, it probably won't increase your future income by enough to pay back the loan. My own view is that U.S. trade deficits reached high enough levels by the mid-2000s that it would have been better for the United States to rely more heavily on domestic sources of capital. In that way, more of the gains from investment would have been paid inside the U.S. economy instead of outside.

When we think about the trade deficit in these macroeconomic terms, some interesting and even unexpected implications appear.

For example, if the trade deficit becomes very large, the national savings and investment identity dictates that something else is changing as well. Maybe the U.S. economy is running large budget deficits, and money flowing in from the big trade deficit is being sucked up by government borrowing. Another possibility is that a big surge in domestic investment in the U.S. economy is pulling foreign investment into the U.S. economy. Or perhaps there's been a sharp drop in private savings rates, with foreign saving flooding in to fill the gap. Any of these could happen; at least one must happen for the national savings and investment identity to hold.

In the 1980s, when the large trade deficits first appeared, the likely cause was that U.S. federal budget deficits were very large. In some cases, the federal government was borrowing directly from abroad; in other cases, the federal government was soaking up the available U.S. financial capital, so when firms wanted money, they turned to foreign investors. That said, trade deficits are not always caused by budget deficits. In the late 1990s, for example, the U.S. budget deficits were small and the economy had budget surpluses for a few years. But at that point, private investment was booming—it was the dot-com era—and private saving was low. In effect, the U.S. economy financed that investment boom with a large inflow of foreign financial capital and large trade deficits. This pattern suggests some commonality between the agenda for fixing trade deficits and the agenda for helping long-term economic growth. After all, reducing the trade deficit—keeping domestic investment high—requires higher domestic savings. Raising the U.S. growth rate also requires keeping domestic investment high through higher savings. Thus, policies aimed at raising growth and maintaining a reasonable trade deficit will be similar: both will attempt to encourage domestic saving.

If the trade deficits are macroeconomic in nature—if they're about national savings rates, national investment rates, government budget deficits, and the like—then many of the most common arguments you hear about trade deficits are misguided. For example, it's common to hear people say, "The U.S. trade deficit happens because of unfair foreign trade practices such as shutting out U.S. products and flooding the U.S. goods market with cheap exports." But from the perspective we've been discussing, those trade practices have literally *nothing* to do with U.S. trade deficits. Again, think about the pattern of U.S. trade deficits over the past few decades. If you think unfair foreign trade practices cause trade deficits, you need to believe that foreign trade was pretty fair in the 1970s, then got deeply unfair in the mid-1980s, then became fairer in the early 1990s, then got unfair in the late 1990s, and even more unfair in the 2000s. While unfair foreign trade practices certainly exist—for example, through taxes and rules that make it harder for U.S. exports to be sold in other countries—there's no evidence that the unfairness fluctuates according to this kind of a pattern. Foreign trade practices about limiting U.S. exports or selling cheaply to the U.S. market are not driving these kinds of swings in the trade deficit.

Similarly, protectionism—that is, the restriction of imports from abroad—isn't going to fix trade deficits. If there's a big gap between national saving and national investment, it's going to show up as a trade imbalance. Protectionism is viewed by most economists as a poor idea because it deprives a nation of the benefits of international trade—which we'll discuss in more detail later—but the point here is that protectionism is unlikely to solve a trade deficit because it doesn't deal with the underlying macroeconomic imbalances.

In addition, trade deficits are not primarily determined by a higher level of trade or by greater exposure to the world economy. In the world economy as a whole, exports are about 25 percent of GDP. But do countries that export more than 25 percent of GDP have bigger trade deficits and surpluses? Or do countries that export less than 25 percent of GDP have smaller trade deficits and surpluses? In short, no. There's no such pattern in the data. For example, in the U.S. economy, exports in recent years have run at about 10 or 12 percent of GDP, yet the U.S. economy has humongous trade deficits. Japan has a similarly low figure for exports—about 8 to 10 percent of its GDP—yet it has huge trade surpluses. Why the difference? Japan has an astonishingly high private savings rate and somewhat lower levels of domestic investment versus the United States. That money has to flow somewhere, and it flows out of the country in the form of trade surpluses.

These days you hear a lot about bilateral trade deficits—for example, the trade deficit the United States has with one other country, such as China or Japan. But bilateral trade deficits have no macroeconomic importance. In economic terms, the United States should be expected to have trade surpluses with some countries and trade deficits with others. There's no economic reason to strive for balance with every individual country.

High-income countries have historically tended to run trade surpluses, and thus have been net investors abroad, investing in low-income countries. But in recent decades, the rest of the world has been investing in the U.S. economy on net. There is no precedent for this situation, and it doesn't seem likely to continue in the long run. At some point, the U.S. economy will need to repay this money. The question for the rest of the world is, how much in U.S. assets are you willing to hold? At some point the world won't be willing to keep adding to its portfolio of U.S. assets, and something will adjust. If less foreign financial capital flows into the United States, either we will have to lower the budget deficit, which means higher taxes and/or less spending; or we will need a higher domestic savings rate, which means less consumption; or firms will have to invest in their own growth. None of these options are attractive. But if the United States keeps running high trade deficits, one of those options—and maybe all three—must come to pass.

CHAPTER 24

Aggregate Supply and Aggregate Demand

Having four separate macroeconomic goals—economic growth, low unemployment, low inflation, and a sustainable balance of trade—can cause confusion when it comes to creating economic policy. Economists and policy makers have to ask themselves if it's possible to reach all four goals at roughly the same time or if there are inevitable trade-offs among the goals. To think about this issue, we need an organizing framework for thinking about the macroeconomy. The most common basic framework is called the aggregate supply and aggregate demand model.

Aggregate supply is the total supply of all products in the macroeconomy. It is limited by potential GDP, which is defined as what the economy can produce if all its resources are fully employed. At potential GDP, cyclical unemployment would be zero, and any remaining unemployment would be accounted for by the natural rate of unemployment. Potential GDP is sometimes referred to as full-employment GDP, which suggests that both workers and machines are fully employed.

Aggregate supply will shift if there is a change in what an economy is capable of producing. The two main causes of aggregate supply shift are technological growth and a sharp change in the conditions of production that affect many firms across the economy. In an economy with rising productivity, potential GDP and aggregate supply will rise gradually over time. However, other changes in the conditions of production can lower aggregate supply. A classic example is the sharp increases in oil prices the U.S. economy experienced in the 1970s and intermittently since then. When the cost of energy rose, it drove up the costs of production for many industries at the same time, which was a negative shock to aggregate supply. While adjusting to this new higher price of oil, the economy was able to produce less than it had before.

Aggregate demand, as you've probably figured out by now, refers to the demand for products across an entire economy. We can define aggregate demand as the combination of the five components we used to determine GDP: $C + I + G + X - M$; that is, consumption plus investment plus government spending plus exports minus imports. Of these components, consumption typically makes up the largest part of GDP. Investment is the most volatile. Government spending is perhaps under the most direct policy control at any given time. Exports and imports are heavily shaped by what's happening in the economies of other countries.

For the economy as a whole, the quantity of aggregate supply must equal the quantity of aggregate demand. But there are differing perspectives about how these factors interact. One theory argues that aggregate supply drives aggregate demand; an alternate theory holds that aggregate demand drives aggregate supply.

Say's law, named for early nineteenth-century French economist Jean-Baptiste Say, states that "supply creates its own demand." This is an oversimplification of Say's views, but it's a useful shorthand. This theory is based on the insight that each time a good or service is produced and sold, it represents income that is earned for someone—a worker, a manager, or an owner, whether at the firm that produced the good or at a supplier somewhere along the production chain. For this reason, a given value of supply in a macroeconomic sense must create an equivalent value of income, and therefore demand, somewhere else in the economy. Modern economists who subscribe to a version of Say's law are typically called neoclassical economists.

The main challenge to Say's law and neoclassical economics is recessions. In a recession, business failures heavily outnumber successes.

If supply always creates its own demand, it's difficult to explain why an economy would contract. After all, if aggregate supply always creates exactly enough aggregate demand, why would a recession ever happen? To be fair to Say, he was perfectly aware of this problem, and it's one of the reasons he didn't completely believe in the law that has been named after him.

The alternative to Say's law is called Keynes's law, named after the twentieth-century British economist John Maynard Keynes. It says, "Demand creates its own supply." Once again, this is a gross but useful simplification of the eponymous economist's views. When Keynes was writing *The General Theory of Employment, Interest, and Money* during the Great Depression, he pointed out that during the Depression, the capacity of the economy to supply goods and services had not changed much. U.S. unemployment rates were higher than 20 percent between 1933 and 1935, but the number of possible workers had not dramatically decreased. Factories had been shuttered, but the machinery, the equipment, and the potential hadn't disappeared. Technologies present during the 1920s were not uninvented in the 1930s. Thus, Keynes argued that the Great Depression—and many ordinary recessions as well—was not caused by a drop in potential supply as measured by labor, physical capital, and technology. Instead, Keynes argued, economies entered recessions because of a lack of demand in the economy as a whole, which led to inadequate incentives for firms to produce. Thus, he argued, a greater amount of aggregate demand could lift an economy out of recession.

What's the main challenge to Keynes's law? If aggregate demand is all that matters at the macroeconomic level, then the government could make the economy as large as it wanted, just by pumping up total demand through a large increase in government spending or enormous tax cuts to push up consumption. But economies do face genuine limits on how much they can produce at any point in time, determined by quantity of labor, physical capital, available technology, and the market structures and economic institutions that bring these factors of production together in markets. These constraints don't disappear just because the government engineers an increase in aggregate demand.

There is a plausible pragmatic compromise between a Say's law approach focused on aggregate supply and a Keynes's law approach focused on aggregate demand: Keynesian statements about the importance of aggregate demand are more relevant for short-run policy, and neoclassical statements about the importance of aggregate supply are more important in the long run. This is probably the majority view among modern economists.

In the long run, the size of an economy is determined by aggregate supply: that is, the number of workers, the skill and education levels of those workers, the level of physical capital investment, the prevailing production technologies, and the market environment in which these factors interact.

But in the short run, aggregate demand may vary. For example, when firms are pessimistic or uncertain about the economic future, they put off some investment projects. Then, when they think the economy's doing better, they may embark on their backlog of projects all at once. Also, big fluctuations in investment patterns can be tied to a nation's financial system. In the Great Depression, for example, many businesses and households were unable to repay their loans, and banks went bankrupt as a result. In fact, of the 24,000 U.S. banks that were in operation in 1929, only about 14,400 remained in operation in 1933. When so many banks went out of business, the availability of loans diminished for firms and households alike. Thus aggregate demand dropped off sharply. The recession of 2007–2009 was also born out of a financial crisis, in this case when the bursting of a bubble in housing prices led to bankruptcies, near-bankruptcies, and waves of financial panic.

If wages throughout the economy are sticky and don't adjust immediately to changes in the economy, these short-run drops in aggregate demand can also lead to unemployment. When demand for products diminishes—that is, when there's a recession—firms don't immediately cut workers' pay. They are more likely to stop hiring workers or to lay off a subset of existing workers, which leads to unemployment and a pattern of aggregate demand that doesn't match the slow, long-term growth of aggregate supply.

Some modern economists have taken the theory of sticky wages and extended it to prices. For example, many companies print catalogs once or twice a year; in this case, they won't be adjusting prices with the market's daily fluctuations. Clearly, their prices are sticky. Adjusting a price is a complicated process; a firm needs to analyze the market demand, the competition, and the costs of production before making any moves. The firm also wants to avoid angering or confusing its customer base with constant fluctuations. In other words, price changes incur costs, which economists call menu costs, so a firm has to plan them carefully. Prices do respond to forces of demand and supply. But from a macroeconomic perspective, the process of changing all the prices throughout the economy—whether up or down—takes time. If the prices in a number of markets do not adjust quickly, you can have widespread surpluses for a time, with goods piling up on shelves, and shortages, in which goods sell out, at least in the short run.

The idea that aggregate demand is more important for the short run and aggregate supply is more important in the long run leaves us, of course, with the problem of linking these two perspectives. Despite a lot of effort, no model for bridging the gap between Say and Keynes has yet gained sway over the economics profession.

What does all this mean in terms of our four macroeconomic goals? Ideally, in the perfect macroeconomy, aggregate supply would grow steadily with productivity, and aggregate demand would follow perfectly from the income being produced by that aggregate supply. Aggregate supply and demand would march in lockstep, so that the economy was always producing at potential GDP, with low inflation and low unemployment. But in the real world, economic growth is not a given, nor is coordination between aggregate supply and aggregate demand. As a result, there are periods of fast and slow growth, as well as recession, unemployment, inflation, and trade imbalances. Of course, these possibilities are what make macroeconomics such a policy challenge.

CHAPTER 25

The Unemployment-Inflation Trade-off

The watchful reader may have noticed the danger of a disconcerting trade-off between the two macroeconomic goals of low unemployment and low inflation. When aggregate demand is less than potential GDP, the economy is likely to be in a recession and have unemployed workers, but at least it won't be experiencing inflation. On the other hand, when aggregate demand begins to bump up against or exceed potential GDP, the economy is likely to have low unemployment, but a rising rate of inflation. Of course, there's also a perfect middle ground. Call it the Goldilocks economy: not too hot, not too cold, just right, in which aggregate demand exactly matches aggregate supply at potential GDP.

Something like the Goldilocks economy occurs now and then—for example, substantial chunks of the 1960s and the 1990s were such a time—but given the complications of the real-world economy, we should expect to see some periods of high unemployment and low inflation and other periods of low unemployment and high inflation. This trade-off is one of the central problems of macroeconomic policy. It's known as the Phillips curve, after an economist named William Housego Phillips, who first provided systematic evidence for such a trade-off. In the 1950s, Phillips looked at annual British data on unemployment and percentage change in wages, which can be thought of as a measure of inflation, over a sixty-year period. Phillips found a distinctive relationship that could be mathematically depicted

A KEYNESIAN PHILLIPS CURVE TRADE-OFF BETWEEN UNEMPLOYMENT AND INFLATION

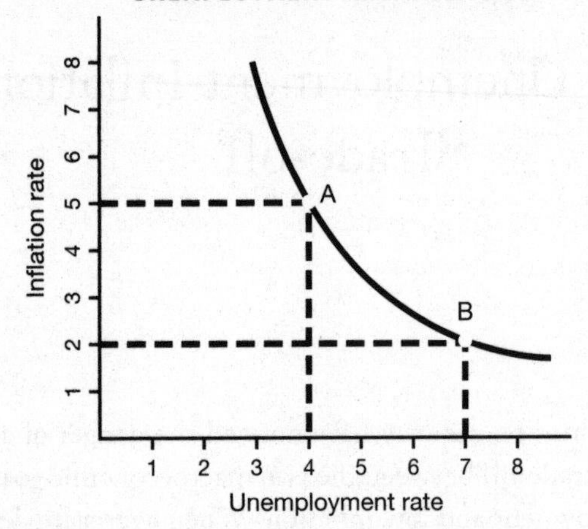

as a curve, with unemployment on the horizontal axis and inflation on the vertical axis of the graph. The curve itself slopes downward, from left to right. In other words, the curve shows that the economy tended to move over time from situations of high inflation and low unemployment to situations of low inflation and high unemployment, and then back again.

What's the economic logic behind the unemployment-inflation trade-off demonstrated by Phillips's data? The aggregate supply and aggregate demand model provides an answer. When the economy is operating at potential GDP, but then aggregate demand increases further, the result is too much money and too much demand trying to chase more than the economy can produce. In that situation, cyclical unemployment is likely to be near zero and unemployment is likely to be low. However, with all that demand, there's a good chance that wages are going to be pushed higher by low unemployment. In the goods market, there are going to be too many dollars chasing too few goods. So, in a situation of full employment, wage inflation and price inflation are more likely to be triggered.

On the other hand, when the economy is operating below potential

GDP, it is in a recession, which means unemployed labor and, in general, underemployed resources. When there's a lot of unemployment, workers are competing for jobs, and wages stay low. In the goods market, there are likely to be lots of surpluses, with too few dollars chasing too many goods. In that situation, there's likely to be hardly any inflation.

After the publication of Phillips's results based on British data, American economists immediately began to look at U.S. data on this same phenomenon. The annual data for the United States on unemployment rates and inflation from the 1950s and '60s, when put on a graph, sketched out a nice clean clear Phillips curve. (It's always nice when the data seem to back up an economic theory!) But it was too good to last. Indeed, in 1968 the famous economist Milton Friedman predicted that the Phillips curve would not hold up in the long run. His argument was deep and thoughtful along many dimensions, but for our purposes, we can boil the key point down to this: in the long run, the economy always reverts to potential GDP and the natural rate of unemployment. Friedman was effectively arguing that in the long run, there wasn't any unemployment-inflation trade-off, just the natural rate of unemployment, and the only question was whether inflation would be high or low at that natural rate. It's worth thinking for just a moment about the raw, intellectual audacity of Friedman's claim. It flew in the face of existing evidence and the main professional consensus of that time. And Friedman turned out to be right.

Just a few years later, in the 1970s, the relationship between unemployment and inflation that had prevailed through the 1950s and '60s collapsed. Remember that the Phillips curve predicts a trade-off between inflation and unemployment. In the 1970s, inflation and unemployment went up at the same time. These were the stagflation years, when inflation and unemployment both nearly hit double digits. In the 1980s both inflation and unemployment went back down. Then, in the late 1990s, inflation and unemployment were both even lower than they had been in the mid-1980s. Instead of a trade-off between unemployment and inflation, the two seemed to be moving in the same direction!

What happened? How can we explain the Phillips curve fitting the U.S. unemployment and inflation data for the 1950s and '60s, but then suddenly not fitting the data in the 1970s, '80s, and '90s? The most plausible explanation is that the Phillips curve is a short-run phenomenon, one that lasts over one or several economic cycles of recession and recovery. But in the long run, these economic cycles and the cyclical unemployment come and go, while the underlying natural rate of unemployment remains. However, the natural rate might be accompanied by either a higher or lower rate of inflation. Recent historical patterns suggest that the natural rate of unemployment in the United States is roughly 5 to 6 percent. Unemployment seemed to return to that level again and again over the past forty years or so, even while inflation fluctuated wildly, from 2.5 percent all the way up to 11 percent. So over a period of a few years, yes, you'll get a Phillips curve trade-off between inflation and unemployment. But over several decades, the economy keeps adjusting back to the natural unemployment rate, and higher inflation in the long run doesn't benefit the economy.

This difference in emphasis between the short run and the long run reflects a division among macroeconomists. Those who champion Keynes's law that demand creates its own supply tend to focus more on the short-run business cycle over a few years, while those who champion Say's law that supply creates its own demand tend to focus more on the long run.

Keynesian economists would emphasize that the macroeconomy sometimes fails to coordinate aggregate demand and aggregate supply; supply grows more or less steadily, but demand fluctuates more because the components of aggregate demand, such as investment and consumption, are subject to all sorts of irrational pressures. Keynes argued that investment was affected by "animal spirits," an impulse to invest or not invest that was unsupported by any kind of careful calculation. Add to this mixture volatility in consumer sentiment, sticky wages, and sticky prices, and you'll have situations of surplus and unemployment. From a Keynesian perspective, the economy looks unstable often on its way either into or out of recession.

Moreover, Keynesians are concerned that the macroeconomy can become stuck below potential GDP for a long time. Even if the economy gradually returns to full employment in the long run without government action, as Keynes famously wrote, "In the long run, we're all dead." Waiting for the long run has large costs; if the economy takes years to readjust, that's a huge chunk out of people's lives and careers. Thus, Keynesian economists tend to support active government macroeconomic policies with the goals of fighting unemployment, stimulating the economy, and shortening recessions and depressions as much as possible.

On the other side, neoclassical economists, who follow Say's law that supply creates demand, tend to emphasize that the economy does adjust toward potential GDP over time. They believe that the modern macroeconomy—leaving aside the Great Depression—is fairly stable. They point to the data for the past four or five decades that suggest the economy always returns to potential GDP, with 5 to 6 percent natural unemployment. Neoclassical economists would certainly admit the Great Depression was a terrible event and that the Great Recession of 2007–2009 was a terrible event. But they also believe that if government actively intervenes in macroeconomic policy, it's as likely to do harm as good, creating even greater economic instability. Neoclassical economists often prefer to see macroeconomic policy conducted with clear rules specified well in advance, both to constrain government discretion and so that markets can take the rules into account.

I don't mean to imply that Keynesian and neoclassical economists disagree on everything. But it's fair to say that Keynesians are more likely to emphasize how government could help the unemployed with programs such as assistance for job searches and retraining or temporary support for unemployment insurance and health insurance. Conversely, neoclassicists are likely to emphasize getting rid of or redesigning rules and regulations that discourage businesses from hiring, rules that mandate providing certain employee benefits or that limit the hours of operation or the locations where they can build new plants.

Both Keynesians and neoclassicists also argue that their particular focus would improve prospects for long-term economic growth. Neoclassical economists emphasize how the stability and predictability of economic policy, together with low inflation, creates an economic environment in which firms can focus on innovation and investment. Remember, the great productivity slowdown of the early 1970s happened at about the same time as the great inflation of the 1970s, and the productivity growth didn't return until inflation had been low for a time. Keynesians often emphasize that recessions tend to be times of high unemployment and low investment in physical capital. Not only does a recession represent short-term economic losses, but workers who fail to gain experience and firms that fail to make physical capital investments will lag behind in long-term growth, too.

Robert Solow (2000, p. 158), the Nobel laureate in economics in 1987, described the dual approach of macroeconomists to the issues of long-run growth and short-run recession fighting:

> At short time scales, I think, something sort of Keynesian is a good approximation and certainly better than anything straight neoclassical. At very long time scales, the interesting questions are best studied in a neoclassical framework and attention to the Keynesian side of things would be a minor distraction. At the 5- to 10-year time scale, we have to piece things together as best we can and look for a hybrid model that will do the job.

Ongoing research in economics continues to pursue that "hybrid model" standing between the Keynesian and neoclassical approaches. In the meantime, we should hold in mind that macroeconomic policy should be concerned with both short-run economic fluctuations and long-run growth.

CHAPTER 26

Fiscal Policy and Budget Deficits

Macroeconomic policy attempts to guide the economy along a course in which, despite the fluctuations and evolutions of the real-world economy, it can achieve all four of the main macroeconomic goals: long-run growth, low unemployment, low inflation, and a sustainable balance of trade. In this chapter, the focus of the discussion shifts to the main tools of macroeconomic policy. This chapter and the two that follow will address fiscal policy: that is, how government tax and spending policy affect the macroeconomy. Subsequent chapters will turn to monetary policy: that is, how the Federal Reserve affects interest rates and the quantity of lending in the economy.

The starting point for understanding the potential power of fiscal policy is that the U.S. federal budget is huge. Roughly speaking, federal government spending has accounted for 20 percent of U.S. GDP over recent decades. The U.S. GDP is approximately one-quarter of world GDP. Thus, the U.S. government's annual budget is 5 percent, or one-twentieth, of world GDP. It's fairly common around the world for government spending to make up one-third, one-half, or even more of a nation's GDP. The sheer size of government spending around the world commands attention.

"Fiscal policy" is the overall term that economists use to cover government tax and spending policy. Although the U.S. federal budget evolves every year, some long-term patterns are discernible.

On the spending side, the main categories of federal spending, which make up about two-thirds of the total, are defense, Social Security, health (especially Medicare and Medicaid), and interest payments on past borrowing. In 2009, for example, 18.8 percent of federal spending was defense spending, 19.4 percent was Social Security, 21.7 percent was health spending, and 5.3 percent was interest spending, leaving about 35 percent to cover everything else in the budget. When I say "everything else," I'm including agriculture, antipoverty programs, benefits for retired federal workers, international spending, space and science, energy, natural resources, commerce, housing, community development, transportation, education and training, veterans' benefits, law enforcement, and the expenses of running government, such as salaries and computers.

Over time, defense spending has declined somewhat as a share of national GDP, falling from about 10 percent in the 1950s to 7 percent in the 1960s and 5 percent in the 1970s. By the mid-1980s, it was up a bit, to about 6.5 percent of GDP, then sagged steadily through the late 1980s and '90s, reaching 3 percent of GDP in 2000. However, in the first decade of the twenty-first century, defense spending has risen back toward 5 percent of GDP. Social Security and health care spending have been steadily increasing as a share of GDP over time.

Some of the hot arguments over federal spending involve amounts that are small by federal government standards. Think, for example, of the argument over funding the National Endowment for the Arts. The total budget for this agency is about $160 million; from the standpoint of a federal budget that totaled $3.5 trillion in 2009, this falls into the category of a rounding error. Foreign aid—which many people seem to think is some humongous amount of government spending—is actually less than 1 percent of the federal budget. Conversely, defense spending is enormous, and it's grown since the terrorist attacks of 9/11, but the biggest single chunk of the federal budget is aimed at the elderly: Social Security, Medicare, and federal retiree benefits make up almost half of the federal budget. This pattern helps explain why it's politically difficult to cut federal spending. Cutting defense, Social Security, and Medicare and other health care spending are all unpopular choices, but they represent much of the spending, and other areas often aren't large enough for cuts to make a significant difference.

What are the trends in overall federal spending over time? First of all, as a share of GDP, federal spending hasn't shown any upward trend over recent decades. Back in the early 1960s, federal spending ranged from about 19 to 22 percent of GDP. It was a little higher than that during Ronald Reagan's military buildup in the 1980s. In the early 1990s, government spending was about 21 percent or 22 percent of GDP. It declined a little bit during Bill Clinton's presidency, so spending was at the low end of the normal range when George W. Bush entered office in 2000. After Bush's first term, federal spending was back in the middle of that 19 to 22 percent range. In the recession of 2007–2009, federal spending rose above its historical range, to about 25 percent of GDP in 2009 and 2010. But these two years of high spending, which occurred under unexpected and exceptional economic circumstances, don't make a long-term trend. At least not yet!

In short, the idea many people have that federal spending has been steadily skyrocketing out of control for decades just isn't true. As a share of GDP, federal spending has been more or less the same for about five decades.

What about the tax side? The main categories of federal taxes, which make up 95 percent of the total, are individual income taxes, corporate income taxes, payroll taxes for Social Security and Medicare, and the excise taxes—that is, taxes on gasoline, cigarettes, and alcohol. For 2009, 43.5 percent of federal taxes collected were individual income taxes, 6.6 percent were corporate taxes, 42.3 percent were Social Security and Medicare, 3 percent were excise taxes, about 1 percent were the estate and gift taxes, and the rest of federal tax revenue was made up of smaller taxes such as customs duties and miscellaneous fees.

Individual income taxes are the single biggest share of federal income, but they are still less than half of all federal revenue. The payroll taxes for Social Security and Medicare are nearly as big. In fact, since income taxes tend to be paid more by people who have high incomes, whereas everyone who works pays the Social Security and Medicare taxes, more than half of U.S. households pay more in payroll taxes than they do in income taxes.

Notice again that some politically controversial taxes, such as the estate tax, don't account for much of federal revenue. Cutting the estate tax may be a good idea, or it may be a bad idea, but it won't substantially change the overall budgetary picture. And as with spending, there hasn't been any upward trend in federal tax collection over the past few decades, either. Since about 1960, federal taxes have typically amounted to 17–19 percent of GDP. That figure was a little bit lower during the 1960s, then pretty constant through the 1970s, 1980s, and early 1990s. In the late 1990s through 2000, federal taxes crept up to 20.9 percent of GDP, the highest level since 1944. Historically, that level of federal taxes was very high, so it's no big surprise that in the 2000 elections, both George W. Bush and Al Gore campaigned on cutting taxes. By 2006 and 2007, federal taxes were a bit above 18 percent of GDP, pretty much at their historical average. But the recession of 2007–2009 slowed down the economy and reduced tax revenues, which fell to about 15 percent of GDP in 2009 and 2010.

Before putting the spending side and the tax side together, let's clear up a couple of side issues. First of all, people sometimes want to leave Social Security out of discussions of the federal budget. After all, it's run with a separate trust fund and separate taxes. But that doesn't change the fact that Social Security involves taxes compelled under law and spending determined by Congress. You can't simply take $700 billion or so in taxes and spending and say, "That's not in my left pocket; it's in my right pocket, so it has no effect on anything else." Social Security—and Medicare—have to be included in any realistic view of what the federal government is doing.

We should also address the matter of state and local budgets for a moment. If you combine the budgets for state and local government, they are roughly 13 or 14 percent of GDP, compared with the roughly 20 percent of GDP that is federal spending. If you add federal, state, and local spending, total government spending in the United States is typically about one-third of GDP. State and local spending, however, is focused on very different priorities than federal spending, especially on education, criminal justice, and infrastructure. For example, state and local government education spending is considerably bigger than the federal defense budget, and considerably bigger than Social Security spending. That said, we're going to stay away from state and local budgets, because they lack the ability to conduct macroeconomic policy. The federal government has the power to run budget deficits; in contrast, state and local governments typically operate under rules that more or less require them to run balanced budgets.

In the federal budget, taxes don't need to match spending in any given year. If the government spends more than it gets in taxes, there's a deficit. If the government taxes more than it spends, it has a surplus. Let's consider the pattern of deficits and surpluses over the past half a century or so. In the 1960s the U.S. government ran mainly small budget deficits, typically around 1 percent or less of GDP; 1969 was the only year in that decade with a budget surplus. In the 1970s there were federal budget deficits every year running around 3 or 4 percent of GDP. The 1980s also had deficits every year, exceeding 5 percent of GDP for several years mid-decade. In the mid-1990s, all of a sudden, deficits started declining, and shockingly—at least to me at that time—from 1998 to 2001, the federal government actually ran surpluses. In 2002, deficits returned, and by the mid-2000s they were typically in the range of 2 to 3 percent of GDP again, roughly the same size as in the 1970s. In the aftermath of the recession of 2007–2009, as already noted, government spending spiked and tax revenues dropped. As a result, budget deficits exploded to historically very high levels of 10 percent of GDP in 2009 and 2010.

When the government spends more than it taxes, where does it get the money? It issues bonds. A bond, as you may remember, is a financial instrument with a certain face value and a promised rate of interest paid over a given period of time. So to meet a budget deficit of, say, $500 billion, the federal government will issue $500 billion in bonds, which it will eventually have to repay.

Every government tax or spending program raises issues of whether it is well designed to accomplish its desired goals at reasonable cost. But here we will set aside discussions about individual policies and instead look at the macroeconomics of federal taxation and spending. In particular, we want to look at how the federal budget affects each of the four main goals of macroeconomic policy.

Our first macroeconomic goal is economic growth, which is affected by factors such as long-term investments in physical capital, human capital, and technology. Government borrowing and saving are linked to physical capital investment as part of what we called the national savings and investment identity. That identity stated that for the economy as a whole, the quantity of financial capital supplied by domestic savings and inflows from foreign investors (the flip side of the U.S. current account deficit) must be equal to the quantity of financial capital demanded for physical capital investment and for financing the U.S. government budget deficit. If the government borrows a lot of money, this could reduce the funds available for private investment. It could also make the government, and the economy as a whole, more dependent on inflows of foreign capital, enlarging the trade deficit. On the other hand, government policies, at all levels of government, are central to building human capital. After all, the government is intimately involved in providing education, and capital for innovation and the development of new technology. If there were more private saving in the U.S. economy—and thus less government borrowing—there could be more spending on things that offer long-term returns, which could help build long-term economic growth.

The second goal: How can fiscal policy be used to address unemployment, whether cyclical or natural? Redesigning specific tax burdens that affect hiring, and redesigning the spending programs that help the unemployed might reduce natural unemployment. Cyclical unemployment, meanwhile, is tied to recessions. In that situation, the appropriate fiscal policy would be more government spending or less taxation. That could pump up aggregate demand and at least hold down the increase that would otherwise occur in cyclical unemployment.

What about the third goal, reducing inflation? Remember, inflation results from too much money chasing too few goods when aggregate demand is so high that it's above the potential GDP. As a result, prices all over the economy rise. In that situation, fiscal policy could be used to reduce aggregate demand through a policy of spending cuts or tax increases, either of which would pull dollars out of the economy and help prevent inflation.

Our fourth goal is a sustainable balance of trade. How can fiscal policy affect the trade balance? Again, government borrowing and saving is part of the national saving and investment identity. In fact, government borrowing is one of the biggest demands for financial capital in the U.S. economy. When the government demands so much capital—say, 3 or 4 percent of GDP each year—that draws in foreign investment. High government borrowing is thus linked to large trade deficits. Once again, more national saving—either in the form of more private-sector saving or less borrowing by the government—would leave the U.S. economy less reliant on inflow of capital from abroad.

These, in broad strokes, are the tools of fiscal policy. But as you've learned, short-term goals and long-term goals for the economy aren't always in sync, so in the next two chapters we will look at these tools in action, first over the short term, then over the long term.

CHAPTER 27

Countercyclical Fiscal Policy

You may have noticed a pattern of addressing macroeconomic issues in two different time frames: a Keynesian, short-term frame and a neoclassical, long-term frame. Here we're going to focus on fiscal policy in the short term, meaning a scale of a few years, typically a period of time from the end of one recession to the start of the next.

Let's back up a half step and remember what is included in aggregate demand: $C + I + G + X - M$, or consumption plus investment plus government spending plus exports minus imports. Of those elements in the equation, three can be particularly affected by fiscal policy. One, obviously, is government spending. But consumption and investment can be strongly affected by tax policy as well. Tax cuts can increase them; tax increases can slow them down. Thus, fiscal policy has the power to shift aggregate demand.

A policy of increasing aggregate demand or buying power in the economy is called expansionary macroeconomic policy. It's also sometimes called a "loose" fiscal policy. Expansionary policy includes tax cuts and spending increases, for example, both of which put more money into the economy. Policies used to reduce aggregate demand, in contrast, are called contractionary policies, or "tight" fiscal policies. A policy of tax increases or spending cuts is considered contractionary, reducing the amount of buying power in the economy. Such a policy can also be used to lean against the cycles of the economy;

such countercyclical fiscal policy aims at counterbalancing the underlying economic cycle of recession and recovery.

The decision about whether to use changes in spending or in taxes to affect demand will depend on specific conditions of that time and place and on political priorities. The emphasis is to get the economy moving, one way or another, by pumping up aggregate demand. In his *General Theory of Employment, Interest, and Money,* John Maynard Keynes (1936) ruminates at one point that the government could "fill old bottles with bank notes and bury them at a suitable depth in disused coal mines, which were then filled up to the surface with town rubbish, and leave it to private enterprise on the well-tried principles of laissez-faire to dig the notes up again." He also points out that it would be more sensible to stimulate the economy in a way that provided actual economic benefits—his example is building houses—but his point is that when you're trying to pump up aggregate demand, exactly how you do it is a secondary concern from a macroeconomic point of view.

If, instead of fighting unemployment, we're trying to fight inflation, we need to think about a tight fiscal policy to reduce aggregate demand. This means lowering spending and/or raising taxes, and the theory doesn't dictate which choice or which mix of the two is best for any given situation or in general. We'll return to a discussion of the choice between tax and spending tools later.

Countercyclical fiscal policy can be implemented in two ways: automatic and discretionary. Automatic stabilizers are government fiscal policies that, without any need for legislation, automatically stimulate aggregate demand when the economy is declining and automatically hold down aggregate demand when the economy is expanding.

To understand how this happens automatically, imagine first that the economy is growing rapidly. Aggregate demand is very high; it's at or above potential GDP, and we're worried about inflation. What would be the appropriate countercyclical fiscal policy in this situation? One option is to increase taxes to take some of the buying power out of the economy. But this happens automatically to some extent because taxes are, more or less, a percentage of what people earn. As income rises, taxes therefore automatically rise. Indeed, the U.S. individual income tax is structured around tax brackets so as people earn more income, the taxes paid out of each additional dollar gradually rise. The same process works in reverse, of course. In a shrinking economy, the taxes that people owe automatically decline because taxes are a share of income. This helps prevent aggregate demand from shrinking as much as it otherwise would. Thus, taxes are an automatic countercyclical fiscal policy, or an automatic stabilizer.

On the spending side, when the economy grows, what countercyclical policy do we want to apply, and what actually happens? As a booming economy approaches potential GDP, the goal of countercyclical fiscal policy is to prevent demand from growing too fast and tipping the economy into inflation. But when the economy is doing well, fewer people need government support programs such as welfare, Medicaid, and unemployment benefits. As a result, in good economic times, spending from the government in these kinds of categories automatically declines, which acts as the desired automatic stabilizer. The same works in reverse. In a shrinking economy or a recession, more people are unemployed and need government assistance. At such times, government spending on programs that help the unemployed and the poor tends to rise, boosting aggregate demand (or at least keeping it from shrinking too much), which is exactly the countercyclical fiscal policy one would want.

Recent economic experience offers several examples of these patterns. During the dot-com economic boom of the late 1990s, there was an unexpected surge in federal tax revenues. President Bill Clinton's proposed budget for fiscal year 1998 predicted a deficit of $120 billion, but when the booming economy produced $200 billion more in tax revenue than expected, it led to a budget surplus of $69 billion. Similarly, Clinton's proposed budget for 1999 predicted a balanced budget in 2000; they actually got a surplus of $236 billion.

Surpluses that existed between 1998 and 2001 led to increased federal tax revenues; federal taxes in 2000 collected 20.9 percent of GDP. These unexpectedly high tax revenues weren't the result of new legislation. They were automatic stabilizers, helping to prevent the economy from expanding too quickly and triggering inflation.

As a counterexample, consider the extremely large budget deficits of 2009 and 2010. President George W. Bush's last proposed budget, which applied to fiscal year 2009, projected that the tax revenues for 2009 would be 18 percent of GDP. But when the recession hit, tax revenues for 2009 turned out to be just 14.8 percent of GDP. A portion of this drop was due to tax cuts passed in 2009 under the incoming administration of President Obama, but most of it was due to the recession turning out to be far harsher than expected. This unexpected drop in tax collections was an automatic stabilizer that helped to cushion the blow of the recession.

More broadly, systematic evidence shows the impact of countercyclical fiscal policy over time. John Taylor looked at evidence from the 1960s up through 2000 and found that, on average, a 2 percent fall in GDP led to an automatic offsetting increase in fiscal policy of 1 percent of GDP.

Given the presence of these automatic stabilizers, and the way in which taxes and spending automatically offset some of the swings in the economy, a controversy then arises: Should Congress go further? Should Congress and the president enact additional discretionary countercyclical fiscal policies that would go beyond the automatic fiscal policies and attempt to stabilize the economy even more? Back in the 1960s and even into the 1970s, a substantial number of economists would have favored using discretionary policy. In the 1980s and '90s, the pendulum swung the other way, toward doubt that such discretionary policy could be useful and effective. However, during the deep recession of 2007–2009, discretionary fiscal stimulus packages made a comeback.

Why are many economists skeptical of discretionary fiscal policies? First, there is a problem of timing. Automatic stabilizers are built into the spending programs and the tax code, so they happen in real time as a recession or recovery unfolds. Discretionary fiscal policy, in contrast, isn't enacted until there's already a problem—at which point it may be too late. Congress doesn't address a recession or inflation until there's already a recession or inflation. Add to that the time it takes to draw up, debate, revise, debate again, revise some more, and finally vote on the federal budget—a process that happens only once a year—and it could be a year or more before the government puts fiscal policy into motion, at which point the economic problem might be different. For example, a stimulus package backed by the Obama administration was passed into law in February 2009. According to the academics at the National Bureau of Economic Research, who date when recessions begin and end, the recession ended in June 2009. Whatever the merits or demerits of the Obama stimulus package, it simply wasn't in place long enough to be a main reason that the recession ended.

A second difficulty with fiscal policy is that it can have undesirable side effects. Imagine the situation of a government running a loose fiscal policy and trying to stimulate the economy, probably boosting the budget deficit via tax cuts and spending increases. But large budget deficits also mean that the federal government might be sopping up much of the money that was otherwise available for domestic investment. Alternatively, the extra demand the government is creating might be directed toward imported products rather than domestic products, pumping up some other nation's economy instead of your own, and leading to a larger trade deficit.

A third difficulty with discretionary fiscal policy lies in the nature of politics. Since the Great Depression and the writings of John Maynard Keynes, many economic policy makers have called for the government to enact countercyclical fiscal policy—that is, to spend in bad times and be tightfisted in good times. But politically, this is tough. Why? Imagine that the economy's growing very quickly. Tax money is flooding in, and economists say, "Don't spend it; build up a really big surplus, cut spending, and raise taxes." That's good countercyclical policy, but it's not an easy sell politically. When the economy is shrinking and money is tight, economists say, "This is a fabulous time for a spending spree. We know there's no tax money; spend anyway!" But many members of the public and politicians will say that if everyone else is tightening their belts in an economic downturn, the government should do so, too. The intuition of contracting the government when the economy is going well and pumping up in bad times is often not common political wisdom.

A fourth concern that applies to both discretionary and automatic countercyclical policy is that these measures can be a little like taking aspirin when you've got a bad case of flu: it numbs the pain so that you feel better, but it doesn't directly address the underlying infection. In the 1970s the U.S. economy was staggered by sharp rises in oil prices. In the late 1990s the U.S. economy was hit by an investment bust after the investment boom of the dot-com years. In the recession of 2007–2009 the U.S. economy was hit by a financial crisis when a bubble of rising housing prices burst. Macroeconomic fiscal policy doesn't address questions such as how to make the U.S. economy less susceptible to oil price shocks, or how to address price bubbles in technology stocks or housing, or how to design a financial system that is less susceptible to crisis. Fiscal policy can ease the pain of a recession, at least somewhat, but the underlying causes of the recession still need to be addressed and worked through by both private markets and the public sector.

Just to throw one final wrench into the macroeconomic works, this discussion has not addressed the monetary policies run by the Federal Reserve. We'll look at these policies in detail later; for now, I'll just say that the Federal Reserve's decision to increase or reduce interest rates offers an alternative policy for the short-term management of aggregate demand. Reduced interest rates help stimulate aggregate demand; increased interest rates hold down aggregate demand. Also, the Federal Reserve can often react more quickly than Congress; interest rate changes are more or less instantaneous compared with the tortuous budget process. So some economists hold that the Federal Reserve and the automatic fiscal stabilizers can mostly handle the short-term issues, while discretionary fiscal policy should be reserved for extreme cases and the long term.

The question of whether to implement fiscal policy through tax policy or spending policy is often made on partisan lines. Conservatives and Republicans often prefer to conduct expansionary fiscal policy with tax cuts and contractionary fiscal policy with spending cuts. Conversely, liberals and Democrats often prefer to conduct expansionary fiscal policy with spending increases and contractionary fiscal policy with tax increases. The theory of countercyclical fiscal policy takes no side in this dispute. Therefore, when economists disagree on how to conduct macroeconomic policy, they often disagree along predictable partisan lines, just like everyone else. The purpose of studying economics is to help you clarify the range of the political choices and the trade-offs between those choices. The political choices themselves remain up to you.

CHAPTER 28

Budget Deficits and National Saving

Federal budget deficits were extremely large in 2009 and 2010—as discussed earlier, roughly 10 percent of GDP. However, a budget deficit that is large for only a few years and then falls dramatically in size—or even turns into a budget surplus—raises very different questions from those raised by budget deficits that remain large over a sustained period of a decade or more. This chapter takes a long-run view of fiscal policy, asking how a pattern of sustained budget deficits might affect the U.S. economy.

Never forget that government borrowing is part of the overall picture of national saving. In the U.S. economy, the federal government is one of the two big demanders of investment funds—the other being private firms who want to borrow for physical capital investment. The two big suppliers of financial capital are private saving and the inflow of foreign capital. So, if the federal budget deficit goes up, some combination of the following three things must happen: private savings must go up, private investment must fall, or inflow of foreign capital must increase. The trick lies in understanding which one, or which combination, is likely to happen.

First, let's look at how likely it is that an increased budget deficit would call forth an increase in private saving. There's an economic theory to cover just about everything, and the theory that private saving rises with an increased government deficit is called Ricardian equivalence, after the nineteenth-century economist David Ricardo.

The theory behind Ricardian equivalence is that when individuals observe large budget deficits, they expect their taxes to increase at some point in the future, and so they increase their saving. At least in a theoretical model, the rise in personal saving could provide the financing for the government deficit–related borrowing. But what's the actual evidence that this happens?

Studies by economists at the World Bank suggest that Ricardian equivalence does hold in certain places and times, to some extent. They estimate that, worldwide, roughly half of the increases in government borrowing are offset by more private saving. But the World Bank's studies also show that in the United States, this theory doesn't hold well at all. For example, the U.S. economy had high budget deficits in the mid-1980s and the mid-2000s, but there was no offsetting rise in private saving in either period. In the 1990s, private saving did drop as budget deficits declined, but private saving has been dropping pretty steadily since the 1980s, so it seems unrelated to the deficit. As the old saying goes, even a stopped clock is right twice a day. Every theory will be correct once in a while, but that doesn't prove it will hold in the future. Ricardian equivalence hasn't held well for the U.S. economy.

The remaining two ways in which the economy can react to a larger budget deficit are either decreased private investment in physical capital or a larger trade imbalance.

The economic theory of "crowding out" holds that as government borrows more and more money to run its deficits, it reduces the funds available to private firms for private investment. Thus, an increase in government borrowing should mean less private investment. Conversely, a drop in government borrowing should mean more funds available for private investment.

Do we actually observe this pattern in the U.S. economy? Over time, private investment tends to be about 14 to 17 percent of U.S. GDP. When the budget deficit turned into surpluses in the late 1990s, around 1998, the investment rate in the U.S. economy also rose. It went from 14 percent of GDP in 1993 to 17.2 percent of GDP in 2000—from the bottom of its typical range to the top. So during that period, it does seem that as the government ran surpluses and borrowed less, more money was invested by private firms. When the deficit returned in the mid-2000s, the private investment rate sank as well; for example, the ratio of investment to GDP dropped to about 14.8 percent by 2003 as the budget deficits swelled. Again, there appears to be an offset between the deficit and private investment, as the theory of crowding out would suggest.

As we discussed previously, sometimes investment is subject to what Keynes called "animal spirits"; it may rise or fall too far and too fast. That probably happened to some extent in the boom years of the late 1990s. But on average, year in, year out, investment in physical capital—in new plants and equipment—is one of the essential elements of economic growth. It's also one of the key ways that new technologies enter the production process. There's reason to believe that if we kept the budget deficit lower, there would be more money available for firms to invest, and it would be easier for firms to adopt new technologies, which would help long-term economic growth. Crowding out of private investment is a negative consequence of large budget deficits.

The third theory we can call crowding in—that is, the idea that large government borrowing can crowd in a trade deficit. We've already discussed how government borrowing can draw in additional foreign investment; to economists, this is the same thing as having a large trade deficit. Remember the overall pattern here: when U.S. budget deficits were very large in the mid-1980s and the mid-2000s, the trade deficits were also very large. Because these budget deficits and trade deficits increased simultaneously, they were sometimes called "the twin deficits." However, the budget surpluses in the late 1990s didn't lead to a trade surplus, so these two deficits aren't always twins. Instead, the extra money from the budget surpluses of the late 1990s went into the 1990s investment boom, so it didn't reduce the trade imbalance. Budget deficits and trade deficits do appear to be linked, but they don't march in lockstep.

In the long run, a series of ever-growing trade deficits just isn't sustainable for any economy. There's a limit to how much of a country's assets foreign investors want to hold. Currently, the U.S. economy is paying hundreds of billions of dollars a year to foreign owners of U.S. assets, and this amount is only going to climb over time. Large trade deficits also carry a risk of economic dislocation. At some point, when the rest of the world becomes unwilling to hold as much in U.S. assets as they currently do, it will be a shock to the U.S. economy. For example, one possibility is a long-lasting drop in the value of the U.S. dollar versus other currencies that could be very unsettling both to consumers who buy imports and to firms that rely on imported products (including oil)—which is, of course, many firms in these globalizing times.

In the short run of a few years, there's not a huge reason to worry about budget deficits, especially if the economy seems to be operating below potential GDP. One might quarrel with how expansionary fiscal policy is carried out (tax cuts versus spending increases) or with how effective it will be in a particular economic situation. But from a macroeconomic point of view, a short-term deficit, especially one emerging from automatic stabilizers, is not a bad thing during a recession.

But what happens when deficits are large and sustained over a long period of time? It's useful here to distinguish between the budget deficit, which is government borrowing that happens in a single year, and the government debt, which is the accumulation of that borrowing over a number of years. Government debt is a useful measure of the sustained impact of deficits over a long period of time. Say, for example, the government has a debt of $4 trillion and then in the next year accumulates a budget deficit of $300 billion. At the end of that year, the total debt would be $4.3 trillion. Conversely, a country with a budget surplus can reduce its amount of outstanding debt.

A standard measure of national indebtedness is dividing the total government debt in any given year by GDP. This calculation gives a sense of the total debt in proportion to the economy and allows useful comparisons over time. During the twentieth century, there were several periods when U.S. government borrowing grew rapidly. The debt-to-GDP ratio rose after World War I and again during the Great Depression, then peaked at 108 percent of GDP in 1946, just after World War II. From that high, the debt-to-GDP ratio slid to about 25 percent by the 1970s. The series of big budget deficits in the 1980s started the debt-to-GDP ratio rising again; it peaked at about 50 percent of GDP in 1994. With the surpluses of the late 1990s, the debt-to-GDP ratio dropped, reaching 33 percent by 2001. With the moderate-size deficits of the mid-2000s, the debt-to-GDP ratio rose slightly, reaching 40 percent by 2008. But under the impetus of the huge budget deficits in 2009 and 2010, the debt-to-GDP ratio reached 63 percent by 2010.

The accumulated U.S. debt-to-GDP ratio by 2010 was high, but not extraordinarily high, by historical standards; however, the long-run projections are dismal. The nonpartisan Congressional Budget Office makes regular budget predictions. The predictions from June 2010, based on what the Congressional Budget Office expects will be the likely course of future legislation, holds that the debt-to-GDP ratio will reach 87 percent by 2020 and 185 percent by 2035. On the tax side, this prediction holds that taxes will creep up only a bit, to 19.3 percent of GDP by 2035—basically within their historical average of 17 to 19 percent of GDP. However, federal spending in this scenario is projected to hit a whopping 35 percent of GDP by 2035, which would be much larger than the historical average. The higher spending levels are driven by three factors: Rising health spending is by far the largest, contributing an additional 5.4 percentage points of GDP in spending from 2010 to 2035. (These projections take into account the effects of the health care reform legislation passed early in 2010.) Higher Social Security spending will contribute an additional 1.4 percentage points of spending between 2010 and 2035. The other big source of higher spending will be the larger interest payments that will begin to accumulate on all this debt.

President Herbert Hoover is reputed to have said, "Blessed are the young, for they shall inherit the national debt." But you don't have to be all that young! If you expect to live another decade or two, the current projections are for a huge national debt within your lifetime.

This budget forecast is not especially controversial. All the long-term projections from the major government accounting offices are broadly similar. If spending on Social Security, Medicare, Medicaid, and other health care programs rises as projected, we're going to face very high levels of government spending. We will pay for this spending either with huge and historically unprecedented tax increases, huge and historically unprecedented budget deficits, or both.

I should emphasize that the single biggest factor driving these dismal long-run budget deficit forecasts is health care costs. I should also emphasize that the long-run budget predictions were already fairly dire before the recession of 2007–2009 and before President Obama took office in 2009. The large deficits that have followed the 2007–2009 recession are making the sharp rise in the debt-to-GDP ratio happen sooner—but it was coming, one way or another.

None of the public policy options here are easy ones. Large increases in taxes are always politically unpalatable. The American political system has shown little ability to hold down health care costs, which have been rising sharply for decades, and little ability to address the long-run funding problems of Social Security, which have been well-known for decades. Slashing everything else the federal government does to accommodate ever-rising costs for health care doesn't seem feasible, either.

One indirect option worth consideration is enacting public policies to increase private saving. If this approach worked, it could provide more financial capital for private investment and also make the U.S. economy less dependent on foreign investment. The United States has tried to encourage private saving over recent decades via various tax breaks, such as IRA plans and 401(k) accounts. The general idea behind these is that the saver delays paying taxes on this money until after retirement, increasing the amount of money available to save and thus increasing the potential rate of return. However, private saving has remained low, even with these accounts in place.

What if we go a step beyond incentives? What if a certain level of saving were legally required? This idea has both politically conservative and politically liberal backers, although they use a different vocabulary to describe it. Conservatives talk in terms of private retirement accounts that would replace part or all of Social Security and Medicare. While the conservative rhetoric tends to emphasize the "private" aspect, implying that this plan gives the individual more choices, if you listen carefully, many of those plans would either require or strongly encourage people to put in more money than they're putting in now. For example, one of the suggested plans is to transfer 1.5 percent of your Social Security payroll taxes into a personal account for workers who also put an extra 1.5 percent of your remaining income into the same account. It's not quite a requirement to save more—maybe more like a bribe—but the hope is to increase personal savings.

On the liberal side, these kinds of proposals are sometimes called liberal paternalism: it's paternalism in that it sets up a default option to encourage private saving, but it's liberal in the sense that you can opt out of the requirement. The general idea is that everyone would be required to have an IRA or a 401(k) account. Everyone would automatically have, say, 5 or 10 percent of their income deposited into that account. You can opt out of this, but the assumption is that most people would accept the default plan, whatever it was, letting the money pile up. Again, such a plan comes very close to requiring people to save more.

The long-term projections for U.S. budget deficits and the accumulated debt burden are grim. The projected budget deficits over time seem unimaginably large. They would eat up a huge share of the available investment capital and hobble economic growth. I can't imagine that current trends will go on. But I also can't foresee what political decisions will be made to taxes or spending that will substantially reduce that deficit. It's almost enough to make an economist humble.

CHAPTER 29

Money and Banking

What is money? It seems a simple question, but the answer is surprisingly complex. Money isn't just bills and coins in your pocketbook; it's not just any of the things used as currency by people at various times and in various places—from beads and shells to livestock. Let's take an example of money that has been used for centuries and is still sometimes used for large purchases in the Yap Islands of the western Pacific. Yappish money took the form of giant cartwheel stones far too heavy for one person to carry, but they worked as money nonetheless because ownership of all those stones was kept clear. If you wanted to buy a house and you offered the owner six cartwheel stones, and the owner accepted, you would simply let all your neighbors know that those six stones that used to be yours now belonged to that other person. There was no need to move the stones. Everyone knew, or could easily find out, to whom they belonged. In one episode, the Yap people tried to transport some of these stones across a bay, and the boat carrying the stones sank. At first this seemed like a catastrophe, but soon the people realized that it didn't matter. They knew how many stones there were and where they were, so they could still say who owned which stone. There was no need to be able to see or touch the stones to use them as money.

You may be thinking that this system of money sounds bonkers. But this is essentially how the money in the U.S. economy worked for a long time. The United States has long kept the bulk of its gold reserves at Fort Knox, in Tennessee. The gold in Fort Knox was only very rarely shipped from place to place. Instead, as with the giant stones of Yap, people simply kept records about which pile of gold belonged to whom: this pile used to belong to bank A, now it belongs to bank B; this other pile used to belong to France, now it belongs to the United Kingdom. It didn't matter where the gold was physically. All that mattered was keeping track of who had what buying power.

But if the large cartwheel stones or the gold in Fort Knox never got moved, the odd truth is that it didn't matter whether they actually existed. Actual money, those coins and bills and checks we use to buy things, can function perfectly well just by our keeping track of who owes what to whom. It doesn't have to have some physical asset such as a pile of stones (even gold ones) backing it up. Economists, therefore, do not define money by its form but as whatever object performs three functions in an economy: as a medium of exchange, a store of value, and a unit of account.

A medium of exchange is something that can be exchanged for whatever is for sale. U.S. paper money, for example, has a statement on it: "This note is legal tender for all debts, public and private." In other words, if you owe a debt, legally speaking, you can pay that debt with these pieces of paper. As the American writer and humorist Ambrose Bierce (1911) wrote, "Money is a blessing that is of no advantage to us, except when we part with it."

As a store of value, money is an object that can be held for a time without losing significant purchasing power. When you receive money, you don't need to spend it immediately, because it will still retain value the next day or the next year. Indeed, holding money is a much better way of storing value than keeping physical goods, such as canned food or refrigerators, and trying to exchange them at some point in the future. This part of the definition does not imply that money must be a perfect store of value. In an economy with inflation, for example, money does lose some buying power, but it remains money as long as it's in widespread use as the way of storing value. In a situation of hyperinflation, money almost ceases to be money because it doesn't store value anymore.

Money's final function is as a unit of account, which means that the price of most items is measured with money. Money is the yardstick of value across the economy, allowing people, businesses, economists, and government statisticians a way to measure and compare the value of everything they encounter in the economy.

For something to be money, it has to fulfill all three of these functions. A house can serve as a store of value in the sense that it builds up value and you can sell it later. But houses do not serve as a medium of exchange; you can't pay that car salesman with a bedroom. Nor do houses serve as a unit of account; you can't calculate how many bathrooms a pound of chicken costs. Thus, houses aren't money.

In a casino, chips might serve as money within the four walls of the casino; inside, you can exchange chips for food and drinks, for a room, or for souvenirs. They can serve as a unit of account and a store of value for everything you're doing within the casino. But once you leave the casino, they're not money anymore, because you can't exchange them for most things.

The great advantage of money is that it avoids the need for barter, the trading of one good or service for another. Barter is an inadequate mechanism for coordinating the wide range of trades that happen in a modern, advanced economy with a highly specialized division of labor. In an economy without money, an exchange between two people requires what economists call a double coincidence of wants, a situation in which each person wants a good or service that the other person can provide. For example, if an accountant wants a pair of shoes, the accountant has to find someone who has a pair of shoes in the correct size and is willing to exchange the shoes for accounting services. If you wandered around looking for trades for everything you wanted in a modern economy, with thousands upon thousands of different jobs and millions of different goods, it would be extraordinarily difficult—and exhausting. Money circumvents this problem. By extension, it allows a far broader division of labor, degree of specialization, and amount of exchange. Money is a kind of lubrication to help the engine of economic exchange work smoothly.

Government statisticians have their own way of defining money. They use a series of definitions that we refer to as M1 and M2. M1 money includes currency (coins and bills) and traveler's checks and personal checking accounts. In 2009 the total amount of M1 money in the U.S. economy was about $1.7 trillion. About half of that was currency and half checking accounts, with only a tiny fraction as traveler's checks.

A broader definition of money, M2, includes everything that's in M1 plus savings accounts. Savings accounts are broadly defined as bank accounts on which you can't write a check directly, but whose money you could easily access in other ways, as at an automatic teller machine or a bank. M2 money includes money market funds, those ultrasafe investment pools, and relatively small (less than $100,000) time deposits, that is, CDs. The point is you can withdraw and spend the money in M2, but it requires a greater effort and perhaps some penalty, whereas M1 can be spent very easily. In 2009 the total amount of M2 in the U.S. economy was $8.5 trillion, a total that includes the $1.7 trillion in M1.

Notice that currency (bills and coins) is only one slice of the total money supply. Currency is only about half of M1 and about one-tenth of M2. Thus, when you're thinking about money in a modern economy, you shouldn't be thinking about bills and coins; you should be thinking about bank accounts.

A common question at this point is "What about credit cards and debit cards? How do they fit into the picture?" They aren't money. A credit card is just a method of short-term borrowing. A debit card is linked to a bank checking account, which is already part of M1. Neither of these card types alters the actual amount of money in an economy, any more than having 300 unused checks in your desk drawer means having more money than if you had 100 unused checks in that drawer. Credit cards and debit cards are methods for making payments, but they are not the money paid.

A key insight here is that money is intertwined with the banking system. Most money in a modern economy is in the form of bank accounts. Thus, to understand money, we need to understand banks and the banking system. In economic terms, a bank is a financial intermediary. A bank accepts deposits and makes loans, so it stands between depositors and borrowers. A bank receives income from making loans, in the form of interest payments, but it pays interest to its depositors and pays for various operating expenses.

In 2009 the U.S. banking industry had a shade over $800 billion in total revenue. Of that revenue, about three-quarters, or $600 billion, came from interest paid to banks by borrowers; the remaining quarter came from fees and charges. Such fees have been a growing part of bank income over time, especially for large banks that are arranging complex loans with complicated terms for repayment. As far as expenses, U.S. banks had a shade under $800 billion in costs in 2009. (With the economy so weak in 2009, profits for the banking industry as a whole were near zero in 2009.) Nearly half of bank costs that year went to operating expenses—that is, salaries, office space, and equipment. About one-third of bank industry expenses were interest payments to depositors. The remaining expenses for the banking industry involved reserves for bad loans and tax payments.

This list of revenues and expenses should help to clarify how a bank might go bankrupt. For example, a bank can go bankrupt if a substantial number of borrowers default on their loans—perhaps because in a weak economy, people lack the income they expected to have. Banks can also suffer if they've made a large number of loans at a fixed rate of interest and the nominal interest rate rises. In this case, the interest the bank receives from borrowers is at the agreed-upon lower interest rate, while the interest the bank pays out is at the higher current interest rate.

In a healthy economy, badly run banks that take losses ought to go out of business just like any other badly run firm. After all, if one bank goes out of business, other banks can continue to take deposits and make loans. But when many banks are in financial trouble all at once, the economy as a whole can suffer. The quantity of loans available drops across the economy, and in a true financial crisis, banks may become reluctant to lend even to one another for short periods, which makes it difficult for money to fulfill its role in greasing the wheels of the economy.

Banks actually create money by the process of making loans. To understand how this happens, think about what happens to the money you get in the form of a bank loan, say for a car or a house. First, you pay the loaned money to someone else. They take the money and deposit it in their bank. What does that second bank do with the money that was deposited? It takes it and makes a loan to someone else. Someone else takes that loan money and hands it over as part of another purchase, and the money is deposited in yet another bank. The banking system is a web of loans and deposits, in which loans are forming the basis for deposits, deposits are forming the basis for loans, and so on and so on. That process creates money because, as discussed earlier, money is what is in bank accounts. Thus, when money is loaned and reloaned, and loaned and reloaned, there's actually more money in the economy.

Banks are legally required to hold a portion of their deposited money as reserves. But when banks are enthusiastically lending money, there will be substantial aggregate demand in an economy thanks to the increased buying power created by these loans. Conversely, if the economy is weak, as in a recession, banks may well decide to make fewer loans because they fear those loans won't be repaid. In that case, the buying power, the aggregate demand, in the economy will decrease. If the amount of lending decreases, that can pose difficulties for the entire rest of the economy.

Because money, banking, lending, and borrowing are so interrelated, the government will want to exert some influence over the quantity of money and lending in an economy. If done well, government policy can help over time in allowing aggregate demand to grow at the same pace as aggregate supply and potential GDP. In this happy situation, the macroeconomy can stay in balance and can approach the Goldilocks economy, in which everything is just right. But if banking, lending, and borrowing get out of whack, and aggregate demand falls out of step with aggregate supply, the result can be recession or inflation. The next chapter discusses the Federal Reserve, the central banking institution that takes the lead in the conduct of U.S. monetary policy. The following chapter then discusses how monetary policy is actually conducted.

CHAPTER 30

The Federal Reserve and Its Powers

Which individual is the most powerful economic actor in the world? The United States has the largest economy of any country in the world, so you might think the most powerful economic actor is the president of the United States. But while the president controls foreign policy in a very direct sense, all tax and spending bills have to proceed through Congress before the president makes a choice about signing them. Maybe the most powerful economic actor is someone like the leader of Saudi Arabia, for the amount of control that person can have over world oil prices; or maybe it's someone in China, with its rapidly growing economy. But even in nondemocratic countries, individual leaders do not control all economic activities and are constrained in various ways by the different groups to which they owe allegiance.

Article I, Section 8 of the U.S. Constitution gives Congress the power to coin money and to regulate its value. In 1913, Congress created the Federal Reserve Bank, colloquially called the Fed, and delegated these powers to it. The chairman of the Fed has great power over the money supply and interest rates, and on a day-to-day or year-to-year basis, that power is not directly limited by Congress or the president. You can make a strong case that the Fed chairman—the head of the central bank of the United States—is the most powerful individual economic actor in the world.

All large economies have a central bank, and most small economies do, too. Some of the other better-known central banks include the European Central Bank, which replaced many national banks across Europe when the European Union adopted the euro; and the Bank of England, since the British do not use the euro but the pound sterling. The Bank of Japan and Bank of China also serve as central banks.

The U.S. Federal Reserve is a quasi-public corporation, which means it mixes government appointees and laws into an organization that is technically owned by private-sector banks. At the national level, the Fed is run by what's called the Board of Governors. The board consists of seven members, each appointed by the U.S. president and confirmed by the U.S. Senate. The members' terms are structured in such a way as to create a degree of political independence. Appointments are for fourteen-year terms, which means that each member's term outlasts the president who appointed that member. The appointments are arranged so that one member's term expires on January 31 of every even-numbered year. Thus, over fourteen years, the entire seven-member board rotates. A person can serve only one full term on the Board of Governors. However, these fourteen-year terms are so long that board members often leave before their term is completed. If a person is appointed to fill out the remainder of someone else's term, that person could still be appointed to a full fourteen-year term of his or her own. One member of the Fed's Board of Governors is designated by the U.S. president as the board's chairman. As a result, although members of the board are appointed by the president and confirmed by the Senate, after being appointed they are insulated from day-to-day politics.

The Federal Reserve's main job is to enact monetary policy—as distinct from the fiscal policy enacted by Congress. Monetary policy is the expansion or contraction of the money supply. Its purpose is to encourage or discourage aggregate demand. The Fed, or any central bank, has three traditional tools for working within the web of banking and money to expand or contract the money supply: reserve requirements, the discount rate, and open market operations. It also has one newly minted tool developed in response to the 2007–2009 recession, called quantitative easing. Let's walk through these tools one by one.

The reserve requirement is the percentage of their deposits banks may *not* loan out. Every bank is required to keep some of its deposits on reserve at the central bank; in effect, they have to deposit that money with the central bank. When the reserve requirement gets higher, each individual bank has less money to lend out. If each individual bank has less money to lend out, the quantity of loans available in the economy diminishes, and aggregate demand shrinks. Interest rates will rise, so that borrowing is less attractive. Conversely, when the reserve requirement is reduced, each bank has more money to lend out. Banks can then expand the supply of lending, which expands aggregate demand. Interest rates should then decline, making the price of borrowing money lower. For example, in 2003 the Fed required that banks hold reserves equal to 3 percent of the first $41.3 million deposited in checking and savings accounts for the bank as a whole. For any amounts deposited above $41.3 million, the bank had to hold reserves equal to 10 percent of that amount. Small changes are made in the reserve requirement almost every year, maybe a few million dollars either way. But changes that have a large effect on bank reserves are actually quite rare. This tool of monetary policy, at least in the United States, is not used often.

The discount rate is another way that the Federal Reserve can encourage or discourage lending. Imagine a situation in which a bank has loaned out most, or perhaps all, of the funds it can possibly loan out, right up to the edge of the reserve requirement. If the bank is right on the edge, it can't be sure until after business closes that day if it has loaned too much or not quite enough; for example, someone could come along just before closing and withdraw or deposit a large sum. If a bank miscalculates such that it can't quite meet the reserve requirement, it needs to borrow in the very short term—literally overnight—to adjust its balance of loans and deposits and meet the reserve requirement. Banks often borrow from one another for this purpose. But if a bank borrows for this reason from the central bank, the interest rate it is charged is the discount rate.

How does the discount rate affect bank behavior? If the central bank raises the discount rate, this will encourage banks to keep money on hand, not to venture too close to the reserve requirement, because if they do need to borrow to make up the reserve, it will cost them more. To keep that little cushion around the reserve requirement, banks will loan a little bit less, reducing the amount of money in the economy as a whole. Conversely, if the central bank reduces the discount rate, banks will be less concerned about skirting close to the reserve requirement, because if they do miscalculate, borrowing the difference isn't that costly. They can lend more money, thus increasing the supply of money in the entire economy.

Although the discount rate is a perfectly good tool of monetary policy, in practice, most of the time the Fed lends little money at the discount rate. Before a bank borrows from the Fed to fill out its reserves, it is common practice first to try to borrow from other banks. But because banks haven't borrowed from the Fed very often in the decades leading up to the Great Recession of 2007–2009, the discount rate doesn't move much; it hasn't been a very commonly used tool of monetary policy.

Up until about 2008, the tool of open market operations was the main method of conducting monetary policy. Open market operations occur when a central bank buys or sells bonds with the goal of decreasing or increasing the money supply. Let's think about how this works. Banks, remember, are holding assets: they've got people's deposits, and they need to invest those deposits one way or another. Some of those deposits are distributed as loans, and banks receive interest when the loans are repaid. But most banks also hold a certain amount of money in bonds, often in government bonds, and they receive some interest from owning these bonds.

The Federal Reserve buys and sells bonds with banks. When the Fed buys bonds from banks, the banks have more money to lend. Remember, bonds are not money. They're not part of M1 or M2. A bank puts depositors' money in bonds, but can't lend out the bonds. When the Federal Reserve buys the bonds, the bank then holds cash instead of bonds, and can increase its lending. The quantity of lending and credit in the economy rises, and aggregate demand rises with it. You can probably intuit the reverse process: If the Federal Reserve sells its bonds to banks, this ties up the banks' money supply, so they can lend out less. Fewer loans means less money circulating in the economy, and the aggregate demand will be diminished.

In recent decades, open market operations have been the most commonly used tool of monetary policy in the United States. One reason for this is that altering the reserve requirement and the discount rate requires guessing how banks will react to a change in the rules. That's a sketchy process; one can never be entirely sure how banks will respond. But with an open market operation, the Fed can order a specific quantity of bonds to be bought or sold. The Fed can see the result in term of interest rates in the market, and then buy or sell more or less as desired.

Decisions about buying and selling bonds through open market operations are made by the Federal Open Market Committee (FOMC) at the Federal Reserve. The FOMC is made up of twelve members, including all seven members of the Fed's Board of Governors, plus five representatives from bank districts all around the country. Thus, decisions about open market operations are made not just by government appointees; there is also input from people who are actually involved in banking all around the country.

The newest approach to monetary policy—known in theory but not used in the United States until 2008—is quantitative easing. It can work in two ways. One is that the Federal Reserve can lend money to participants in financial markets. These loans are typically short term, so during 2008 and early 2009 this approach was a way to ensure that big players in the financial markets had access to cash during a financial crisis, when usual sources of lending may have dried up. This kind of quantitative easing policy phases itself out as the short-term loans are repaid. The other approach to quantitative easing is for the Fed to purchase longer-term financial securities. In 2009 and 2010 the Fed purchased U.S. Treasury bonds and, in addition, more than $1 trillion in financial securities backed by payments from home mortgages. This approach to quantitative easing seems to have helped stabilize financial markets in 2009 and 2010, but how it will work in the longer term—when the Fed eventually decides to stop purchasing such securities or to sell some of the securities it holds—remains uncertain.

Remember, banks create money through the web of loans. One bank makes a loan; it's deposited in another bank, where it provides the basis for an additional loan, and so on. The tools of monetary policy all work because they make banks either more or less eager to lend—or, to put it a little differently, more or less able to lend. To nail down this point, let's talk about how monetary policy influences lending, aggregate demand, and interest rates.

If the Fed wants the money supply to be larger, it has four options: It can lower the reserve requirement, lower the discount rate, buy bonds from the banks, or buy financial securities related to borrowing. All these steps can be referred to as expansionary, or loose, monetary policy. They all tend to reduce interest rates and encourage lending. In terms of our aggregate supply and aggregate demand model, they increase the quantity of aggregate demand in the economy.

Conversely, if the Fed wants to reduce the money supply, or at least restrain the rate of growth in the money supply, it enacts a contractionary, or tight, monetary policy, using some combination of its tools: a higher discount rate, a higher reserve requirement, the selling of bonds to banks, or the selling of financial securities it holds back into the market. All these would tend to tighten the money supply; they would raise interest rates and discourage lending. In terms of our aggregate supply and aggregate demand model, all these steps would reduce aggregate demand, or at least limit the rise in aggregate demand.

News reports about the Federal Reserve often refer to the Fed raising or lowering interest rates. At this point, however, you should understand that the Fed doesn't have dictatorial powers to say, "We declare that interest rates must rise" or "We declare that interest rates must fall." Instead, the Fed uses its policy tools to affect the supply of funds that banks are willing and able to lend. With expansionary policy and an increased supply of funds, banks are more willing to lend, and interest rates fall. With contractionary monetary policy and a decreased supply of funds, banks are less willing to lend, and interest rates rise. Through its open market operations, the Fed actually targets one specific interest rate, called the "federal funds rate." The federal funds rate is the interest rate at which banks make short-term overnight loans to other banks. As this interest rate goes up or down, other interest rates—such as the rate on your car loan or home loan—move up or down more or less in sync with it.

Although enacting monetary policy is the main task of a central bank such as the Federal Reserve, and the one that gets the most media attention, it's not the only job for the Fed. A central bank must ensure that enough currency and coins are circulating through the financial system to meet the demands of the public. For example, each year the Federal Reserve has the responsibility of increasing the amount of currency available in banks around the Christmas shopping season and then reducing that amount of currency again in January.

In the months before January 1, 2000, there was a fear that the so-called "Y2K bug" would cause computer breakdowns all over the United States and the world economy, including the banks. As it turned out, the fears were greatly exaggerated, although some mishaps did occur: The U.S. government lost touch with a set of spy satellites for four days; a number of airports experienced short-term glitches in their air traffic control systems; seven nuclear power plants experienced computer problems; and about 4,000 small businesses around the country found that their systems for processing credit cards didn't work. But before January 1, 2000, the Federal Reserve announced that it would have $200 billion in currency on hand, just in case the financial system crashed and everything needed to run on cash for a little while. People's demand for currency did surge right around January 1, 2000, probably out of fear that something might happen. But the increase in the demand for currency was only about $20 billion; and by the end of January 2000, that extra $20 billion in cash had been deposited back into the banking system. Part of the Fed's job, therefore, is to be ready for situations that might lead to fluctuations in the demand for cash.

The Federal Reserve also acts as a bank for banks, so it plays a central role in clearing checks. When you write a check from your own bank, and the person who receives that check deposits it in another bank, the check (or a digital image of the check) needs to be returned to your bank, and money needs to be transferred from your bank to the other bank. The Fed transfers funds from bank to bank as needed to reflect the flow of checks. Actually, the Federal Reserve contracts out a substantial amount of the work of collecting, sorting, photographing, and transmitting checks to different private firms, but it is technically in charge of and responsible for the process.

The Federal Reserve is also involved as one of the regulators of the financial system. In the system of deposit insurance, for example, banks pay into the system to protect their individual depositors' assets up to $250,000, should the banks go broke. In many countries, deposit insurance is run by the central bank; in the United States it is managed by the Federal Deposit Insurance Corporation (FDIC). A bank pays premiums to the FDIC, which pays the depositors directly if the bank goes broke. The insurance premium is based on a bank's level of deposits, adjusted according to the riskiness of a bank's financial situation. The FDIC determines a bank's level of risk by looking at the value of its loans, how many of the loans are being paid off, what the conditions are of those loans, how much the bank owes—basically, the bank's overall financial health. In 2009, for example, a fairly safe bank might have paid from $0.07 to $0.24 in deposit insurance premiums for every $100 in bank deposits, depending on the underlying riskiness of its financial investments, while a risky bank might have paid $0.40 to $0.77 in deposit insurance premiums for every $100 in bank deposits.

The FDIC provides deposit insurance for about 8,000 banks in the United States. Even if a bank goes broke, and the executives of the bank lose their jobs, and the bank vanishes, deposit insurance and the federal government still guarantee that depositors will get their money up to $250,000. This is enough for almost all individuals, but not for some businesses. The Federal Reserve, along with the U.S. Department of the Treasury, plays a key role in auditing the country's banks in an attempt to make sure they have sufficient financial assets and aren't making overly risky loans. Within the U.S. Department of the Treasury is the Office of the Comptroller of the Currency (OCC). It has a national staff of bank examiners who conduct on-site reviews of the 1,500 largest national banks and savings and loans. Another organization, called the National Credit Union Administration (NCUA), looks at credit unions, which are nonprofit banks owned and technically run by their members. The Federal Reserve also has some responsibility for supervising bank holding companies, large firms that own banks along with other financial companies such as insurance firms or brokerage companies.

When you bring all these regulatory responsibilities together, you get alphabet soup: the Federal Financial Institutions Examination Council (FFIEC) includes the FDIC, the NCUA, the OCC, and the Fed. Basically, the FFIEC is an umbrella organization that makes sure that all these bank regulators communicate with one another and use similar standards when they're evaluating the riskiness of the banks. Of course, the succession of financial crises during the recession of 2007–2009 raised harsh questions as to whether this oversight was being adequately performed.

A central bank such as the Fed also has a role as a lender of last resort. That is, when a financial system is potentially endangered by a major financial crash, the central bank provides short-term loans so the financial system won't explode or implode. Financial panics can build on themselves and create an avalanche, as seen in well-known movies such as *Mary Poppins* and *It's a Wonderful Life*. These avalanches are called bank runs; people literally run to the bank to grab their money. We don't have bank runs anymore. People know their bank deposits are safe, thanks to deposit insurance. But there's still a chance, for various reasons, that the financial system could go into gridlock. During the stock market crash in October 1987, for example, the value of U.S. stocks fell by 25 percent in a single day, and no one quite knew where they stood. What if you were a financial institution that had a relationship with a company or a financial firm that held a lot of stock? You knew that other institution had absorbed a lot of losses. Was that institution broke? Would your loans be repaid? How were the losses distributed through the financial system and the economy? No one quite knew. On that day, the Federal Reserve was out there effectively saying, "For anyone who needs money, we will loan it to you short term, at the discount rate, and in an almost unlimited amount." It made this promise so that the financial system could keep working while the banks and institutions sorted everything out. The quantitative easing approach that makes short-term loans available to financial market participants is similar to the "lender of last resort" task—although it happened in the face of a financial crunch that lasted for more than a year, rather than a single salient event such as a bank run.

Central banks have both the power and the responsibility to conduct monetary policy and to participate in the soundness and safety of the banking system. In the next chapter, we'll focus on the actual monetary policy choices, which can be a source of considerable controversy.

CHAPTER 31

The Conduct of Monetary Policy

When recession hits, the Federal Reserve is the first line of defense for the macroeconomy. During a recession, a looser monetary policy will reduce interest rates, stimulate aggregate demand toward potential GDP, and thus reduce cyclical unemployment. Therefore, the standard prescription during a recession is for the Fed to cut interest rates; the Fed should have an expansionary, loose monetary policy. The Federal Reserve cut interest rates eleven times during the recession of 2001. The federal funds interest rate—the rate at which banks make overnight loans to other banks—fell from 6.2 percent in 2000 to 1.7 percent by 2002. When the recession hit in 2007, the Federal Reserve cut the federal funds interest rate ten times, dropping it from 5.25 percent in mid-2007 to the range of 0 to 0.25 percent by the end of 2008.

Clearly the Fed acts aggressively in the face of a recession to encourage more aggregate demand. Indeed, the new quantitative easing policies adopted by the Federal Reserve starting in 2008 arose out of the Fed's desire to find a way to increase lending at a time when it had already, through its open market operations, pushed the federal funds lending rate down to near-zero. By making short-term loans to participants in financial markets at a time when those markets were under particular stress and by purchasing both U.S. government bonds and mortgage-backed financial securities, the Fed hoped to keep financial markets operating and to improve the willingness of banks to lend. The combination of low interest rates and quantitative easing was clearly not enough to keep cyclical unemployment from rising to near 10 percent in 2009 and 2010, but without the Fed's actions, unemployment might well have climbed even higher.

Expansionary or loose monetary policy does not reduce the natural rate of unemployment. Remember, whereas cyclical unemployment is a symptom of recession, the natural rate of unemployment is determined by the supply and demand for labor in a dynamic marketplace. It is affected by incentives for working and hiring. It's attributable to all the factors that affect supply and demand for labor in a dynamic marketplace, such as welfare and unemployment benefits that affect workers' behavior and rules and regulations that affect the cost of hiring and, thus, employers' behavior. When an economy is at or near potential GDP, the natural rate of unemployment is basically all the unemployment that remains in the economy, because cyclical unemployment will be virtually zero; in such situations, expansionary monetary policy can't reduce unemployment further.

Tighter monetary policy can fight inflation by raising interest rates and reducing aggregate demand in the economy. A tighter monetary policy reduces the amount of money that's circulating in the economy, thus reducing the willingness of banks to lend. As that happens, the amount of loanable funds in the economy shrinks and the interest rate goes higher. A higher interest rate, in turn, means less aggregate demand—less borrowing for big purchases such as cars, houses, and industrial plants and equipment. That means fewer dollars chasing goods and a lower inflation rate.

A classic example of this in action happened in the United States in the late 1970s and early 1980s. At that time, inflation was running into the double digits. The Federal Reserve, under Chairman Paul Volcker, was determined to break that inflation, so it ran a very tight monetary policy. The Fed pushed interest rates up into the double digits. It pushed interest rates so high, and the fall in aggregate demand was so severe, in fact, that the U.S. economy actually suffered back-to-back recessions over a three-year period from 1980 through 1982. But by the mid-1980s, the Fed had slain the inflation monster.

The Fed keeps a vigil against inflation, and a few times since the 1980s it has tweaked the federal funds interest rate up a bit when it feared a resurgence of inflation. But in the aftermath of the 2007–2009 recession, inflation is less of a concern—with the economy growing so slowly and with unemployment remaining so high—than is deflation.

Deflation occurs when the rate of inflation is negative; that is, instead of money having less purchasing power over time, money is actually worth more over time. Having the buying power of money increase may not sound so bad, but when deflation interacts with interest rates, it can cause recessions that are difficult for monetary policy to address.

The real interest rate is the nominal interest rate minus the rate of inflation. If the nominal interest rate is 7 percent and the rate of inflation is 3 percent, then the borrower is effectively paying a 4 percent real interest rate. Now let's imagine that the nominal interest rate is 7 percent and there's deflation of 2 percent (that is, inflation is negative 2 percent). In that situation, the real interest rate is actually 9 percent—higher than the nominal rate. In this way, unexpected deflation raises the real interest payments for borrowers everywhere in the economy. An unexpected deflation can lead to an unexpectedly high number of loans not being repaid. Banks face unexpected losses, and become less able and less eager to make new loans. The web of money and credit begins to contract, and as aggregate demand declines, the economy can easily end up in a recession.

Here comes the double whammy: after deflation causes a recession, it can then make it difficult for monetary policy to work. Let's say the Fed sees a recession happening and wants to use expansionary monetary policy. It cuts the nominal interest rate, and cuts it, and cuts it—all the way down to nearly zero percent. But if an economy has 5 percent deflation, then even if the nominal interest rate is zero, the real interest rate is 5 percent. The central bank can't make the nominal interest rate negative, and as a result, even the most aggressive possible open market operation can't reduce the real interest rate below zero during a period of deflation. In the early 1930s, for example, deflation was 6.7 percent in the United States, so real interest rates were very high. This is part of what made the Great Depression so terrible. Many borrowers had to default on their loans; many banks ended up bankrupt. The economy was trapped in a cycle of fewer and fewer banks, fewer and fewer loans, less and less aggregate demand. The fear of deflation is one of the reasons that the Federal Reserve started experimenting with policies of quantitative easing in 2008.

Not all episodes of deflation end in severe depression. Japan, for example, has been experiencing mild deflation, typically about 1 percent per year, since 1998. While its economy hasn't done especially well over this time period, it has grown by about 1 percent per year on average. There are even some historical examples of deflation coexisting with rapid growth. The U.S. economy experienced deflation of about 1.1 percent per year over the quarter century from 1876 to 1900. Deflation was the normal state of affairs in that period. But during that time, real GDP also was expanding at a rapid clip of about 4 percent per year. Even in an environment of deflation, banks, firms, and consumers can make adjustments.

A central bank needs to be on guard against deflation. In fact, many central banks aim at an inflation rate of about 2 percent, rather than zero, because they want a little wiggle room to avoid possible deflation. But except in severe cases such as the Great Depression, when nearly everything that could go wrong did go wrong, deflation does not guarantee economic disaster.

Monetary policy can also be used to encourage economic growth. The main determinants of economic growth, as discussed earlier, are investments in human capital, physical capital, and technology interacting in a market-oriented environment. The long-term planning that facilitates investment is most likely to occur when the economic environment has low and stable inflation and interest rates. The central bank wants to foster an economic environment in which firms make profits by greater productivity and innovation, not by playing games with inflation or trying to outguess the financial markets. The great productivity slowdown of the 1970s happened at about the same time as the great inflation buildup of the 1970s. While it's difficult to draw a tight statistical connection between the two, there is a suspicion among many economists that in a developed market economy, rising or variable inflation works as a distraction for firms and households from the kinds of efforts and investments that lead to long-term growth.

There's controversy over whether monetary policy should be used to address financial bubbles such as the buildup in the U.S. stock market in the late 1990s or the buildup in the U.S. housing market in the mid-2000s. It's probably useful to take half a step back here and define what economists mean by "bubble." A bubble occurs when prices rise not because of any characteristic of the good itself, but because investors expect prices to keep rising. A bubble creates its own momentum, because many people buying all at once will tend to drive up the price. But that momentum can't go on forever, and when enough people recognize that the bubble is unsustainable, prices will burst.

It can be difficult to spot a bubble when it's happening. In the U.S. stock market in the late 1990s, for example, some people attributed the huge rise in stock prices to the Internet and related new technologies creating the possibility of enormous future profits. Others said the prices were high only because investors were assuming they'd get even higher. In the mid-2000s some economists argued that the increase in housing prices was sustainable up to about 2004, but then it turned into a bubble in 2005 and 2006. Deciding in real time just when a price increase goes beyond reasonable and turns into a bubble will almost always be controversial.

When bubbles in asset prices pop, it can be difficult for an economy. However, central banks have not historically paid much attention to asset bubbles, for several reasons. One is that, as we said earlier, it's hard to say when something is a bubble and when it isn't. Do we really want to give the Fed the power to decide when, say, stock prices are too high and ought to decline? Moreover, popping a bubble requires contractionary monetary policy and higher interest rates; it might even cause a recession. Is it worth the risk of recession to pop a bubble? After the bubble pops and recession looms, the Federal Reserve can use monetary policy at that time to fight the recession. Before the recession of 2007–2009, central banks steered away from making decisions about asset bubbles. But since the recession, economists at places such as the International Monetary Fund have begun to propose that, in some way, central banks should be taking asset bubbles into their calculations.

We discussed earlier a difference between automatic and discretionary fiscal policy. There's a similar division in monetary policy: Should monetary policy be conducted at the discretion of the central bank, or should it be guided by specific rules?

The case for discretionary monetary policy is that the economy is unpredictable. The central bank has experts who study the economy 24-7. Thus, the argument goes, the central bank should have the flexibility to diagnose the economy and to react to it as it sees fit. But discretionary monetary policy has some practical problems: time lags, risks of overshooting, and what economists call "pushing on a string."

First, the time lag problem is that monetary policy involves a chain of events. A central bank must perceive a situation in the economy, hold a meeting, and make a decision to act. That change then needs time to percolate through the banking system—and then businesses and consumers must react to banks' behavior. All this takes time. The full effects of a monetary policy that, say, sharply reduced interest rates may not be felt for twelve to eighteen months.

Second, the risk of overshooting means that monetary policy can create more economic fluctuations than it resolves. Alan Blinder, an eminent Princeton economics professor who served on the Federal Reserve Board of Governors, has offered a useful analogy: Say you go to a hotel room in the evening and the room feels very cold. You turn the thermostat up, but nothing seems to happen. It's late, you're tired, so you turn the thermostat way up and go to bed. Later that night, you wake up in a room that feels like a sauna. So you stagger out of bed and turn the heat down. You wake up in the morning, and the room is like a refrigerator. The lesson is that when reactions take some time to become evident, it's easy to go too far. In your hotel room, this isn't a tragedy; in the conduct of monetary policy, overreaction can mean a macroeconomic disaster.

A third issue is that monetary policy might be better at contracting an economy than at stimulating it. Just as you can lead a horse to water but can't make it drink, a central bank can buy bonds from banks so banks have more money to lend, but it can't force banks to lend that additional money. If banks are unwilling to lend because they're afraid of too many defaults, monetary policy won't be much help in fighting a recession. In the aftermath of the 2007–2009 recession, banks and many nonfinancial firms were holding substantial amounts of cash, but given the level of economic uncertainty, they were reluctant to make loans. Central bankers have an old saying to capture this problem: Monetary policy can be like pulling and pushing on a string. When you pull a string, it moves toward you, but when you push on a string, it folds up and doesn't move. When a central bank pulls on the string through contractionary policy, it can definitely raise interest rates and reduce aggregate demand. But when a central bank tries to push on the string through expansionary policy, it won't have any effect if banks decide not to lend. It's not that expansionary monetary policy never works, but it's not always reliable.

Finally, a central bank may have different priorities as a result of pressure from politicians or citizens, who may disagree over what policy goal is most important or how aggressive monetary policy should be. Discretion means the central bank, rather than someone else, has the freedom to make those choices.

These issues, perhaps especially the risk of overshooting, have led to interest in developing rules that central banks must follow. Around the world, perhaps the most common method of setting monetary policy is called "inflation targeting." In more than twenty countries, the central bank is legally required to focus above all on keeping inflation low. Indeed, the legislation that established the European Central Bank, which controls the euro, set price stability as its primary goal and defined it as an inflation rate of 2 percent per year. The advantage of inflation targeting is that it makes the central bank accountable and transparent. But the U.S. Federal Reserve is an exception: it is legally required to pay attention to both unemployment and inflation. In practice, this seems to mean that the Fed should reduce interest rates during recessions and raise interest rates if inflation appears to threaten.

No high-income nation conducts its monetary policy through the legislative or the executive branch of government. Instead, they all have set up their central banks as agencies that are somewhat independent of politics. Why is monetary policy conducted in this manner? After all, elected representatives conduct fiscal policy of taxes and spending, why not monetary policy, too?

On the flip side of this argument, insulating the central bank from day-to-day politics gives its members the freedom to make tough decisions fairly quickly multiple times in a given year, which could be more difficult if such decisions went through Congress. Indeed, day-to-day democratic control of monetary policy seems impractical. Further, there is concern that politicians would always be seeking more loans and lower interest rates; after all, politicians are unlikely to accept unpopular realities such as the natural unemployment rate, or the fact that monetary policy alone can't quickly fix the aftermath of a housing bubble or a financial crisis. Political control over monetary policy could easily lead to an economy biased toward higher inflation.

The debate over democratic control of monetary policy isn't going away, but the most common trend worldwide in the first decade of the 2000s has been toward writing specific rules for central banks to follow, such as targeting inflation, and then leaving it up to the central bank to achieve that goal, rather than moving toward greater democratic control of the central bank.

CHAPTER 32

The Gains of International Trade

Most economists favor free international trade. I do, too. But even though I believe that trade is beneficial as a whole, it still poses both benefits and costs that need to be considered.

Let's start with some basic perspective: How much globalization—to use one of the buzzwords of our time—has occurred in recent decades? One simple metric considers exports as a share of world GDP. In 1950, world exports were about 7 percent of world GDP. Now world exports are about 25 percent of world GDP, so exports have more than tripled. There's a similar pattern in the U.S. economy. In 1950, exports were about 3 percent of U.S. GDP. In the mid-2000s, exports were about 12 percent of U.S. GDP. Again, the level of trade has more than tripled. When people talk about globalization, this is, in essence, the trend they're talking about.

There are several reasons why international trade can offer a win-win situation for all the countries that participate. The potential gains from trade can be split into three main categories: absolute advantages, comparative advantages, and dynamic gains over time. In international terms, one nation has what economists call an absolute advantage over another nation in the production of a certain good if it can make that good with higher productivity—either a higher rate of output per hour or fewer inputs needed to make that output. As an example, imagine a world that has just two countries: call them the United States and Saudi Arabia. Let's say—and this is plausible enough—that the United States has an absolute advantage over Saudi Arabia in growing wheat, and Saudi Arabia has an absolute advantage in producing oil. That's not to say there's no cropland in Saudi Arabia or no oil in the United States; it's just that productivity for the specified good is greater in one country over another. In this situation, both sides can produce their desired output of wheat and oil at lower cost if they play to their absolute advantage and trade with each other. Both countries are better off if they play to their strengths.

This idea of gains from trade is pretty straightforward, but let's now imagine a more difficult case, in which one country has an absolute productivity advantage in all areas and the other country has an absolute disadvantage in all areas. The example I sometimes use here—which isn't quite fair or accurate but works for illustrating the argument—is the United States and Mexico. In a wide range of goods and services markets, the United States has more educated workers; better and newer capital equipment; and a better infrastructure of communications, electricity, and transportation than Mexico does. Yet, perhaps counterintuitively, it's still possible to see trade between the United States and Mexico as benefitting both countries. The theory of comparative advantage explains why.

A nation has a comparative advantage for producing a good or service for which it has either the largest productivity advantage or the smallest productivity disadvantage. Consider an analogy: Let's say I have two main jobs, editing economics articles and typing memos. Let's also say that I have a secretary, and I'm faster at both of these jobs than my secretary is. I have an absolute advantage in both areas. Does it then follow that I should do both jobs? Of course not. Presumably I have a big advantage in editing economics articles compared with my secretary, but I have only a smaller advantage in typing over my secretary. I've got only so many work hours in each day. It follows that more total work will get done if I focus on editing, where my productivity advantage is greatest, and hire a secretary to do the typing.

Let's return to the United States/Mexico example. Say that the

United States is much better at producing computers and a bit better at producing textiles than Mexico is, in the sense of higher productivity. Does it therefore follow that the United States should produce all its computers and all textiles and have no trade with Mexico in either area? No, for the same reason that I shouldn't do both the editing and typing. If the United States focuses on computers and Mexico on textiles, total output of the two goods can be higher, the two nations can then trade with each other, and both nations end up better off.

Both absolute and comparative advantages are about trade between countries with different productivity levels selling different products. However, well over half of world trade happens between countries that are fairly similar. I'm thinking particularly here of the high-income economies of the world, such as the United States, Canada, Japan, Australia, and countries of the European Union. Much of the trade between these countries involves buying and selling very similar products. The United States imports cars from Europe and exports cars to Europe; Japan exports computers to the United States and imports computers from the United States; and so on. Moreover, the high-income countries that are trading with one another have, in a big-picture sense, roughly similar wages.

How can this kind of trade of very similar goods benefit the economies of both countries? A first advantage is that it allows even smaller countries to take advantage of economies of scale. If a medium-size economy such as the United Kingdom had a whole bunch of car companies and no international trade, each company would need to be fairly small, because there are only so many British car buyers. Such companies would be unable to take advantage of economies of scale—that is, the fact that large car companies can produce at a lower average cost. However, when a few large auto production plants in the United Kingdom can produce for both domestic consumption and exporting, they can take advantage of economies of scale.

A second advantage of this kind of trade is a gain in variety. Again, imagine that in a small economy such as the United Kingdom's, one big car plant can provide all the cars the country demands in a year. But because of economies of scale, that one big plant may be able to do only one thing really well—say, producing small, efficient city cars. If the British market wants lots of different kinds of cars—city cars, family cars, sports cars, SUVs, what have you—it could get that variety through international trade.

A third advantage: trading similar goods allows a greater degree of specialization within industries. This is sometimes called "breaking up the value chain." For example, a car is made from many separate pieces. There are low-tech pieces, such as the fabric covering the seats; there are higher-tech pieces, such as the computers and the engines; and there is an assembly process. When trade occurs between similar countries, some pieces of the car are made in one country, some are made in other countries, and the car may be assembled in still another country. If this process allows each party to focus on specific, specialized tasks, they can all be more productive.

A fourth advantage: trade in similar goods can encourage a flow of knowledge and skills. Several decades ago, Japanese companies invented something called just-in-time inventory management, in which inventories were kept very low and supplies were delivered to the factory only as needed. It turns out that in a number of industries, this is a very effective way of organizing manufacturing. The United States learned this idea from Japan and adopted it. There was a flow of ideas, not just of goods and services.

Finally, trading similar goods across national borders provides greater competition for domestic producers. As we know, competition provides better incentives for low prices and innovation.

There is a strong empirical correlation between countries that expand their international trade and countries that have good economic growth. What's more, there are literally zero examples of countries that have gotten very rich without expanding trade. The World Bank published a study several years ago on this subject. They split the world economy into two groups: globalizers, countries whose ratio of exports to GDP doubled in the 1980s and '90s; and nonglobalizers, whose ratio of exports to GDP declined in that period. Globalizers included China, India, Mexico, and most of the high-income countries of the world, for a total of three billion people. Among globalizers, per capita GDP rose 5 percent per year in the 1990s. Among nonglobalizers, including much of Africa, the Middle East, and Russia, per capita GDP declined an average of 1 percent per year in the 1990s.

That said, international trade is only one of many factors that contribute to economic growth, and it probably isn't the most important factor. A country with poor education, low investment, nonexistent transportation and communications infrastructure, high corruption, and a weak rule of law is not going to save its economy by expanding international trade. Moreover, the gains from globalization are real, but they result from restructuring industries and orienting your economy toward the global economy.

How far has globalization actually gone? How close is the world economy to a borderless market? The perhaps surprising answer is that, even in the twenty-first century, national borders still seem to matter a great deal. Let me offer some of the evidence.

One way to measure how much national borders matter is to compare trade between metropolitan areas, states, or regions within national boundaries and across national boundaries. If borders don't matter, then the trade going back and forth across the national borders should be more or less the same as the trade between regions of one country. For example, a 1995 study by John McCallum, of the Royal Bank of Canada, compared trade between provinces of Canada and states of the United States. It found that, after you adjust for distance and the size of the local economies, Canadian provinces trade maybe twenty times as much with each other as they do with comparable U.S. states. Later estimates reduced that multiple somewhat, but nonetheless, it is common to find that in the world's highest-income countries, trade between cities or regions within a country is often three to ten times higher than trade between similar cities or regions across national borders. National borders matter a lot.

Another test of a borderless world: Do things cost pretty much the same in one country as they do in another? Think about some tradable good that's common across markets, such as televisions or cars or blue jeans. They'll cost about the same in, say, Minneapolis, Chicago, and St. Louis. But will they cost the same in Minneapolis, Moscow, and Mumbai? A lot of detailed surveys say no. One way to see such differences in action is to look at what happens to prices when exchange rates shift. If prices are the same across national borders, they should shift in proportion to exchange rates. But it turns out that only about half of changes in the exchange rate filter through to prices in different international markets.

Why do national borders matter? While we often think of ourselves as living in a globalized economy, transportation and communication networks are usually developed within a country, with national borders in mind, not to facilitate movements across national borders. Whenever business crosses a national border, it must deal with different legal and tax systems. It often must deal with different languages and cultures, with different currencies, labor laws, safety regulations, accounting rules, and trade laws. Efforts to estimate the costs of factors suggest that they could add up to 40 percent to the price of a good when it crosses a national border. In short, the costs of crossing national borders are still important, and for better or worse, we are not yet close to a borderless world.

International trade seems likely to continue rising in the future, for a variety of reasons. International trade agreements such as those made under the World Trade Organization encourage an expansion of trade. New technologies are bringing transportation costs down and making the costs of communication and information exchange quite minuscule. This not only makes it easier and cheaper to coordinate international trade, but it also facilitates trade in services that can be performed from other countries, which includes everything from the work done at call centers to preparing tax returns to looking at diagnostic X-rays. Major economies that have not previously been a substantial part of world trade, including China, India, and Brazil, are enthusiastically entering global markets—and many other nations around the world, such as those in Africa, would like to do so.

The public discussion over free trade is often a matter of labels and seems to hang on the notion of fairness. Some Americans and Europeans feel that it's "unfair" to try to compete with production from China or India or Mexico or Poland, countries with lower wage levels and different laws about pollution control and workplace regulation. But fairness is a concept that economists often have a hard time discussing; it often seems as if "fairness" is just code for "I don't think we should import stuff from other countries." The arguments for limiting imports can be evaluated on more concrete grounds—such as concerns over jobs, wages, and the environment—and we'll do so in the next chapter.

CHAPTER 33

The Debates over Protectionism

Although most economists are supportive of the forces of free trade, they readily admit that it can cause dislocations in and disruptions to an economy. As a result, political pressure often arises to limit imports. Such steps are known generically as "protectionism," because the stated intent of laws restricting imports is to protect domestic industries from foreign competition.

There are several ways to implement protectionism. Import quotas put a numerical limit on imports. Tariffs are a kind of tax that raises the costs of imports. Countries may enter voluntary export restraint agreements, which are sometimes not so voluntary; they are instead negotiated under the threat that if one country doesn't "voluntarily" reduce its exports, the other country will institute a quota or tariff. In the 1970s and '80s the United States entered this sort of agreement with Japan to restrict Japan's export of steel to the United States. Finally, there are nontariff barriers, a catchall category that includes any bureaucratic or regulatory process set up, explicitly or implicitly, for the purpose of restricting imports. For example, imagine a hypothetical rule that all television sets imported to the United States must be unpacked and inspected, one at a time, at one warehouse in the middle of Kansas. The costs of time and inconvenience imposed by a rule like that would certainly discourage imports.

A protected industry faces less competition from foreign producers. As a result, it can charge higher prices and earn higher profits.

Thus protectionism, in economic terms, is just a way for a government to provide an indirect subsidy to a domestic industry, paid for by higher prices to domestic consumers. Sometimes, as in the case of steel and other raw materials, it's not individuals who consume the raw goods but other firms who will use them to make a finished good. Still, consumers of the finished good ultimately pay a higher price, as the costs are passed along to them.

Perhaps the most prominent arguments for subsidizing industry are about how protectionism could benefit domestic workers. This argument actually comes in four different varieties, some more persuasive than others: imports might affect the total number of jobs available for domestic workers; imports might affect the average level of wages; imports might create disruption from workers having to change jobs; and imports might lead to greater inequality of wages across the economy, even if the average wage goes up. Let's look at these arguments in turn.

There's no question that protectionism is a subsidy that can help retain jobs within a certain industry; however, there is no reason to believe that protectionism increases the overall number of jobs in an economy. To put the same point in reverse, there is zero evidence that international trade diminishes the total number of jobs. One vivid illustration of this occurred when the North American Free Trade Agreement was being discussed in the early 1990s. Presidential candidate Ross Perot, arguing against the treaty, liked to say, "If there's free trade between the United States and Mexico, there would be a giant sucking sound of jobs heading south." Well, the North American Free Trade Agreement passed in 1994. It was followed by seven of the best years for job growth in U.S. history. The giant sucking sound never happened.

Economic theory also suggests that international trade has very little to do with the nation's overall employment level. Cyclical unemployment is tied to recessions and growth, while natural unemployment is tied to labor market incentives. Either way, it's not about trade. Imagine the extreme case: Would shutting out all imports from other nations solve unemployment? Of course not. On top of that, other countries would retaliate; we would lose export jobs. Other countries wouldn't want U.S. dollars if they couldn't sell here; they couldn't buy exports. Without trade, the overall unemployment rate would probably be much the same as before.

What about protectionism as a way to keep wages high? Protectionism is a subsidy to an industry, so it can certainly help wages in that industry. However, that doesn't mean higher wages for the economy as a whole. The higher wages in the protected industry are coming at the cost of higher prices for the good, so everyone else pays. Ultimately, wages are going to depend on productivity. If free trade increases productivity, it will also contribute to a gradual increase in average wages over time.

The argument that imports can create disruption between industries by causing domestic industries that compete with imports to lose production and causing those that export to increase production is completely true. Indeed, this sort of disruption is precisely the mechanism through which trade brings economic gains to an economy. But even here it's important to put the effects of international trade in the context of the typical churning and turmoil of the U.S. economy. Jobs are being gained and lost all the time in the enormous U.S. economy because some firms fail and contract while other firms succeed and expand. Most of that churning in the economy is due to domestic competition, the quality of management and workers in these companies, whether sales of certain products are rising or falling, and other factors that have nothing in particular to do with international trade.

Can protectionism reduce the amount of inequality in an economy? There's a dispute over how much the rise in inequality of income that happened in the United States between the 1970s and the mid-2000s was caused by trade. The consensus seems to be that globalization does contribute somewhat to inequality, but it's not the biggest factor. Factors such as how information and communication technology have improved the productivity of high-skilled labor seem more important, along with other factors discussed in the earlier chapter on inequality. Globalization is a much smaller cause, in part because so much of U.S. international trade is with other high-wage economies and in part because roughly two-thirds of jobs in the United States aren't in competition with imports at all. American lawyers don't compete much with Japanese lawyers. A real estate agent selling a home in New York isn't in competition with a real estate agent selling a home in London. If you need your car fixed, you're not going to take it from Florida to Brazil for the job. Many jobs are not in competition with imports and can't be outsourced to foreign producers. So while trade has some effect on wage inequality, it's not the main cause. Also, there are better solutions to wage inequality (discussed earlier in the chapter on inequality) than restricting trade.

Some argue that trade has contributed to a growing income gap between the richest and poorest countries of the world. Over the past century, the richest countries of the world have been getting steadily and steadily richer, while the poorer countries haven't made much progress at all, so there's been a divergence in per capita GDP. However, the wealth of the richest countries is not built on keeping sub-Saharan Africa, or parts of India, or western China poor. Those places aren't poor because of trade; they aren't much involved in trade. If anything, they're poor because of a lack of trade. This rising gap in world incomes exists not because globalization is harming the poorest countries of the world, but because they aren't participating in globalization. The leading success stories in economic development, such as Japan, South Korea, China, and now India, have typically used foreign trade as one of their main engines of growth.

What about other arguments for protectionism? It's sometimes argued that new industries, called "infant industries," need to be sheltered from foreign competition until they build up enough size and expertise to compete in world markets. In theory, this argument makes sense. But in practice, these infant industries often never grow up and become able to compete—and in the meantime, the economy suffers from supporting them. A classic example arose in the 1970s, when Brazil decided to protect its own infant computer industry from import competition. By the later part of the 1980s, the Brazilian computer industry was about ten years behind the times, which in computer years is an eon. This wasn't a problem only for the computer industry. Think of all the other Brazilian industries that use computers: finance, industry, communications—they were all trying to survive in the world economy with computers that were ten years out of date. An outdated and uncompetitive computer industry was bad enough, but in protecting that industry, Brazil hobbled its other industries as well.

An example of infant industry protection working pretty well occurred in South Korea, where the government subsidized certain industries such as heavy construction equipment manufacture, but if that industry didn't reach a certain level of international sales within a preset time frame, all subsidies were cut off. Thus, short-term protectionism was accompanied by a predetermined deadline for competing in world markets. That said, for South Korea and other countries in East Asia, the fundamental reason for their economic growth is not infant industry policy, but high rates of investment in physical capital, education, and the adoption of new technology. While these countries protected a few infant industries, they gave even more help to old, aging industries such as agriculture.

Yet another argument given for protectionism is the concern that foreign producers might have an unfair advantage because their nations have lower environmental standards versus the United States, and thus lower production costs. This argument is frail. Environmental costs are only a small share of total costs, maybe 2 percent in most U.S. industries. Also, as countries get richer—which is part of what happens from international trade—they tend to make their environments cleaner. After all, they have more resources to spend on cleaning up their environment. In fact, multinational producers often lead the way in reducing pollution in other countries because they bring pollution-control technology developed in Europe or the United States to their plants in the lower-income countries. The notion that reducing trade would lead to a cleaner environment is deeply misguided.

Another concern over international trade is the problem of predatory pricing, sometimes called "dumping": the practice of selling below cost to drive out competition, then raising the price once you have a monopoly. This accusation has been hurled at a lot of international competitors in the U.S. market, perhaps especially at producers of imported steel. It's easy to find cases, such as in the manufacture of cars, steel, or television sets, in which foreign competitors caused U.S. firms great difficulties or even drove them out of business. However, it's impossible to find a case in which the foreign firms were then able follow up by earning monopoly profits. After all, the foreign producers still had to compete with one another. For example, Japanese cars do very well in the U.S. auto market, but Honda and Toyota still compete fiercely with each other, and with other firms. Dumping, by definition, isn't just a matter of hurting the domestic producer; if no monopoly charging high prices emerges, no dumping has occurred.

Sometimes people argue for protectionism on the grounds that certain products such as oil are vital to national security, so we shouldn't rely on foreign suppliers. The logic of this position escapes me. Oil is a vital resource. In this case, doesn't it make more sense to import as much of it as we can now and stockpile it, rather than using up our domestic resources? Shouldn't we conserve our own vital resources for when we need them? If the vital product is a new technology, surely it makes sense to have the best available technology here as soon as possible, to learn about it, and to be able to produce it domestically in the future. Moreover, the national security excuse for restricting imports is easily abused. The U.S. government started providing subsidies for mohair producers in the 1950s, on the national security grounds that it was needed for soldiers' uniforms. In the twenty-first century, we still subsidize mohair, although it has not been used for decades in making uniforms.

There are lots of arguments for protectionism, but few of them are compelling—and for those arguments that are compelling, there are always better ways to address the problem than cutting back on imports.

It's worth remembering that the world economy experienced a sharp decline in international trade during the interwar years of the twentieth century—that is, between World War I, through the Great Depression, and up to World War II. After that time, governments realized that the constriction of trade was bad for all. So an international treaty called the General Agreement on Tariffs and Trade (GATT) was signed in 1947. In 1995, GATT morphed into the World Trade Organization. Regional free trade agreements such as NAFTA and the European Community exist all over the world; in fact, some people say that regional trade agreements are a spaghetti bowl of agreements, with all the strands reaching back and forth from one country to another. In general, this pattern of trade agreements has been successful. The typical tariff has dropped from 40 percent in the 1950s to about 4 percent today, thus making trade between countries much easier. The mission of these international trade agreements has also expanded to cover trade in services (as opposed to goods), environmental issues, and labor issues.

Countries sign international agreements to support free trade for much the same reason that people join a health club and sign up for exercise classes. Countries know that they will be under constant temptation to lean toward protectionism. There are always going to be certain industries that are particularly challenged by foreign competition and thus hostile to it. Those industries are going to organize and lobby politicians for protectionism. In the U.S. political system, it isn't uncommon for a well-organized special interest with a large stake in the outcome, such as an industry looking for protectionism, to win out when the costs are spread broadly over an unorganized, if larger group such as consumers. When countries sign free trade agreements, they tie their hands in a way that makes protectionism harder to adopt.

The trend toward a more globalized economy will surely continue, driven by technological developments in communications and transportation that make global economic links easier, by international treaties that reduce legal barriers to trade, and by the surging and internationally oriented economies of China, India, Brazil, and others. Every major economic change brings its own challenges and disruptions, and globalization is no exception. But the overall direction of globalization is to increase the standard of living in the United States, and throughout the world.

CHAPTER 34

Exchange Rates

In 1995, Ken Kasa, a research economist at the Federal Reserve Bank of San Francisco, wrote the following lines:

> If you asked a random sample of economists to name the three most difficult questions confronting mankind, the answers would probably be: 1) What is the meaning of life? 2) What is the relationship between quantum mechanics and general relativity? 3) What's going on in the foreign exchange market? [Not necessarily in that order.]

Anyone who has traveled abroad has dealt with foreign exchange rates, but explaining why exchange rates are at their current level, why their value changes, and what, if anything, should be done about it can be difficult. Let's start by clearing away some of the rhetorical underbrush, because the subject of exchange rates is typically discussed with terminology that can be deeply misleading.

For example, everyone knows that "strong" is good and "weak" is bad, right? That in financial matters, "appreciation" is good and "depreciation" is bad, right? In the case of exchange rates, both of those statements are wrong. When it comes to prices, whether "high" is good or bad depends on which side of the transaction you're on. Producers like high prices for what they produce; consumers like low prices for what they buy; and most of us play both roles—as producers when we work and as consumers when we buy. An exchange rate is just a price at which one currency can be traded for another. A strong dollar means that the U.S. dollar can buy more of other currencies. A weak dollar means that U.S. currency buys less of other currencies. So if you're buying imported products, you like a strong dollar that can purchase lots of other currency. If you're exporting a good from the United States, you prefer a weak dollar, so that when you convert your export earnings from foreign currencies back into dollars, you are better off.

The international currency market is—as you'd probably expect—a matter of supply and demand. Who's on the supply side of a foreign exchange market, and who's on the demand side? Let's answer this question in terms of the market for the U.S. dollar. If you are an American tourist traveling abroad, you are supplying U.S. dollars; that is, you give U.S. dollars and receive foreign currency in exchange. Foreign firms that sell in the U.S. market earn U.S. dollars, but they need to end up with their home currency, so that they can pay workers and suppliers and investors back in their home country. Thus, foreign firms that sell in the United States are suppliers of U.S. dollars and demanders of their home currency. U.S. investors who want to invest in other countries are suppliers of U.S. currency in foreign exchange markets, and if they want to invest in, say, Germany, they demand euros.

Who's demanding U.S. dollars in the foreign exchange market? The counterparts to the three groups just mentioned, naturally. Foreign tourists in the United States supply their own national currencies and demand U.S. dollars. U.S. exporters earn foreign currency, but they need to trade it for U.S. dollars to produce goods and pay workers in U.S. plants. Finally, foreign investors who want to buy into U.S. assets—stocks, bonds, or real estate—start off with their home currency and demand the U.S. dollars needed to buy U.S. assets.

When the U.S. dollar is stronger and can buy more foreign currencies, those who supply dollars are going to benefit and those who demand dollars are going to suffer. When the U.S. dollar is weaker and can buy less of foreign currencies—or equivalently, foreign currencies can buy more of U.S. dollars—those who supply dollars benefit and those who demand dollars suffer.

What does this mean in concrete terms? If you're a U.S. tourist abroad, a stronger dollar is great because it's buying more foreign currency, so you can spend more on your trip. But if you're a foreign tourist coming to the United States, you want your home currency to buy a lot of U.S. dollars, so you would prefer that the dollar be weak.

Foreign firms that produce what the United States imports prefer a strong U.S. currency because they are earning U.S. dollars, which they can exchange for much more of their own currency. Indirectly, this means that U.S. consumers of imports should also like a stronger dollar, which enables them to buy more goods from all around the world. On the flip side, U.S. firms that export prefer a weak U.S. currency and stronger foreign currencies because they are earning in the foreign currency but paying expenses in U.S. dollars. In effect, a weak dollar holds down the firm's expenses while keeping its earnings high. As a result of this pattern, a stronger dollar tends to hurt exporters and help importers, while reducing a trade surplus or raising a trade deficit. A weaker dollar, on the other hand, encourages exports, discourages imports, and reduces a trade deficit or causes a trade surplus.

What about foreign investors in the U.S. economy? They like a strong dollar because the U.S. dollars they earn with their investment are worth more; when they trade them for their home currency, they get more money. However, a strong U.S. dollar can hurt U.S. investors abroad, because they are earning foreign currency, and when they convert that back into dollars, they get less money. Thus, a strong currency encourages a net inflow of foreign financial capital; a weaker currency discourages such inflows. I mentioned that a strong currency tends to discourage exports, raise imports, and lead to a trade deficit; in terms of investment, strong dollars encourage capital inflows. These two statements are essentially the same: trade deficits, after all, indicate an inflow of foreign capital. To put this another way, a strong dollar encourages foreigners to invest in U.S. assets instead of buying U.S. goods. Conversely, a weaker dollar encourages foreigners to buy U.S. exports instead of investing in U.S. assets.

The world has more than 150 different currencies. Alphabetically, they range from the Afghanistan afghani and the Albanian lek to the Zambian kwacha and the Zimbabwean dollar. But the currencies that matter the most to the U.S. economy are those of our main trading partners, such as the Canadian dollar, the Chinese yuan, the European euro, and the Japanese yen.

From the end of World War II until the early 1970s, foreign exchange rates were fixed. The Bretton Woods Agreement, in July 1944, created the International Monetary Fund (IMF) and the International Bank for Reconstruction and Development, which is usually called the World Bank. One of the jobs of the IMF was to fix exchange rates in place; all currencies were convertible into gold at a certain rate. However, trying to hold exchange rates at a fixed level, when economic forces wanted them to adjust, ultimately proved impossible, and since 1973, exchange rates have been allowed to float, meaning that supply and demand primarily determine exchange rates, with occasional government intervention.

Floating exchange rates have proven fairly volatile, often rising and falling by 30 percent or more over a period of a few years. The Federal Reserve calculates an average exchange rate for the U.S. dollar, weighted according to how much trade each country does with the United States, so the currency of big trading partners gets a bigger weight than little trading partners. Based on that average, the U.S. dollar rose 30 percent in value from 1981 to 1984. Then from 1985 to 1988, it fell 25 percent. From 1999 to 2001, it was up 10 percent. From 2003 to 2008, it was down 10 percent. Short-term movements of exchange rates—within a day or a few months—against individual currencies have been considerably larger than this.

In the long run, however, economists believe that exchange rates move toward the "purchasing power parity" exchange rate, sometimes called the PPP exchange rate. A group of economists at the International Comparison Program, part of the World Bank, calculate the PPP exchange rate for all countries by using a basket of internationally tradable goods—things such as televisions, wheat, and oil. Think about buying a certain group of internationally tradable goods in the United States, with the price measured in dollars, and then buying the same basket of goods in another country, measured in the currency of that country. The purchasing power parity exchange rate is the exchange rate that makes the cost of purchasing this basket of goods the same in either country's currency.

The argument for why exchange rates will eventually head toward the PPP exchange rate is that any other situation is inherently unstable. If internationally traded goods were much cheaper in one country than in another, somebody could make money by buying in the cheap country and selling in the expensive one. Eventually, that process would alter the quantities demanded and supplied in such a way that moved the exchange rate toward the PPP. This theory also implies that exchange rates will adjust for differences in inflation between countries; after all, PPP is linked to the actual purchasing power of goods and services. If your country, say, had 5 percent higher inflation in this group of internationally traded goods every year, your money would buy 5 percent less every year relative to other countries.

However, in the short and medium runs, exchange rates are often not near the PPP level, nor moving toward it. Instead, exchange rates can fluctuate quite dramatically. This fluctuation is largely driven by changing expectations about rates of return. Total global exports in the world economy are something like $15 trillion per year, while the total value traded on foreign exchange rate markets in 2007 was calculated at $2.3 trillion *per day*. Clearly, a lot of currency is being traded for reasons that have nothing to do with international trade in goods and services. These foreign exchange trades are tied to financial investment in one form or another. When international investors want to know where they'll get the best rate of return—an investment in the United States, Europe, Brazil, Russia, wherever—the answer depends not only on the rates of return of the investment, but also on currency exchange rates, now and in the future.

For example, if I'm a U.S. investor, a 20 percent rate of return from a Brazilian investment doesn't do me any good if Brazil's currency depreciates by 30 percent over time. Thus, when people think about investing in other countries, they're thinking, "Do I expect the exchange rate in that other country to get stronger or weaker?" That behavior sets up a cycle of self-fulfilling expectations. If people think a country's currency is going to strengthen, they're going to invest in that country. As they invest, the greater demand for that currency strengthens it. But this self-fulfilling cycle of expectation—that a currency will rise, leading to a currency that actually rises, leading to additional expectations for a rising currency, and then further actual rise—can't go on forever. In the case of the goods market, we call this kind of behavior a bubble, and the exchange rate markets are full of small and larger bubbles expanding and popping all the time. At some point, the exchange rate will eventual return toward PPP.

Some believe the market should determine the exchange rate. Indeed, this is U.S. exchange rate policy most of the time. The opposite opinion points to the volatility of the exchange market compared with other markets. Even if the mammoth U.S. economy can more or less let its exchange rate fluctuate in the market, smaller countries—which are importing and exporting half or more of their GDP—have a hard time taking a hands-off attitude. Big changes in exchange rates have too disruptive an effect on too much of their economy.

If a government wants to manage its exchange rate, it should generally seek a stable or a slowly moving exchange rate to help create a stable business environment for trade and long-term investment. The logic here is similar to the reasons for keeping inflation low: the goal of economic policy should be to encourage firms to focus on increasing productivity and their comparative advantage in global markets. No country should want its firms to spend a disproportionate share of their time worrying about how to protect themselves against exchange rate movements or focusing on how to profit off these fluctuations instead of from producing and selling.

The first goal might be to keep the currency somewhat stable. It's sometimes proposed that a nation should depreciate (that is, weaken) its currency to help its exporters become more competitive and create more jobs in exporting industries. While underlying economic factors will sometimes cause a currency to depreciate, a depreciating currency is not a road to sustained economic growth. After all, a weaker currency not only makes exporters more competitive, it also makes all imports more expensive, both for consumers and for all the firms that are purchasing imported products, such as imported oil—and there are a lot of firms in that category. As a long-term strategy, a nation can't continually depreciate its currency.

A government might seek to control exchange rates. For example, contractionary monetary policy can raise interest rates, which strengthens the exchange rate because investors around the world will seek to invest in your currency for the higher rate of return. Conversely, an expansionary monetary policy can reduce interest rates, which will make your currency less attractive to foreign investors and weaken your exchange rate. However, if a nation uses monetary policy to affect exchange rates, it can't simultaneously use monetary policy for fighting inflation or unemployment. For example, imagine that a country suffers a negative economic shock of some kind, and so its exchange rate starts falling. If that country wants to keep its exchange rate up, it will need a contractionary monetary policy to make interest rates high, and make its exchange rate and currency more attractive. But that contractionary monetary policy will take the negative shock the economy has already experienced and make it worse. Faced with that trade-off, most countries will try to help their domestic economy, rather than stabilize their exchange rate.

An alternative method for affecting exchange rates is for a country to buy and sell its own currency directly on foreign exchange markets. A country that wants to strengthen its currency could buy its own currency on foreign exchange markets. A country that wants to weaken its currency could sell its own currency on foreign exchange markets. But this direct approach has its limitations. When a country sells its own currency, it gets foreign exchange reserves of some other currency. Thus, a country can sell its own currency only as long as it is willing to continually build up foreign exchange reserves. When a country buys its own currency, it needs to have foreign exchange reserves of some other currency to make the purchase. Thus, a country can keep buying its own currency only if it has the foreign exchange reserves to do so—and at some point, those reserves will run out, so you can't buy your own currency forever. Attempts to buy and sell one's own currency tend to be a short-term fix, not a long-term policy.

All government attempts to manage exchange rates run into two practical problems. First, foreign exchange markets will attempt to outguess the government. For example, if foreign investors expect a government to cause a currency to fall, they'll sell that currency and it will start falling immediately. If the government changes its mind, investors may buy again, and the currency will rise. Beliefs about how a government might intervene in exchange rates can themselves make the exchange rate quite volatile.

The other problem is that it's hard for governments to choose a realistic exchange rate. In the long run, a currency needs to reflect PPP; it needs to reflect what the currency can actually buy. If the government tries to fix the currency at an unrealistic level, high or low, it's going to create imbalances and financial stress. If the government tries to keep the currency too strong, over time that country will have weak exports and huge trade deficits over a sustained period. If the government keeps the currency too weak, it will have large trade surpluses and a continual outflow of investment capital. Again, speculators will begin to anticipate that the currency is going to move; the government will then have to step in and use either interest rates or direct buying and selling to discourage the speculators. Holding an exchange rate fixed, against the tides of foreign exchange markets, is a tricky business.

Conventional wisdom among economists in recent years has been that an economy can either choose to let its exchange rates float or fix them, but it probably shouldn't hang out in the middle ground, sometimes letting exchange rates move and sometimes not, in an unpredictable manner. The result of such middle-ground policy is often that exchange rates remain steady for a time, but then move violently, in a way that can severely jolt a small or midsize economy.

The U.S. economy has not had to be deeply concerned with exchange rates. After all, the overwhelming majority of the U.S. economy happens within the borders of the country, and the common currency across the fifty United States is a type of permanent fixed exchange rate. A California dollar is equal to a New York dollar is equal to a Texas dollar. This fixed exchange rate across the United States greatly facilitates trade within the U.S. economy. But nations in Asia, Latin America, and Africa—and across much of Europe until the introduction of the euro—need to set exchange rate policy in a context of dealing with many different currencies. As the spread of globalization links the U.S. economy more tightly with the rest of the world, exchange rate issues will certainly matter more in the United States, too.

CHAPTER 35

International Financial Crashes

Every few years, the news headlines feature a story about a national economy stricken by an international financial crisis. Back in the 1980s many countries in Latin America had overborrowed in global financial capital markets and couldn't repay the loans. In the 1990s, Mexico was unable to repay its debts. International financial crises struck countries across East Asia in 1997, Russia in 1998, Turkey in 2001, and Argentina in 2001 and 2002. In the aftermath of the recession of 2007–2009, no country has yet defaulted on its debts, but there has been considerable turmoil surrounding whether what have become known as the PIGS countries—Portugal, Ireland, Greece, and Spain—might default on their borrowing. Alarmingly, looking a decade or two down the road, the U.S. government appears to be on a path of borrowing that, if not changed, could prove difficult to repay.

What happened in these situations? The problem combines a number of elements we've talked about so far: the growing size of international financial capital flows; changes in exchange rates and the difficulty in fixing exchange rates; and banking system collapses. The twist on the situation, however, is that governments are having trouble repaying their financial obligations, not just a person or a firm.

Countries that have experienced financial crashes have certain things in common. Typically, they've suffered extremely large drops in GDP. For example, in 1995, Mexico's economy contracted by 6 percent; Indonesia's economy contracted by 13 percent in 1998; Argentina's economy contracted by 11 percent in 2002. One reason that the U.S. recession of 2007–2009 was so much longer and deeper than the preceding recessions in 2001 and 1990–1991 was that it was triggered by a financial crisis.

Here is the general pattern of an international financial crisis—although of course the specifics differ from case to case. Countries that have experienced financial crashes also experienced a substantial net inflow of foreign financial capital before the crisis occurred—in many cases, often about 4 to 7 percent of GDP. These economies had become popular destinations for foreign financial investment, and as foreign capital flooded their banking and financial systems, bank lending expanded substantially. As a result of some very loose lending practices, these countries reached a point where a high share of bank loans were not being repaid on schedule. A similar effect happened in these countries' stock markets; that is, the inflow of foreign investment capital, the much greater demand, drove up stock market values very quickly. (The stock market might increase by 50 percent over a fairly short time horizon of maybe a few years.) Then, this inflow of foreign financial capital, which was driving the extra bank lending and the higher stock markets, stopped or reversed itself.

It's hard to know just what causes international capital flows to turn in this way. It's like asking what causes an avalanche. Sometimes a small incident can trigger a big event. In the 1980s, Latin American countries borrowed heavily when interest rates appeared low, but then they couldn't repay when interest rates went up. In the 1990s there was a vogue for investing in East Asian countries for a few years, but that bubble eventually burst. More recently, Greece overborrowed to finance high government spending, while Ireland overborrowed to build more houses than anyone wanted to live in. When an international flow of financial capital reverses direction, it can turn hard and quickly. Financial markets do have some tendency to chase trends. When the stock market in these little countries is rising, it looks like a good idea to lend to those countries, and money floods in—more than the local economy can handle in a useful way. Economists sometimes call this process "overshooting." Then, at some point, it becomes apparent that the local economy can't actually handle this amount of money. Lots of bank loans aren't being repaid; the prices of companies in the stock market look extraordinarily high. When the money starts flooding out again, the process often overshoots in the opposite direction.

As the money floods into these economies and then floods out, the economies can experience sharp movements in exchange rates. As foreign financial investment floods into an economy, lots and lots of people want to buy that currency, and the currency gets stronger in a hurry. When that financial investment pulls out, everyone's trying to sell the currency, which drives the exchange rate way down. For example, the Argentinean peso was worth about one U.S. dollar on January 1, 2002. Only six months later, after the international financial capital flooded out, it was worth twenty-eight cents. It is common in these crises for the value of a country's currency to fall by half or even more. Remember, exchange markets can be affected by self-fulfilling expectations.

Exchange rate fluctuations can bring on an even bigger problem. In developing economies, most borrowing in the international market is done in a major currency, typically U.S. dollars, but sometimes in European euros or Japanese yen. So, when Thailand is borrowing money, the banks in Thailand will borrow funds in, say, U.S. dollars, but will lend in Thai baht. To see the problem that can arise, say a bank borrows $1 million in U.S. currency, converts it at an exchange rate of 40 baht to the dollar, then lends it to a Thai firm. The firm repays the bank in baht; then the bank converts the baht back to U.S. dollars to repay the original loan. So far, so good, but what happens if the baht loses half its value before the firm repays the bank? That 40 million baht, instead of being worth $1 million, is worth only $500,000. The bank won't have enough money to repay its loan. Now imagine that this happens all over the Thai economy; essentially all of Thailand's largest banks would go bankrupt simultaneously. It gets worse. Imagine Thailand's government has deposit insurance, as most countries do. When the bank goes broke, the government is responsible for repaying bank deposits. These payments can be huge—10 percent of GDP or more. So the government faces a massive budget deficit, too.

Many low-income and middle-income countries do want a steady inflow of foreign financial investment, which not only brings in money for physical capital investment but often is accompanied by management expertise, international business contacts, sophisticated worker training, and improved technology. The trick for such nations is to make investment attractive to foreign investors but reduce the risk of a sudden U-turn in international financial flows, followed by economic collapse. What policy options do these countries have?

For one thing, the International Monetary Fund is empowered to give loans to countries that are experiencing a financial crash in order to soften the blow. The IMF is an international institution, officially an agency of the United Nations founded in 1945 to encourage stable exchange rates. When a country is in a financial crisis, the IMF stands ready to make loans—not just temporary or short-term loans, but long-term loans that can help countries adjust to these changes. The IMF has a Board of Governors made up of representatives from all over the world that meets once a year. It also has a twenty-four-person Executive Board that meets several times a week. The Executive Board always includes members from the United States, Japan, Germany, France, the United Kingdom, China, Russia, and Saudi Arabia. The other sixteen seats are elected by the members of the IMF. Technically, the importance of each vote varies by the size of a nation's economy, so the United States has more voting power than other countries, but most day-to-day decisions are effectively made by consensus. The IMF loans often come with conditions: for example, that a government must take steps to reduce certain kinds of subsidies, or reduce its budget deficits, or install more financial regulations. In some cases, the IMF has arguably gone too far, crossing the line from useful advice to dictating controversial details of economic policy. The difficulty is that the IMF is a little like the fire department: it's useful, but it shows up only after the crisis has happened. It would be better to avoid starting the fire in the first place. But how? One possibility is government controls preventing foreign money from flowing out of the economy, but such laws are hard to enforce. If a country is involved in the global economy, if it's importing and exporting, it has to let money move in and out of the country. It's no simple task to figure out whether any given outflow is linked to good, healthy trade or is investment capital fleeing the country. Accountants are very good at creating categories to conceal those sorts of distinctions. Besides, in a world of international bank accounts, if a government even hints that it might prevent money from leaving the country, money floods out immediately, thus creating or worsening the problem the government is trying to avoid.

Perhaps the best kind of government control—which worked to some extent for Chile in the 1980s—is to worry less about money leaving and worry more about what kind of money arrives in the first place. Broadly speaking, foreign investment can be divided into two types: direct investment, when a foreign capital buys a firm or a factory—something solid—and portfolio investment, when foreign investment capital buys a financial instrument such as a bond. Direct investment is less likely to flee the country in a hurry, because it's hard to sell a factory on the spur of the moment, and direct investors are more likely to seek a long-term payoff. Thus, if a small or medium-size country is going to try to impose controls on foreign investment, encouraging direct investment is probably the best route.

Countries can also reduce their risks of a financial crash through better regulation of their banking and financial systems. Banks that recognize their own foreign exchange risks, for example, will be better at hedging their bets to reduce the size of the risks they face. In some of the crisis countries we mentioned at the start of this chapter, governments had, for some time, been holding the exchange rate at pretty much the same level. A fixed rate wasn't official policy, but for about ten or fifteen years, their banks and firms had begun to assume that the exchange rate wasn't going to move. When the exchange rate did move, they were unprepared. Government financial regulators can require banks to be prepared for exchange rate fluctuations; governments can also let the exchange rate move to some extent on a regular basis, so that being prepared for such fluctuations is the norm. Governments can also mitigate their own financial risk in a crash by limiting deposit insurance to individuals and letting firms look after themselves. This also provides an incentive for firms to be aware of the risk they face from fluctuating foreign exchange rates and to find ways to address it.

Some economists have proposed an international mechanism that would work as a sort of bankruptcy court for countries going through a financial crisis. The hope is that if foreign investors know they will be treated fairly, with some predictable procedure, they won't be quite so quick to pull their funds. Such a mechanism would require a lot of international treaties, and it's not quite clear how courts could enforce rulings. A milder alternative would be to add to the fine print of international bond agreements more details about what will happen if a country is unable to repay, so the process becomes more transparent and investors can take the risks into account. By the mid-2000s, a number of countries had started doing this. Overall, countries are getting smarter about holding more reserves of international currency, about pushing banks and companies to recognize the risks of exchange rate fluctuations, and about writing more detailed debt contracts.

How vulnerable is the United States to an international financial crash? The situation in the United States is quite different from that in many smaller economies, in part because the U.S. economy can borrow in its own currency, so its banking system is less vulnerable to being whipsawed by fluctuating exchange rates. Indeed, if the exchange rate of the U.S. dollar does fall, it reduces the cost of the debts that U.S. companies owe to foreign investors. The U.S. economy has handled substantial falls in the value of the U.S. dollar in the past without dramatic ill effects. Much of the inflow of foreign financial capital to the United States is in the form of assets with a variable return, such as stock and real estate, which in contrast to borrowed money are not forms of investment that require fixed payments, and so can lose value but not actually default.

However, while fluctuations in exchange rates can make an international financial crisis worse, they are not necessary for such a crisis to occur. Portugal, Ireland, Greece, and Spain—the PIGS—were able to borrow during the mid-2000s in their shared currency of euros, which helped to insulate them from exchange rate risks. However, Greece used its borrowed money to run up huge government deficits. In Ireland, foreign financial investment flowed through Irish banks, which used the money to make real estate loans. When Ireland's real estate bubble burst, the country's banks found themselves bankrupt, and the Irish government stepped in to guarantee that all investors, whether foreign or domestic, would not lose their money. This guarantee prevented a financial panic, but at a huge cost.

The U.S. financial crisis that led to the recession of 2007–2009 is fundamentally homegrown rather than international. The wave of subprime lending, the housing bubble, and the bursting of that bubble are all U.S. experiences. But the U.S. economy has been running large trade deficits throughout the 2000s, reflecting large net inflows of international capital. Trade deficits have often been in the range of 4 to 5 percent of GDP—$500 billion a year or more. Foreign central banks—especially in Japan, China, and elsewhere in East Asia—have been building up enormous reserves of U.S. dollar assets. In 2009 and 2010, the U.S. government started running budget deficits that, as a share of GDP, were enormous by historical standards. The huge demand for financial capital from the borrowing of the U.S. government is being met, in substantial part, by international lending from the rest of the world. The rest of the world will not be willing to increase its holdings of U.S. dollar assets in perpetuity.

Even if the United States is unlikely to experience an outright financial crash, the experience of foreign investors gradually becoming less willing to park their funds in the U.S. economy could contribute to a long-term, slow-motion disruption. If the U.S. economy experienced a slowdown or even a reversal of the inflows of foreign financial investment capital, it would have to adjust. The national savings and investment identity points out that the adjustment would happen in one of three ways: either more private saving sufficient to offset the drop in foreign investment capital, which doesn't seem especially likely given the U.S. history of relatively low rates of private saving; less government borrowing, which means some combination of spending cuts and tax hikes; or less private-sector investment in physical capital and new technology, which would harm long-run growth. Because even the mammoth U.S. economy cannot rely on foreign investors being perpetually willing to increase their holdings of U.S. dollar financial assets, some combination of these three options will eventually come to pass. Finding a way to reduce the projected long-term parade of budget deficits or to increase private saving is a relatively attractive option; in contrast, crowding out investment and reducing the long-term growth rate would be a painful price to pay.

CHAPTER 36

A Global Economic Perspective

The world is becoming economically more integrated. The World Trade Organization and other institutions are reducing legal barriers to trade and financial flows. Communication and information flow are getting easier and cheaper, making global production easier to coordinate. The costs of moving goods are falling—the costs not just of shipping physical output by plane, truck, or boat but also of sending digital output and services over the Internet. The global economy is becoming less oriented to national boundaries, and more to globalization.

When reviewing the global economic scene, it's useful to start with world GDP and world population, then to compare GDP and population for groups of countries. A standard breakdown is first to separate out the high-income economies (the United States, Canada, the European Union, Japan, and a few others), then to divide the world into regions (East Asia and the Pacific; Eastern Europe and Central Asia; Latin America and the Caribbean; the Middle East and North Africa; South Asia and sub-Saharan Africa). The World Bank categorizes the nations of the world along these lines, and provides international data that allow us to take a quick tour of the world economy.

World GDP was about $58 trillion in 2009 (as measured in current U.S. dollars). World population that year was 6.8 billion. Thus, per capita GDP for the world was approximately $8,500. The high-income countries combined included about 16 percent of world population, but they produced 72 percent of world GDP, with a per capita GDP of roughly $37,000. Each of these high-income economies faces various issues and problems, including unemployment, budget deficits, and how to pay for an aging population. But this group of countries as a whole has seen its economies grow by 2 to 3 percent on average, decade after decade. These countries' economies have been staggered by the global financial crises of 2007–2009, but over the longer run, they have enormous fundamental strengths. They have well-educated workforces and good human capital; they have strong rates of investment in physical capital; they are good at developing and using technology; and they have well-functioning market institutions.

The largest economies in the East Asia and Pacific region include China and the countries sometimes called the East Asian "tigers," including Indonesia, South Korea, and Thailand. These countries have about 29 percent of world population, with China accounting for roughly one-fifth of world population all by itself. These countries as a group produce about 11 percent of world GDP. Per capita GDP for the region is about $3,300, something like one-twelfth the per capita GDP of the high-income countries. Nonetheless, this region is the major economic success story of the past few decades, first with the rapid economic growth in the tiger nations in the 1970s and '80s and then the rapid growth of China's economy over the past three decades. The bulk of the long-term growth in this region can be attributed to good fundamentals: a very high savings rate, very high domestic investment rates, and a major effort to build human capital through expanding public education. These countries have had a great willingness to import technology and learn to use it well. They have had a great willingness to adopt market-oriented incentives for their producers and to integrate into the world economy. Even China has moved away from a planned, centralized economy and into a market-oriented economy.

The largest economy in the region of Eastern Europe and Central Asia is Russia, but Poland and Turkey are substantial as well. This region has about 6 percent of world population but produces about 4.5 percent of world GDP. Thus, per capita GDP is about $6,400. The area covers a very broad range of countries, from Poland and the Czech Republic in the west, through the Russian Federation and Turkey in the center of the region, and all the way to countries such as Kazakhstan, Tajikistan, and the Kyrgyz Republic in the east. Generalizations about this huge area are hazardous. I still look back in wonder at the time between the 1950s and the late 1980s when people talked about the economy of the U.S.S.R. as if it were roughly comparable to the economy of the United States or Western Europe. Many people—even economists—were fooled by the Soviet Olympic and chess champions, and the space program, and the well-developed parts of Moscow. But all that time, the old Soviet bloc as a whole had an economy in per capita terms a lot closer to that of Mexico or Brazil than to the United States. The countries in this region typically have well-educated populations by world standards and good ties to the high-income economies of Europe. But they are still working through the transition away from decades of built-in government subsidies and dysfunctional legal institutions inherited from their communist past.

The next region on our whirlwind global tour is Latin America and the Caribbean. The biggest economies in this region are Brazil, Mexico, and Argentina. This region holds 8.5 percent of world population and produces 7.2 percent of world GDP, giving a per capita GDP of about $7,200. In the 1970s and '80s, many of the countries in this region had some extraordinary problems: enormous government debts, financial crashes, inward-looking protectionist trade policies that damaged long-term growth, and horrendous inflation—sometimes verging on hyperinflation. Now, a decade into the twenty-first century, these countries have more or less shaped up their macroeconomic policies. They have tamed and then banished hyperinflation. They have largely, although not entirely, given up on protecting infant industries and privatized some government-owned industry. They've reduced price controls. Their economic performance has picked up. One of their highest current priorities must be to address their enormous inequalities in education levels and health care, as these inequalities create a breeding ground for corruption and populist policy that only hinders growth. Latin America and the Caribbean also need to get serious about competing in the world economy. These countries still have far too many barriers to markets and to trade, even within the region itself.

Our next region is the Middle East and North Africa. The largest economies in that region are Saudi Arabia, Iran, and Egypt. (For the record, Israel is counted in the high-income countries of the world, as are a few of the small oil-exporting countries such as Kuwait and the United Arab Emirates.) This region has about 5 percent of world population and 2 percent of world GDP; per capita GDP is about $3,200. Given the geopolitical importance of this region—in a word, oil—it's always a shock that in economic terms, the region isn't very big. If it weren't for oil, it would barely play a role in the world economy at all. The long-term economic prospects for this region appear shaky. Human capital investment has historically been low. It's not a well-educated region, especially for women. Other than the oil industry, investment in physical capital has also been low. Market institutions, such as the financial and legal underpinnings of a market economy, are not well developed. Political freedom is limited. Rates of population growth have been high. Over the next few decades, the region will experience a very large infusion of young workers with low levels of education, and it is not at all clear how these workers can be absorbed. The oil industry is very capital intensive; it's not going to hire them. The governments already have budget deficits; they're not likely to provide government jobs. The private sector in this region hasn't shown an ability to expand and draw workers in.

In the South Asia region, the largest economy by far is India, but other large countries include Pakistan and Bangladesh. This region has about 23 percent of world population, but produces only 3 percent of world GDP. Per capita GDP in this region is about $1,000. The region is extremely poor, but there are some encouraging signs. In particular, India seems to be reducing the heavy level of regulation in its economy and moving more toward market incentives and a global orientation. India is a nation of economic extremes right now: as one economist put it, part Silicon Valley and part sub-Saharan Africa. On average, India remains a low-income country, but there is some real strength in certain parts of its economy, especially related to trade in high technology and services.

In sub-Saharan Africa, comprising forty-eight countries, the largest economy by far is South Africa, and the most populous country is Nigeria. The region has 12 percent of the world's population, but it produces less than 2 percent of world GDP, with a per capita GDP of roughly $1,100, similar to South Asia's. However, in recent years Africa has shown some intriguing glimmers of hope. Levels of education and measures of health in Africa have improved substantially in recent decades. Since about 1960, for example, the childhood mortality rate has fallen by more than half. In 1960 around 1 or 2 percent of the population attended secondary school; in many countries that figure is now 30 or 40 percent. Parts of Africa have shown genuine growth; South Africa, in particular, is a middle-income economy by world standards. But many people in Africa continue to eke out a subsistence living in countries that are ill-governed at best and in turmoil and civil war at worst.

After this whirlwind tour, I want to take a moment to discuss the specific situations of China and India, the two countries with the largest populations in the world. China had about 1.3 billion people in 2009; India had over 1.1 billion. Together they have over one-third of the world population. Both countries are still very poor; China had a per capita GDP of about $3,700 in 2009; India, about one-third that level. However, both countries have also experienced robust growth in recent years. China's real GDP has grown at about 9 percent per year since the 1980s. India's real GDP has been growing at 6 to 8 percent per year over the past decade. Remember the power of rapid growth rates. At a 9 percent annual rate of growth, China's economy has been doubling in size every eight years. At a 7 percent annual growth rate, India's economy doubles each decade.

The single biggest change for the very poorest people in the world in the past few decades is the explosive economic growth of these two countries, which has lifted more people out of the lowest subsistence poverty levels faster than any other event in human history. Intriguingly, each nation is achieving this growth in a different way. China has focused on manufacturing and has a relatively free market economy with an undemocratic political system. India has focused more on the technology and service sectors within a democratic political system that's reforming itself toward a greater market orientation. Given those differences, I wouldn't be stunned if India's economic future over the next few decades turned out to be brighter than China's.

What are the major dangers the world economy faces, not in the short run of a few years, but over the next few decades?

For example, could a trade war cripple the global economy? Economic historians teach that there was a previous age of globalization between the end of the nineteenth century and the start of World War I. That age ended in a series of world wars, political reactions against trade, and the Great Depression. Could that all happen again? Well, the general momentum toward free trade seems extremely difficult to stop. The costs of trade keep falling; communication keeps getting easier. Global businesses, international law and finance, and international transportation are getting easier to manage over time. Also, the economic gains from taking advantage of trade are only going to continue.

What about an energy shortage? Over the next thirty to forty years, prices of oil and natural gas may well rise substantially, but there's little reason to expect an outright shortfall. As prices become higher, it becomes economically viable to use existing technologies to search out and use other sources of fossil fuels, such as oil shale and tar sands. Emerging technology may uncover new energy sources or more efficient ways to make use of current resources—substitutes of one kind or another. It's worth noting that a lot of the economic gains of recent years, such as in information and computer technology, are not largely dependent on heavy energy use the way old industries used to be. I don't think an energy crunch will derail the world economy in the next few decades.

Will an environmental crisis stop long-run growth? The U.S. economy pays approximately 2 to 3 percent of GDP on costs related to keeping the environment clean. This cost seems to be more or less constant; it's not increasing over time. Thus, as the economy grows, we can continue to make things cleaner without committing ever more resources. The other good news is that rapidly growing economies, such as those of China, India, and Mexico, have become much more aware of the environment than the U.S. was, say, a century ago. The quality of air and water in those countries, while often not at all good by U.S. standards, is typically improving. In general, a richer world will be more willing to spend resources on environmental protection. In fact, taxing energy sources as an incentive for reducing pollution would also reduce the risk of an energy crisis. Combining economic growth with environmental progress will be an ongoing challenge, but it is certainly economically possible—if there is sufficient political will behind it.

Will population growth outstrip world economic growth? This worry was especially common in some popular bestselling books of the 1960s and '70s, but current thinking focuses on the idea that countries go through a demographic transition, in which birth rates drop and life expectancy rises. In Japan and across Western Europe, this demographic transition has been so strong that populations are expected to decline substantially in the next half century. Even in many low-income countries, birth rates are way down compared to the 1960s and '70s. As my wife likes to note, it's pretty amazing what happens when women get more education and when contraception becomes widely available. The current projections are for world population to top out at 9 billion around 2050 and then be flat or decline after that. Feeding this global population will be a challenge, but with appropriate investments in agricultural research and development, it should be possible.

Sometimes when you listen to political discussions about economic policy, it sounds like *everything* is a threat. But the future economy will offer remarkable opportunities along with its challenges and disruptions. The world economy is not a zero-sum game with a fixed amount of growth. The U.S. economy is not growing at the expense of other nations, or vice versa. Instead, it is an essentially cooperative venture, in which all countries can grow more quickly if they work together in networks of trade, production, technology, and knowledge that reach around the world. But within this network, each nation remains responsible for its own destiny. If nations undertake policies that lead to building human and physical capital, creating and diffusing new technology, and improving legal and financial infrastructure for supporting markets, their economies will grow. Nations that can't put together a successful set of policies will see their growth rates fall behind.

There are certainly reasons to be concerned about the future competitive position of the U.S. economy. We need to work on education at the elementary, secondary, and college and university levels. We need to address our culture of overborrowing, both at the individual and government level. We need to create incentives for investment in physical capital and in the ongoing development of technology. We need to prepare for our aging population and confront the rising costs of health care. These issues are all real ones, but they're also problems that the United States will ultimately face by itself, whatever happens in the economies of Europe or China or India or Latin America. Our future is really in our own hands.

Thomas Jefferson once wrote, "An enlightened citizenry is indispensable for the proper functioning of a republic." The economy is a robust institution, but also one that needs thoughtful support from knowledgeable citizens, both in their private-sector roles as workers, managers, consumers, savers, investors, and entrepreneurs, and in their public roles as citizens, voters, and politicians. This book has sought to develop a spirit of respect for the power of market forces, but also a clear awareness of where those market forces may fall short; a belief that government policy may sometimes be highly useful, but also an understanding that it can in some cases be useless or even counterproductive; a perspective over time that encompasses both short-run needs and the ingredients for long-run success; and the ability to see economic issues both within U.S. borders and around the world. The concepts and insights of economics offer a powerful vocabulary for enunciating both the promises and the potential trade-offs that are sure to arise in the evolving U.S. and world economy. Economic analysis will not dictate a single correct answer in many situations, but it can guide the way to better-informed and more thoughtful answers.

References

Bierce, Ambrose. 1911. *The Devil's Dictionary.* Available at www.alcyone.com/max/lit/devils/.

Downs, Anthony. 1957. *Economic Theory of Democracy.* New York: Harper.

Heilbroner, Robert. 1968 [2009]. *The Making of Economic Society,* 12th ed. Englewood Cliffs, NJ: Prentice-Hall.

Hicks, John. 1935. "Annual Survey of Economic Theory: The Theory of Monopoly." *Econometrica* 3.

Jefferson, Thomas. 1813. "Thomas Jefferson to Isaac McPherson." August 13. In *The Writings of Thomas Jefferson.* Edited by Andrew A. Lipscomb and Albert Ellery Bergh. 20 vols. Washington: Thomas Jefferson Memorial Association, 1905. Volume 3, Article 1, Section 8, Clause 8, Document 12. Available at press-pubs.uchicago.edu/founders/documents/a1_8_8s12.html.

Kasa, Kenneth. 1995. "Understanding Trends in Foreign Exchange Rates." Federal Reserve Bank of San Francisco. *FRBSF Weekly Letter.* 95–22. June 9. At www.frbsf.org/publications/economics/letter/1995/el1995-22.pdf.

Malkiel, Burton. 1973 [2003]. *A Random Walk Down Wall Street.* New York: W.W. Norton.

Marx, Karl. 1875. "Critique of the Gotha Program." Available at www.marxists.org/archive/marx/works/1875/gotha/ch01.htm.

Mill, John Stuart. 1848 [1878]. *Principles of Political Economy,* 8th ed. London: Longmans, Green, Reader, Dyer.

Read, Leonard. 1958. "I, Pencil." *The Freeman.* December. Available at www.econlib.org/library/Essays/rdPncl1.html#I,%20Pencil.

Robinson, Joan. 1978. *Contributions to Modern Economics.* New York: Academic Press.

Smith, Adam. 1776 [1994]. *An Inquiry into the Nature and Causes of the Wealth of Nations.* New York: Modern Library.

Solow, Robert M. 1986. "James Meade at Eighty." *Economic Journal,* 986–88.

———. 2000. "Toward a Macroeconomics of the Medium Run." *Journal of Economic Perspectives* 14:151–58.

Stein, Herbert. 1991. "The Washington Economist: What Economic Advisers Do." *American Enterprise,* 6–9.

Wilde, Oscar. 1891. "Lady Windermere's Fan." Available at www.classicbookshelf.com/library/oscar_wilde/lady_windermere_s_fan/.

Index